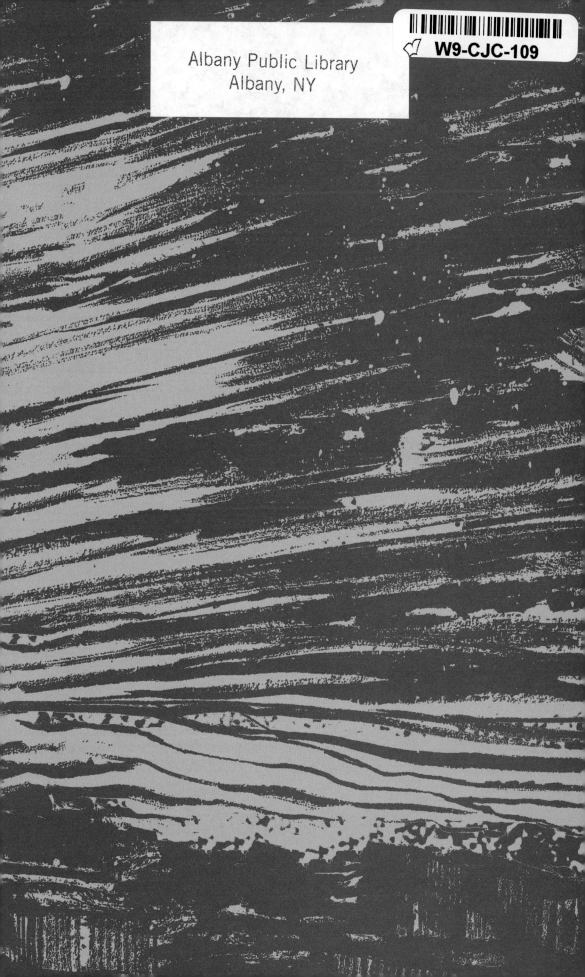

W9-CJC-109

SWORD DAUGHTER

script
BRIAN WOOD

art
MACK CHATER

colors
JOSÉ VILLARRUBIA

lettering
NATE PIEKOS OF BLAMBOT®

cover art
BEN OLIVER

chapter break art
MACK CHATER

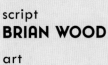

Dark Horse Comics

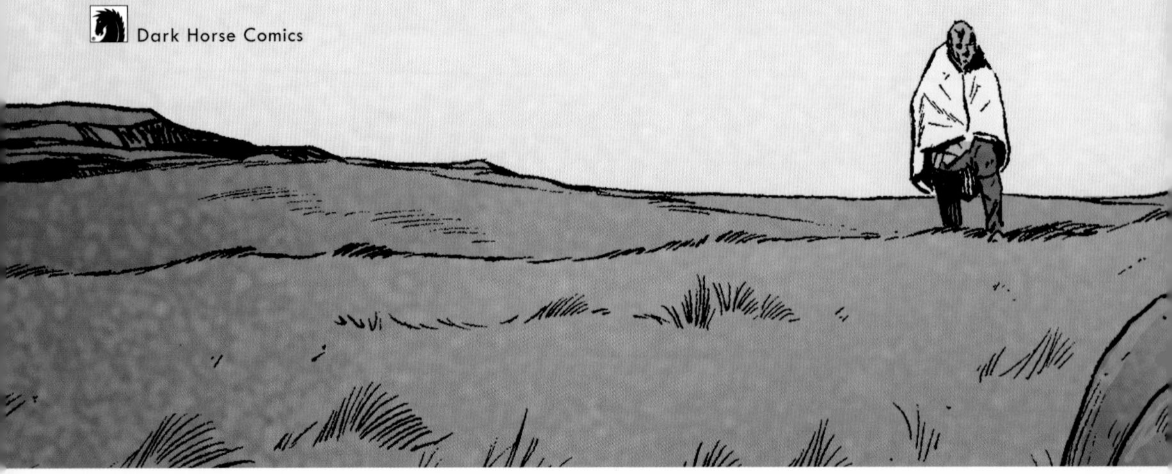

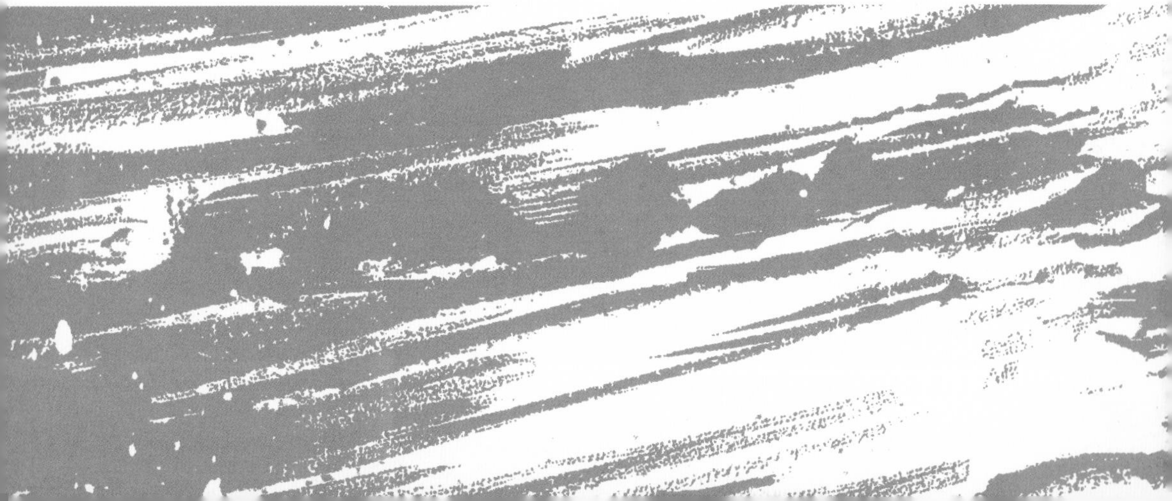

SWORD DAUGHTER

3: ELSBETH OF THE ISLAND

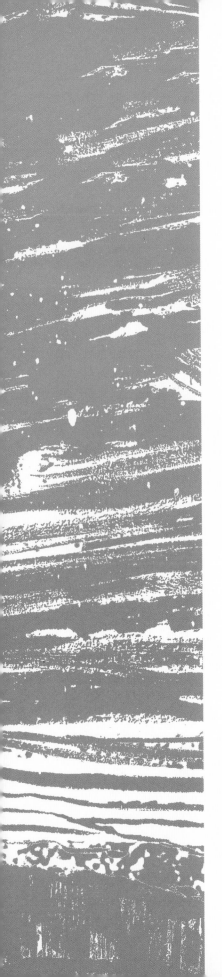

president and publisher **MIKE RICHARDSON**

editor **SPENCER CUSHING**

assistant editor **KONNER KNUDSEN**

collection designer **ANITA MAGAÑA**

digital art technician **JOSIE CHRISTENSEN**

SWORD DAUGHTER VOLUME 3: ELSBETH OF THE ISLAND

This volume collects the Dark Horse comic book series *Sword Daughter* #7–#9, originally published June 2019–January 2020.

Published by Dark Horse Books
A division of Dark Horse Comics LLC
10956 SE Main Street
Milwaukie, OR 97222
DarkHorse.com

To find a comics shop in your area, visit comicshoplocator.com

Neil Hankerson, Executive Vice President ¦ Tom Weddle, Chief Financial Officer ¦ Randy Stradley, Vice President of Publishing ¦ Nick McWhorter, Chief Business Development Officer ¦ Dale LaFountain, Chief Information Officer ¦ Matt Parkinson, Vice President of Marketing ¦ Cara Niece, Vice President of Production and Scheduling ¦ Mark Bernardi, Vice President of Book Trade and Digital Sales ¦ Ken Lizzi, General Counsel ¦ Dave Marshall, Editor in Chief ¦ Davey Estrada, Editorial Director ¦ Chris Warner, Senior Books Editor ¦ Cary Grazzini, Director of Specialty Projects ¦ Lia Ribacchi, Art Director ¦ Vanessa Todd-Holmes, Director of Print Purchasing ¦ Matt Dryer, Director of Digital Art and Prepress ¦ Michael Gombos, Senior Director of Licensed Publications ¦ Kari Yadro, Director of Custom Programs ¦ Kari Torson, Director of International Licensing ¦ Sean Brice, Director of Trade Sales

First edition: April 2020
ISBN 978-1-50670-784-6

10 9 8 7 6 5 4 3 2 1
Printed in China

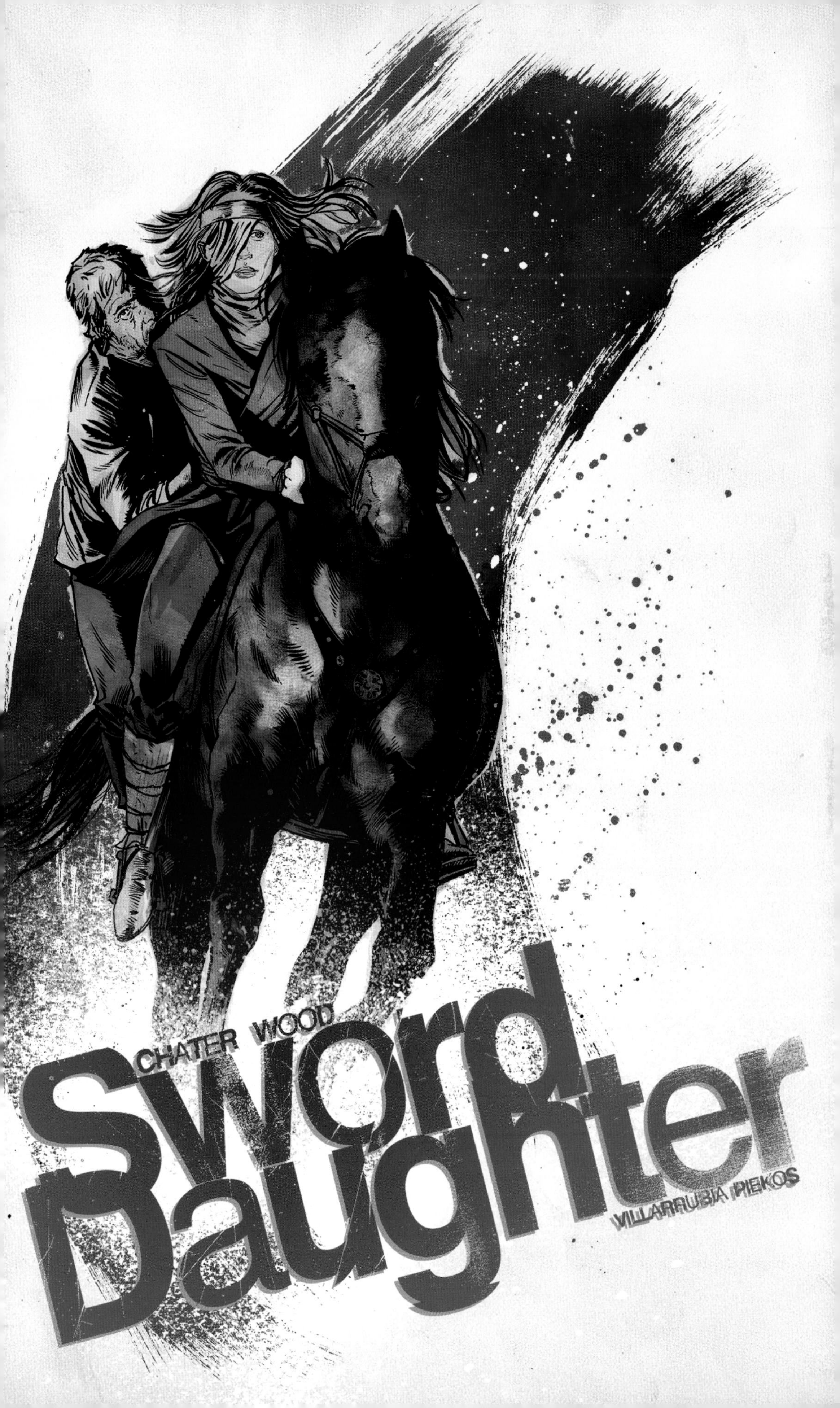
CHATER WOOD
Sword Daughter
VILLARRUBIA PIEKOS

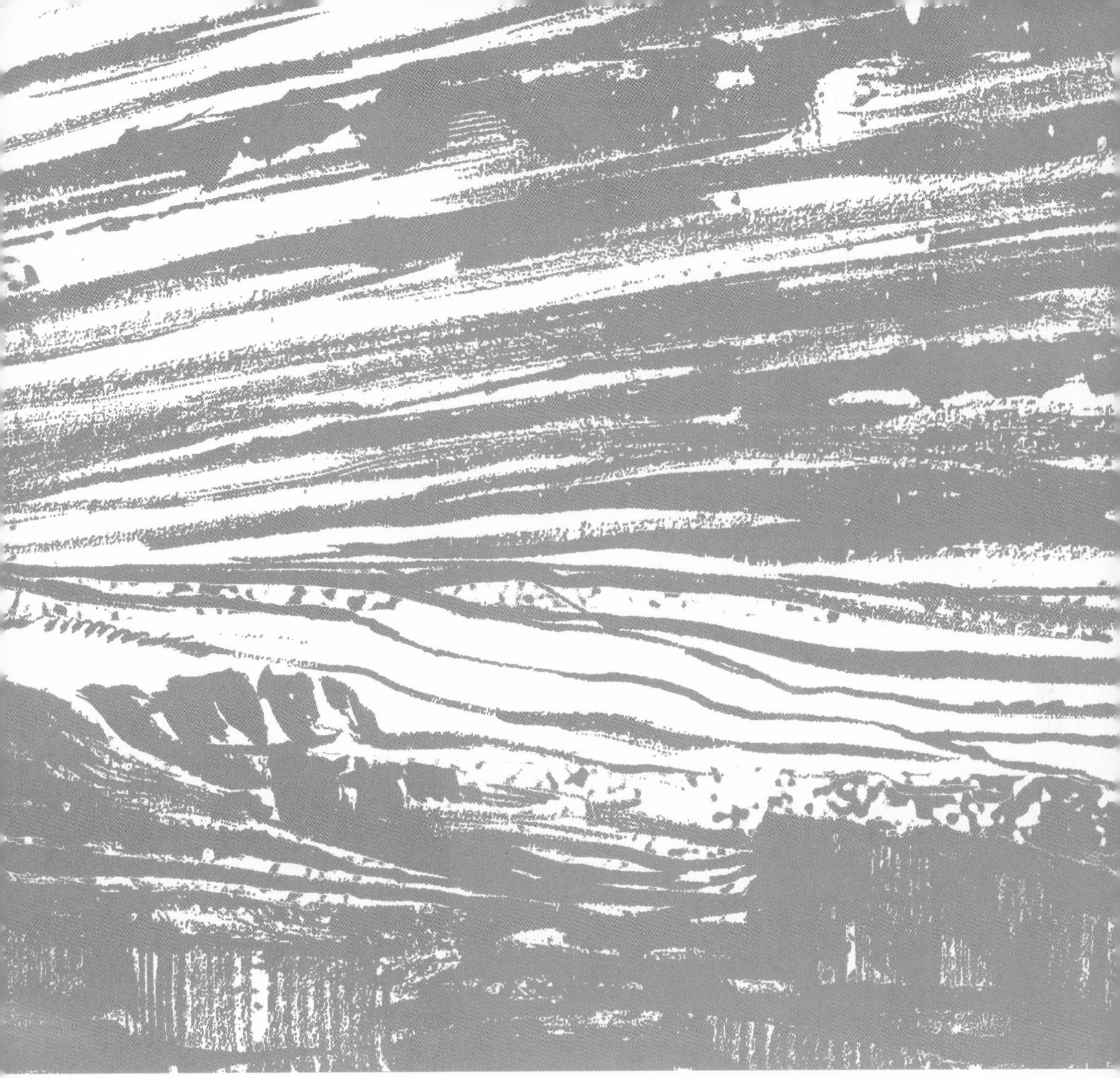

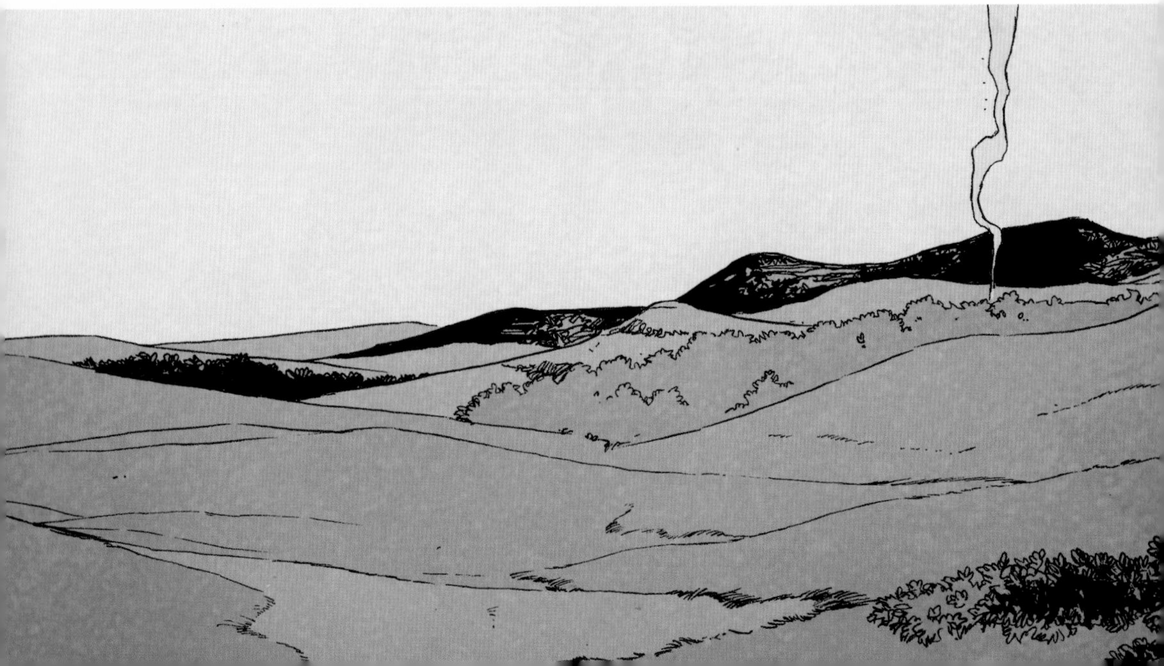

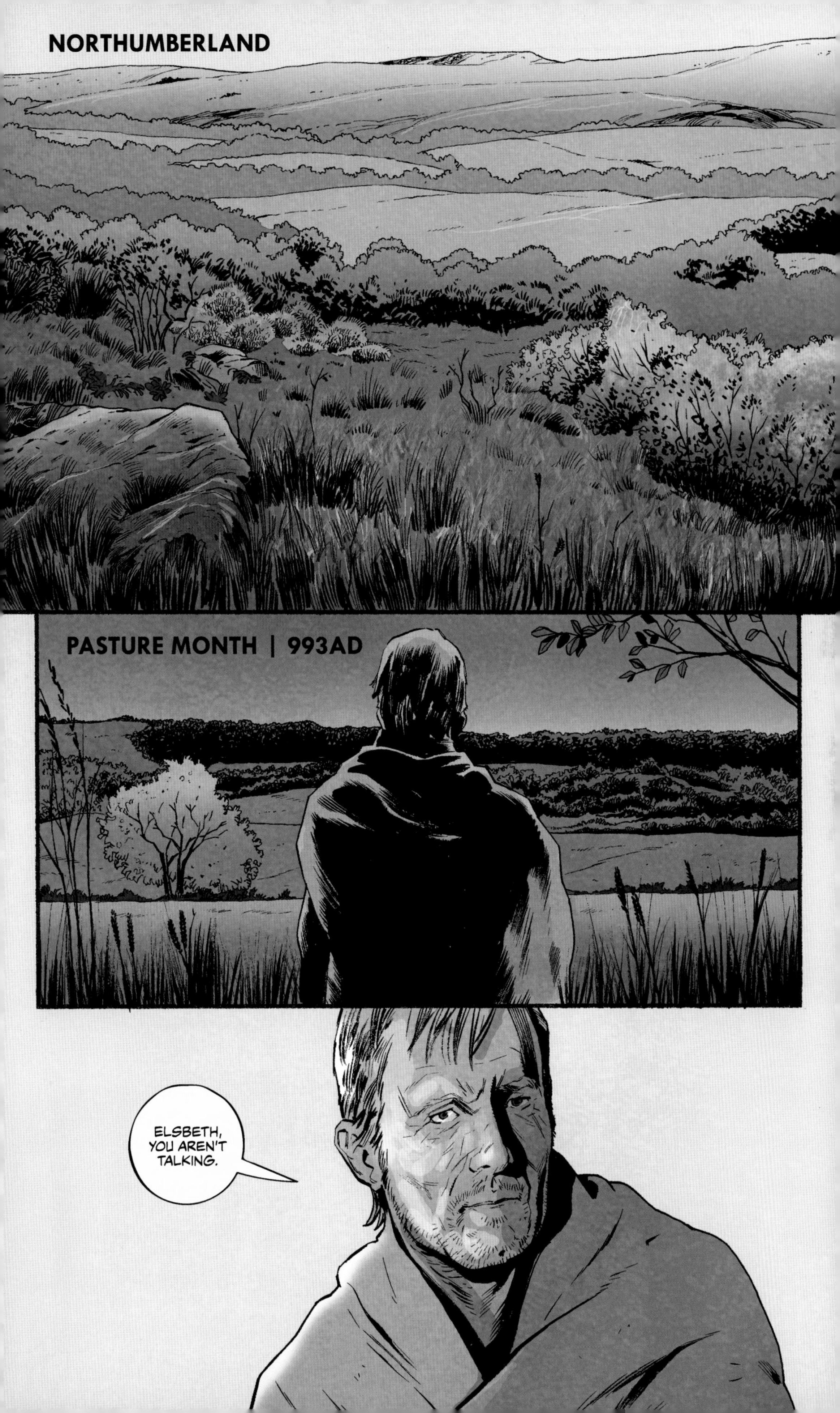
NORTHUMBERLAND
PASTURE MONTH | 993AD
ELSBETH, YOU AREN'T TALKING.

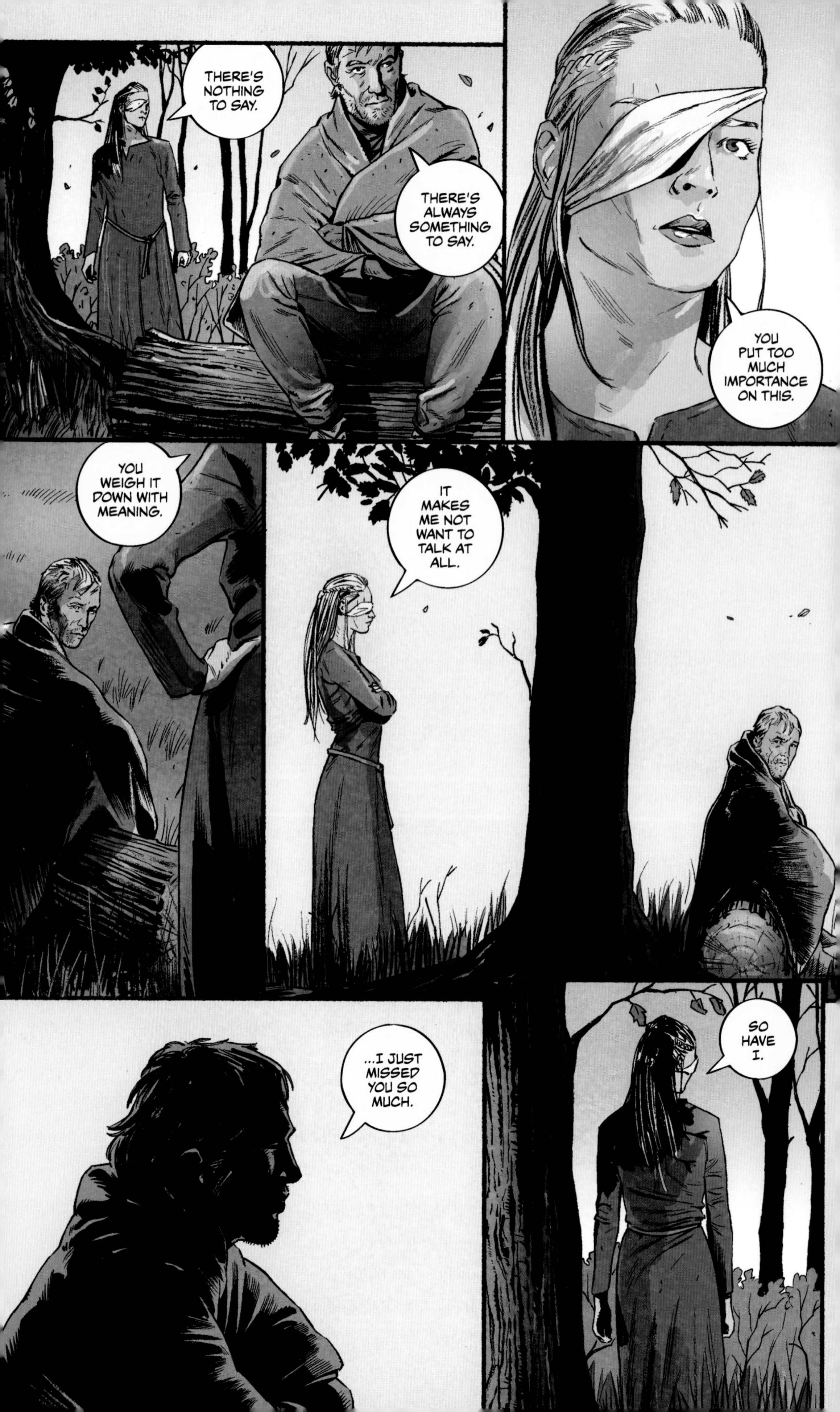
THERE'S NOTHING TO SAY.
THERE'S ALWAYS SOMETHING TO SAY.
YOU PUT TOO MUCH IMPORTANCE ON THIS.
YOU WEIGH IT DOWN WITH MEANING.
IT MAKES ME NOT WANT TO TALK AT ALL.
...I JUST MISSED YOU SO MUCH.
SO HAVE I.

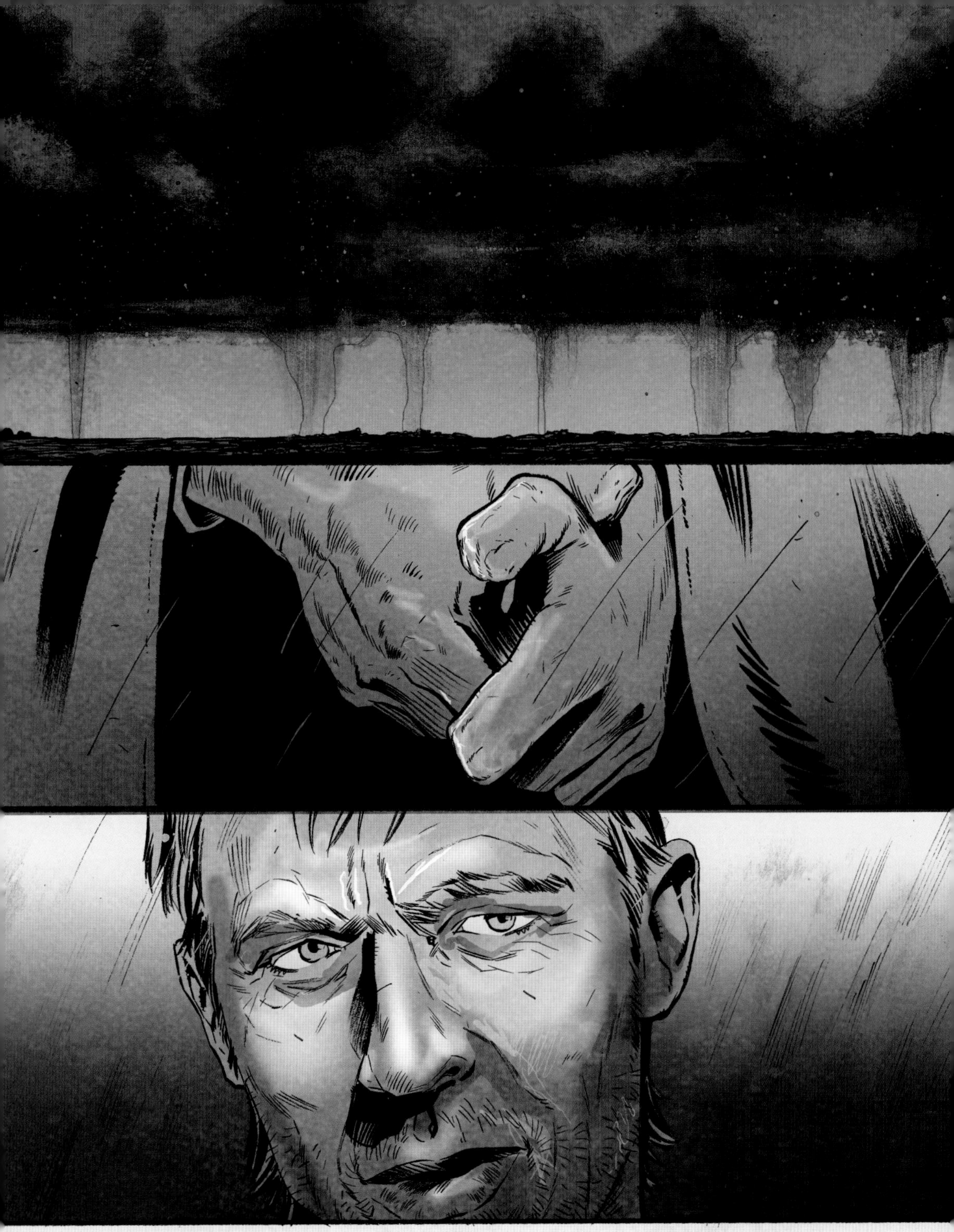

SWORD DAUGHTER
COLD RAIN

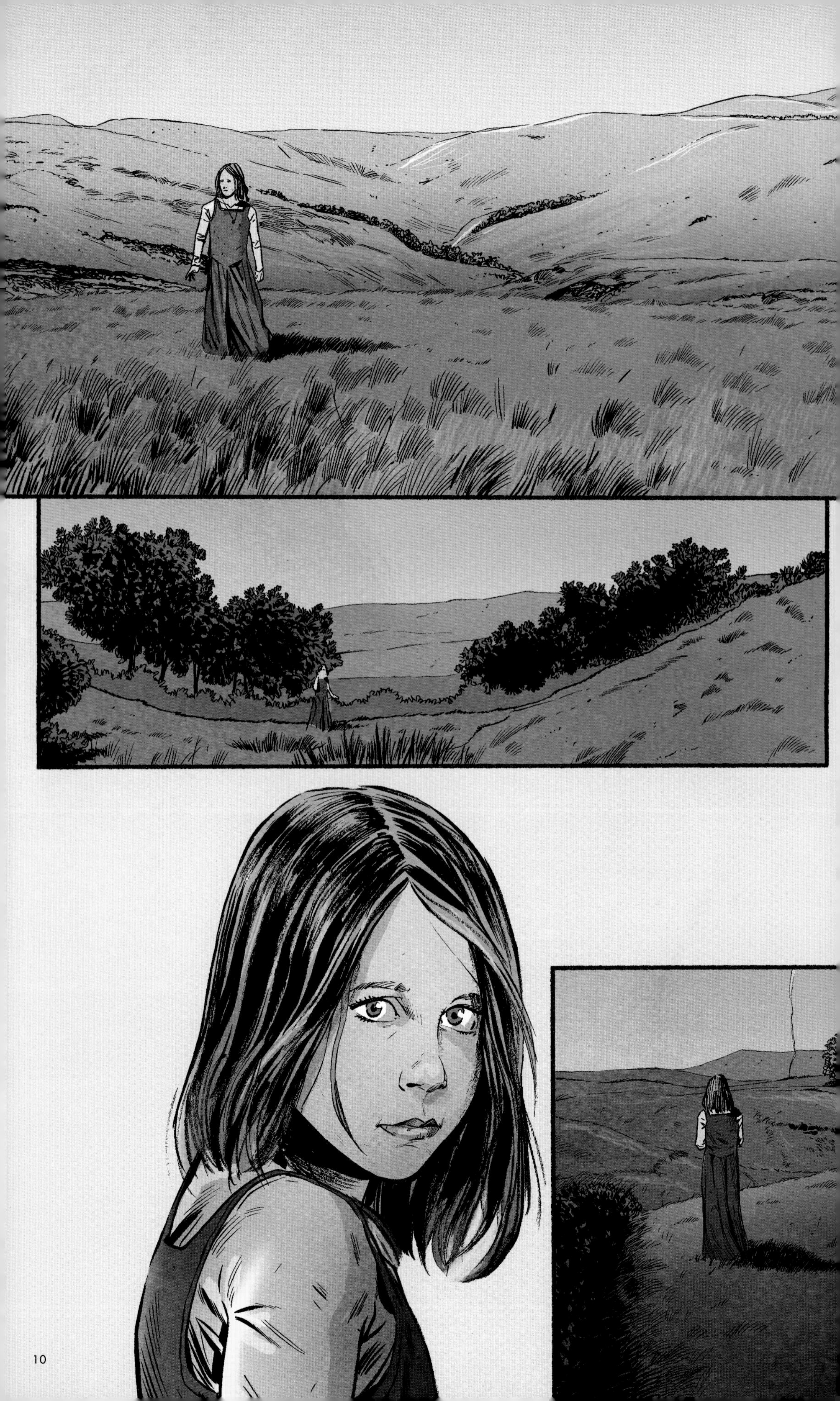

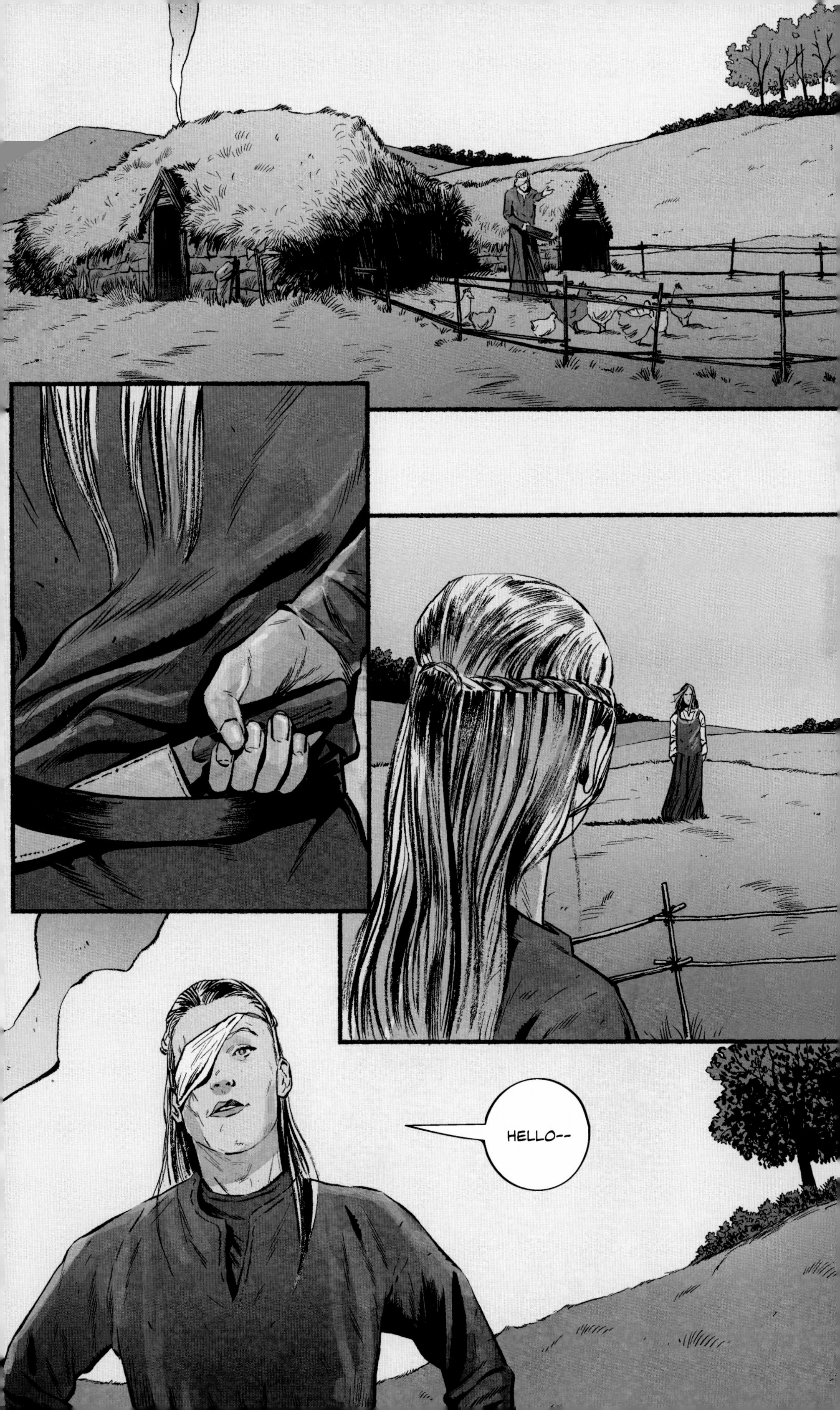
HELLO--

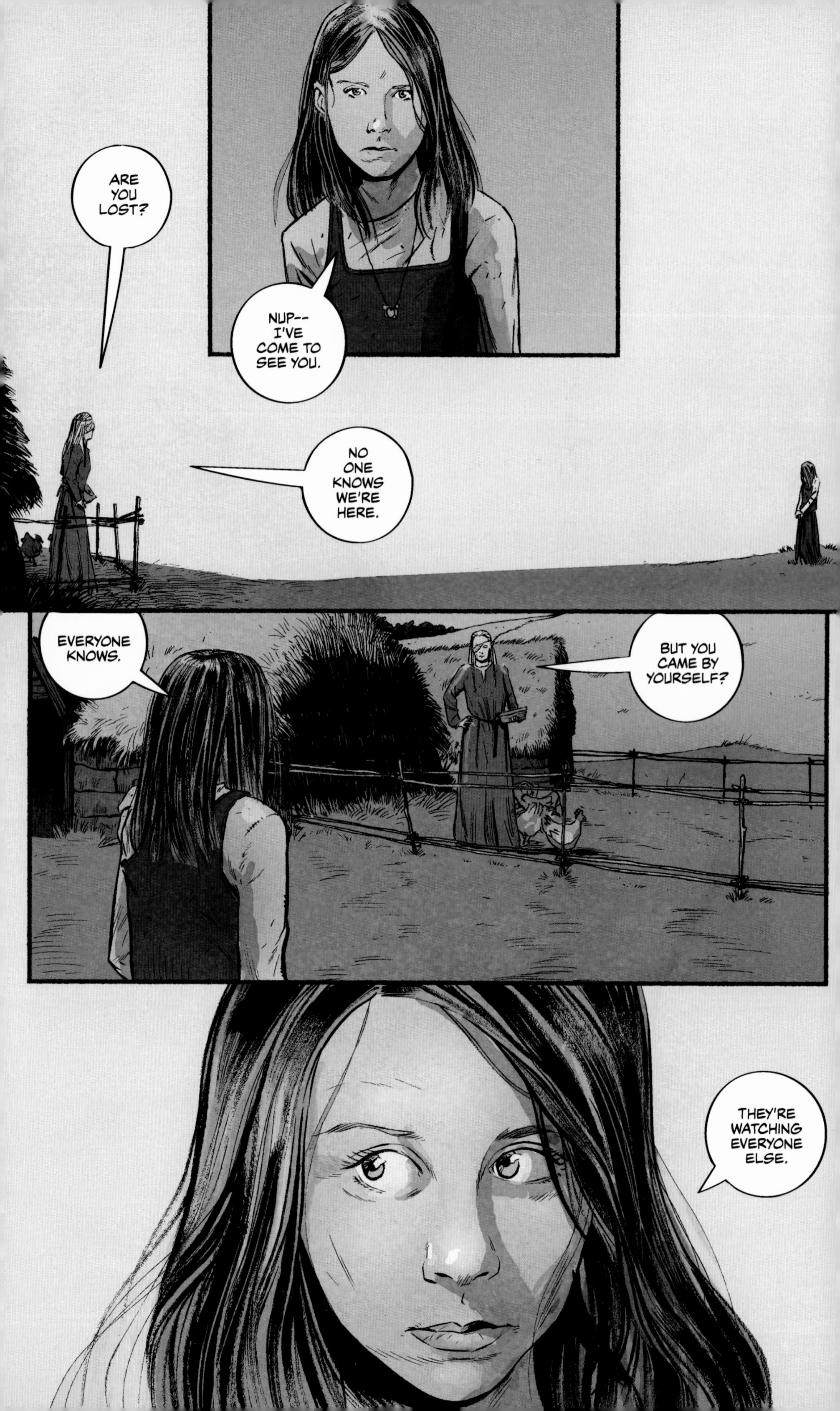
ARE YOU LOST?
NUP-- I'VE COME TO SEE YOU.
NO ONE KNOWS WE'RE HERE.
EVERYONE KNOWS.
BUT YOU CAME BY YOURSELF?
THEY'RE WATCHING EVERYONE ELSE.

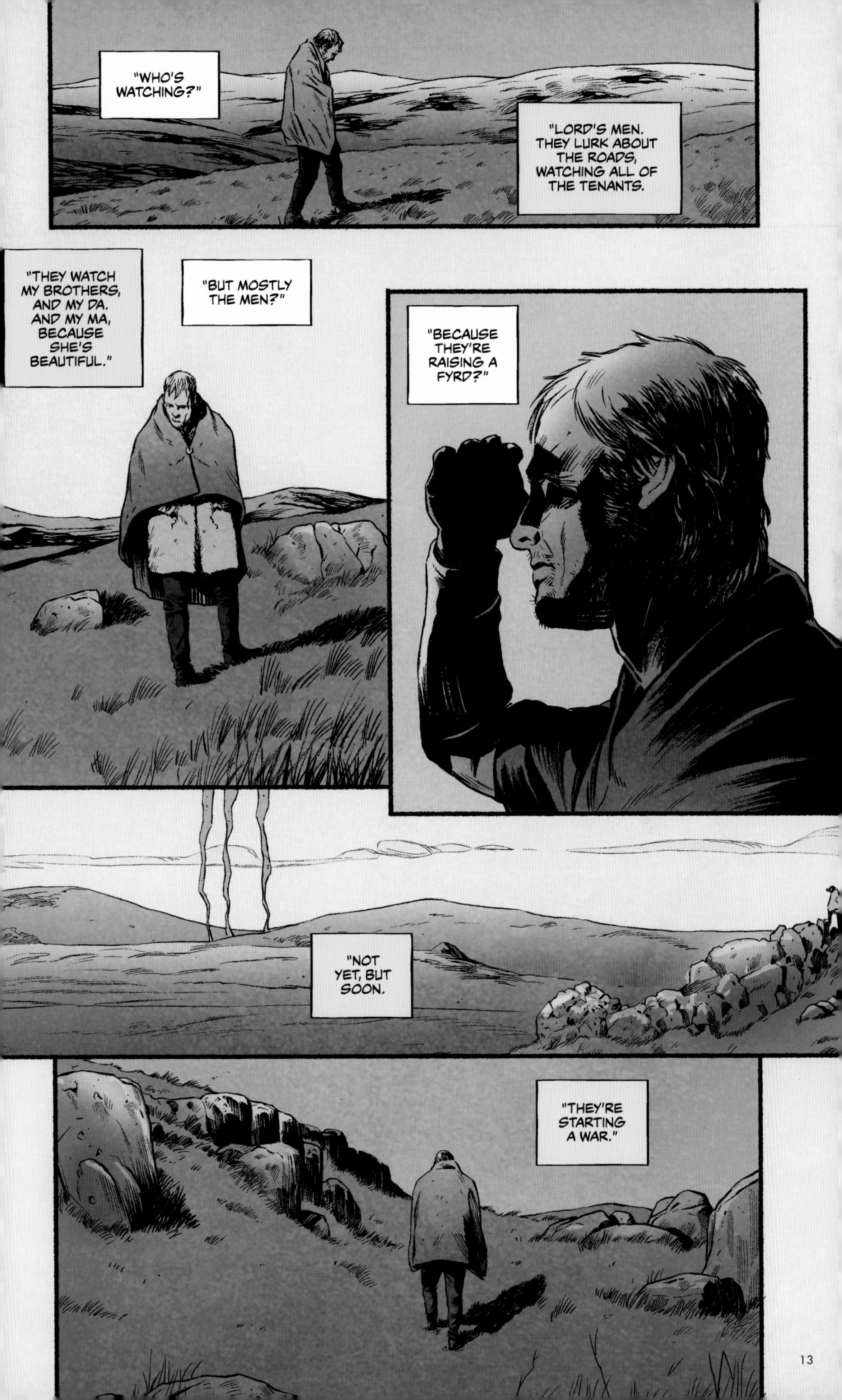
"WHO'S WATCHING?"
"LORD'S MEN. THEY LURK ABOUT THE ROADS, WATCHING ALL OF THE TENANTS.
"THEY WATCH MY BROTHERS, AND MY DA. AND MY MA, BECAUSE SHE'S BEAUTIFUL."
"BUT MOSTLY THE MEN?"
"BECAUSE THEY'RE RAISING A FYRD?"
"NOT YET, BUT SOON.
"THEY'RE STARTING A WAR."

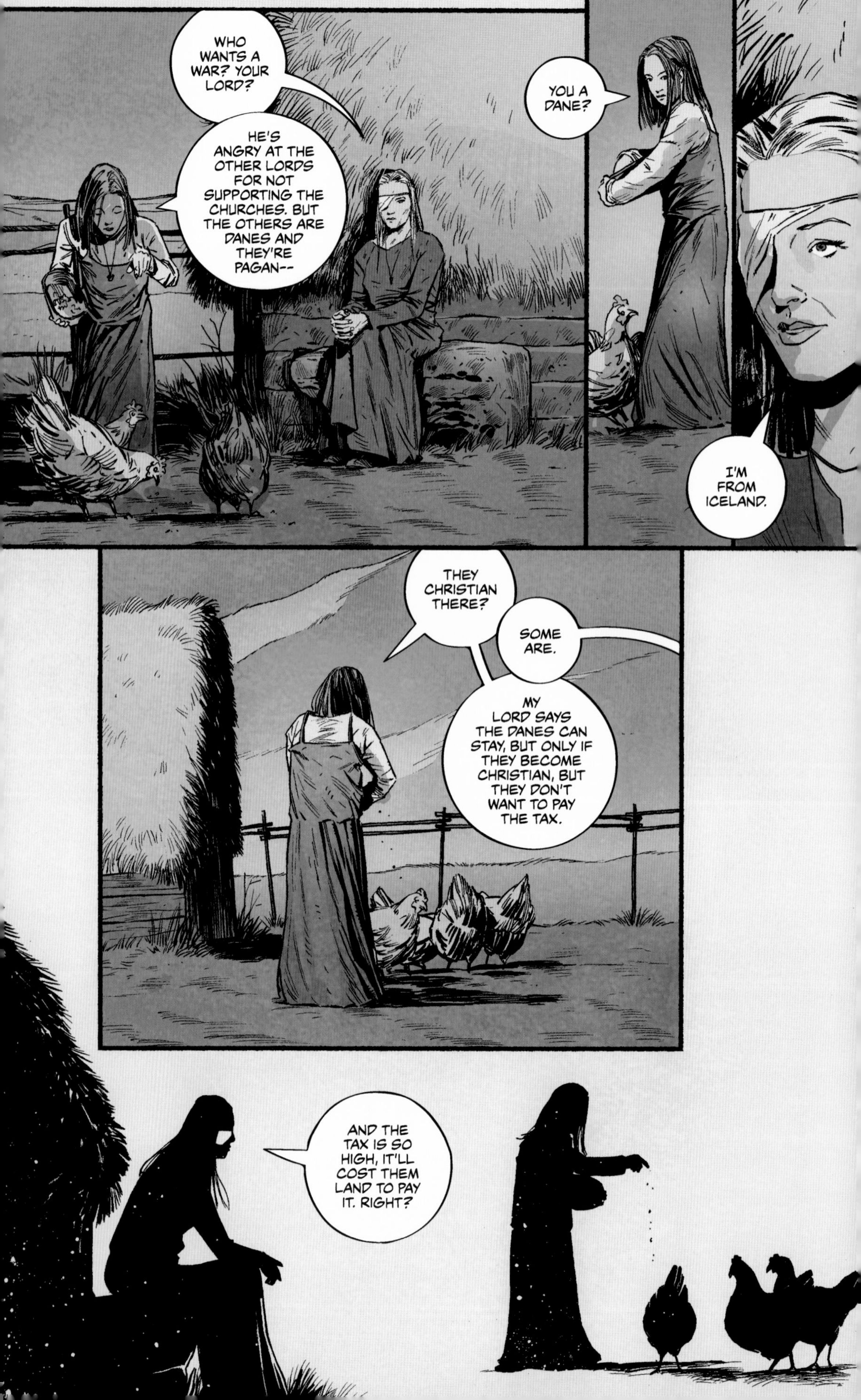
WHO WANTS A WAR? YOUR LORD?
HE'S ANGRY AT THE OTHER LORDS FOR NOT SUPPORTING THE CHURCHES. BUT THE OTHERS ARE DANES AND THEY'RE PAGAN--
YOU A DANE?
I'M FROM ICELAND.
THEY CHRISTIAN THERE?
SOME ARE.
MY LORD SAYS THE DANES CAN STAY, BUT ONLY IF THEY BECOME CHRISTIAN, BUT THEY DON'T WANT TO PAY THE TAX.
AND THE TAX IS SO HIGH, IT'LL COST THEM LAND TO PAY IT. RIGHT?

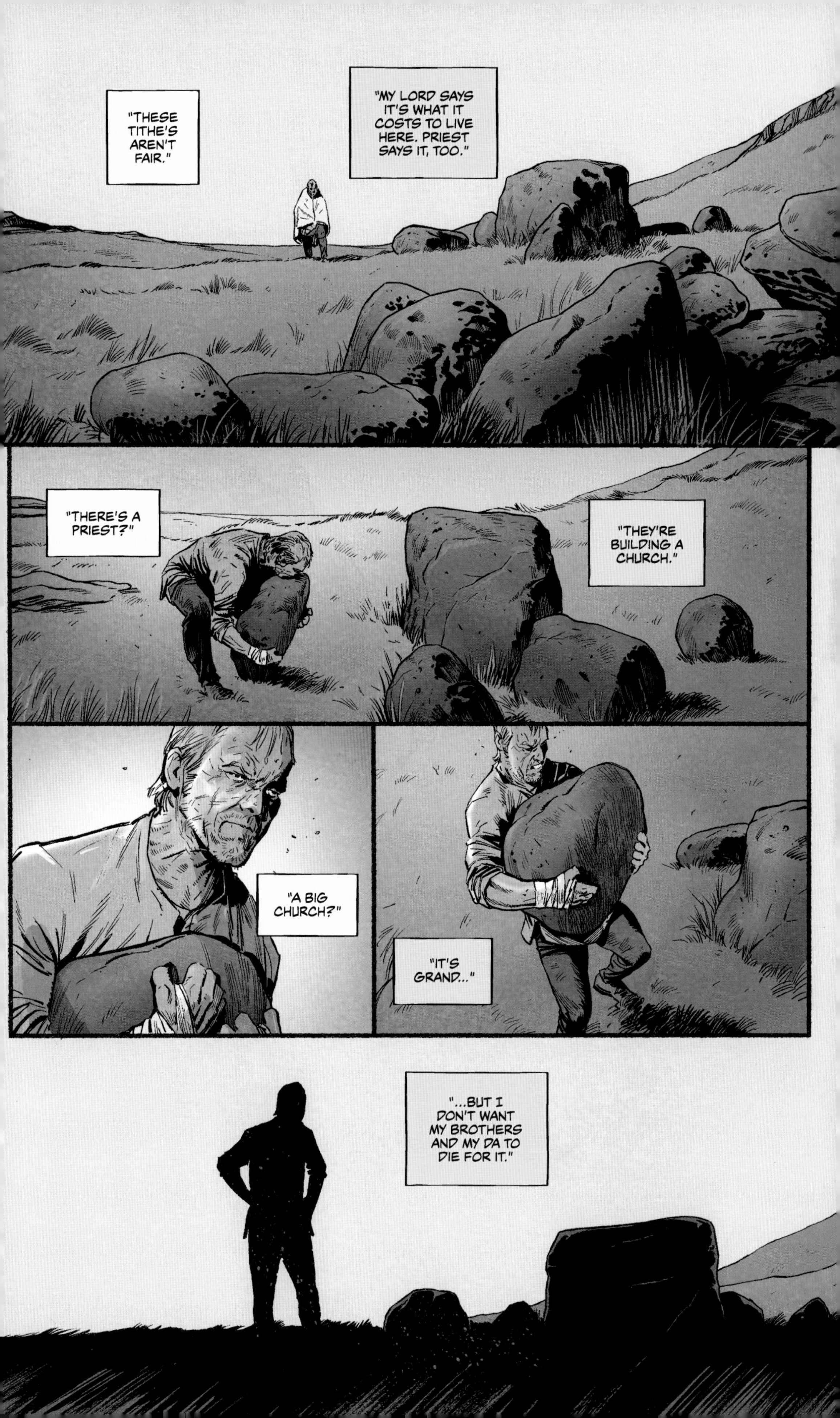
"THESE TITHE'S AREN'T FAIR."
"MY LORD SAYS IT'S WHAT IT COSTS TO LIVE HERE. PRIEST SAYS IT, TOO."
"THERE'S A PRIEST?"
"THEY'RE BUILDING A CHURCH."
"A BIG CHURCH?"
"IT'S GRAND..."
"...BUT I DON'T WANT MY BROTHERS AND MY DA TO DIE FOR IT."

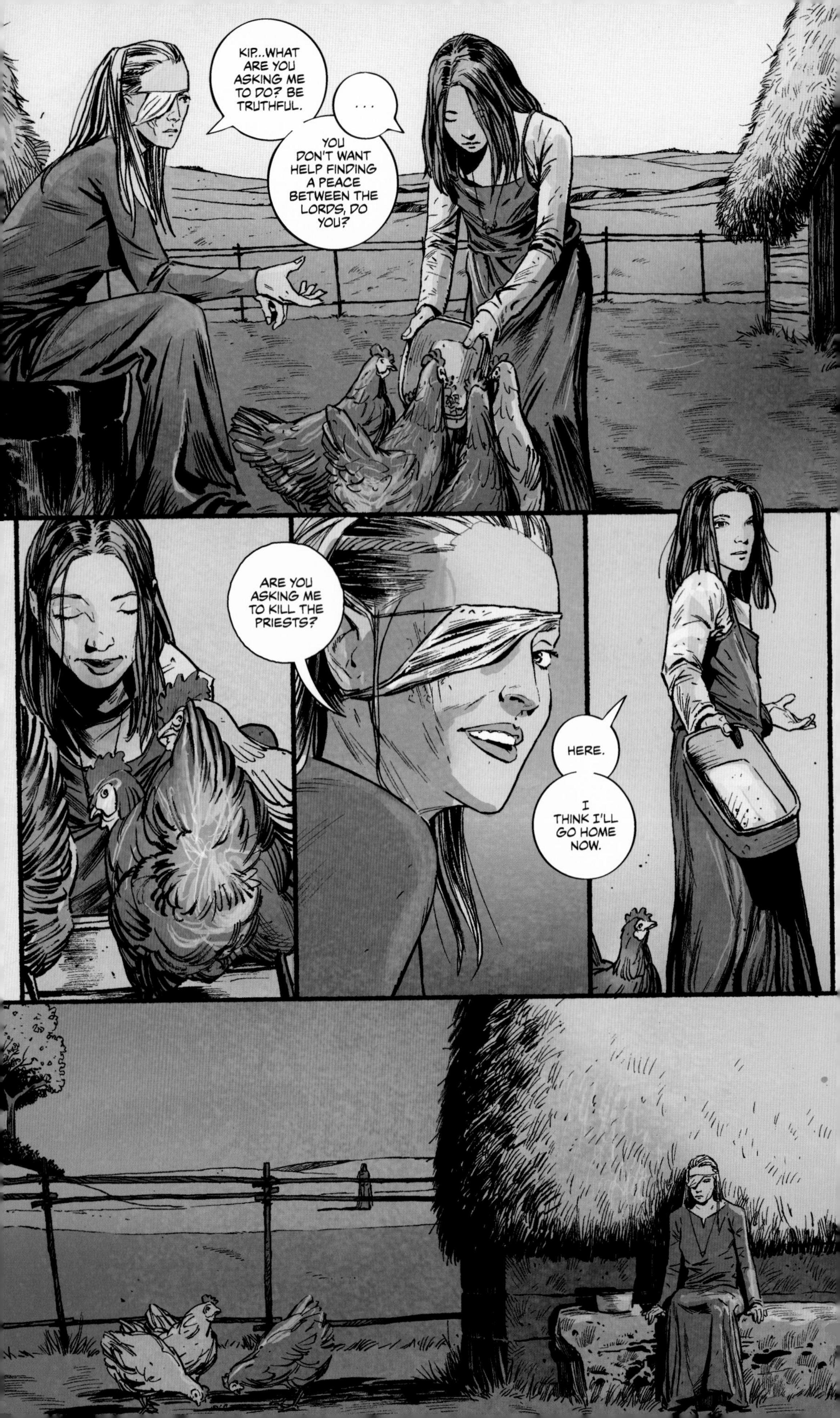
KIP...WHAT ARE YOU ASKING ME TO DO? BE TRUTHFUL.
. . .
YOU DON'T WANT HELP FINDING A PEACE BETWEEN THE LORDS, DO YOU?
ARE YOU ASKING ME TO KILL THE PRIESTS?
HERE.
I THINK I'LL GO HOME NOW.

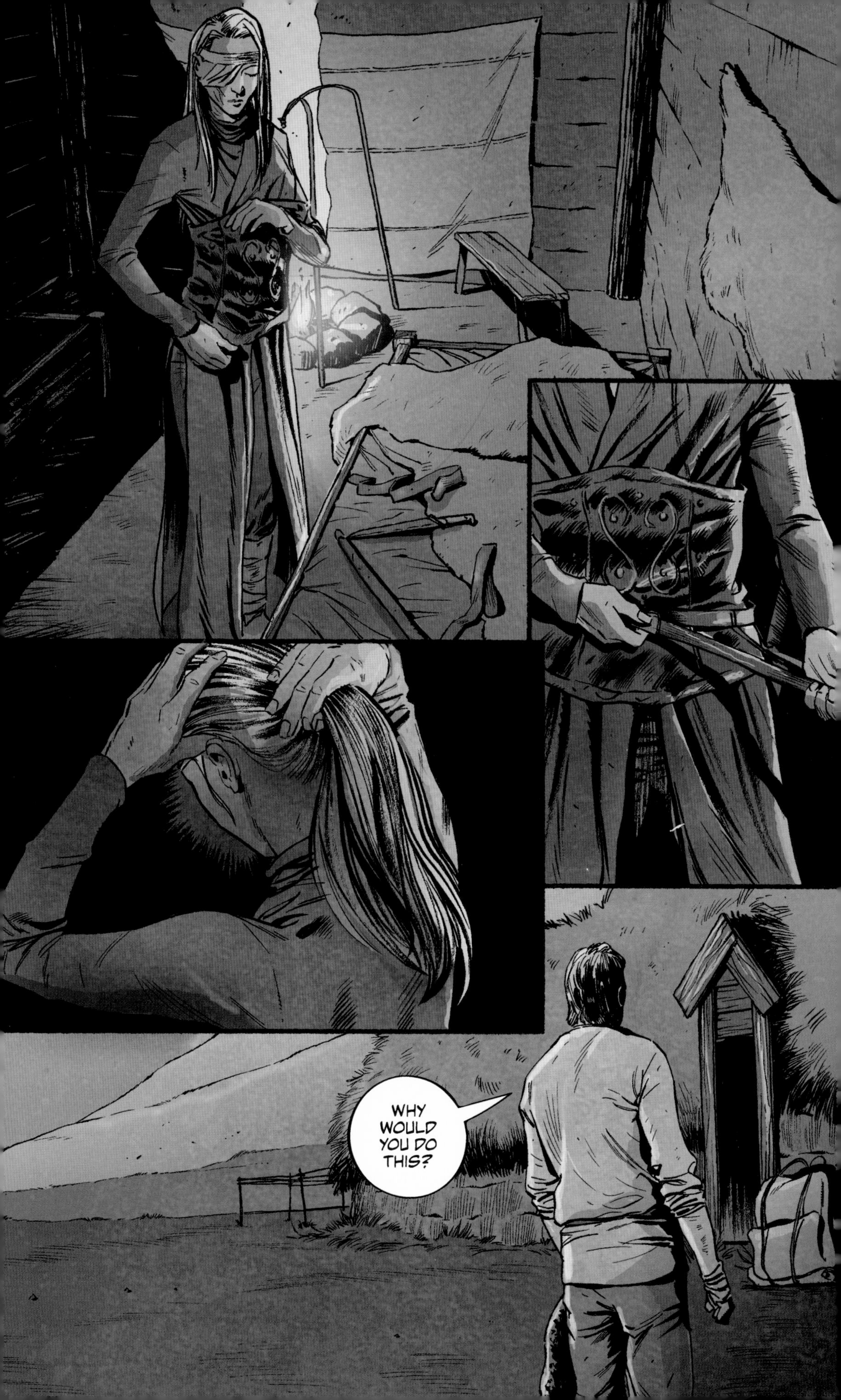
WHY WOULD YOU DO THIS?

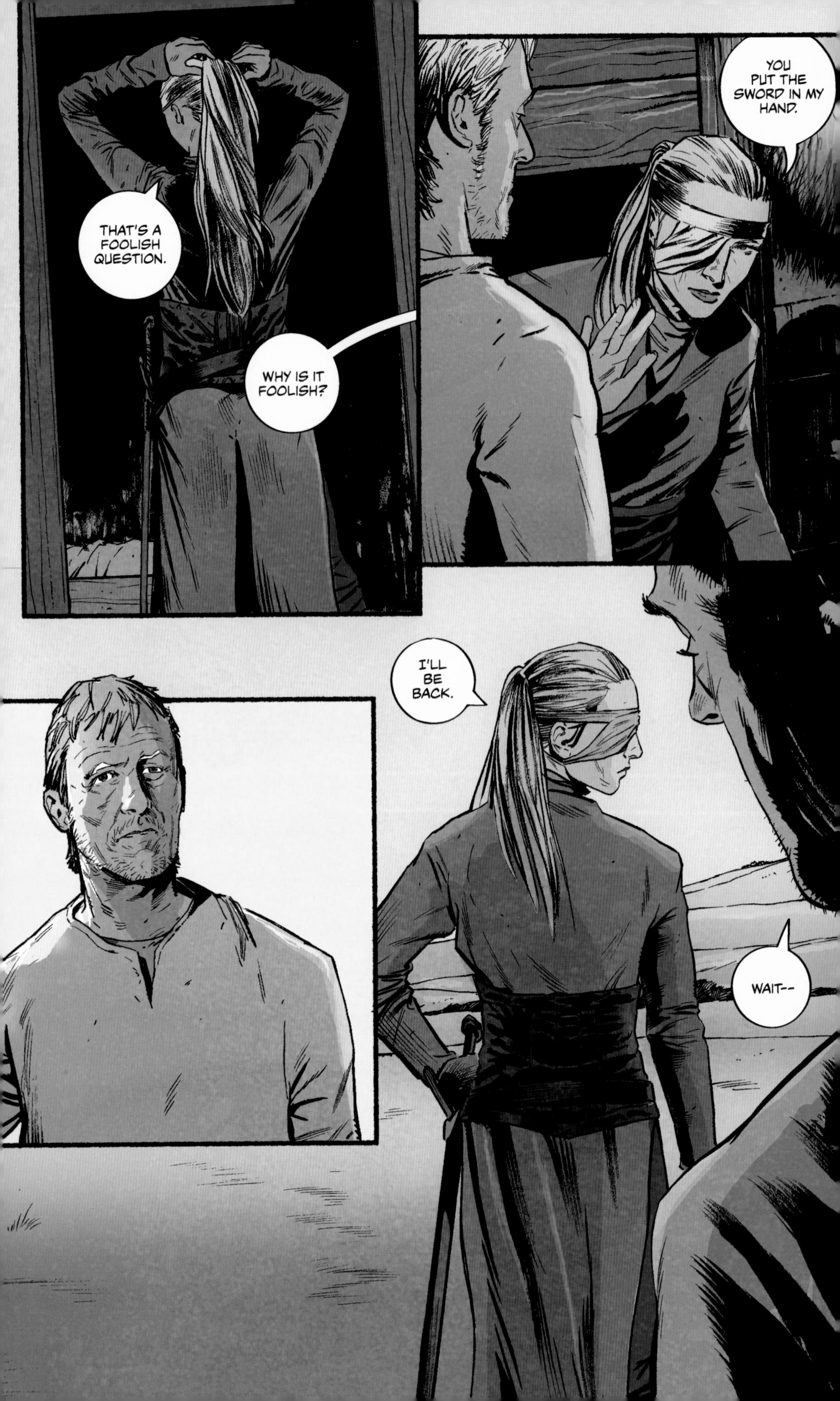
THAT'S A FOOLISH QUESTION.
WHY IS IT FOOLISH?
YOU PUT THE SWORD IN MY HAND.
I'LL BE BACK.
WAIT--

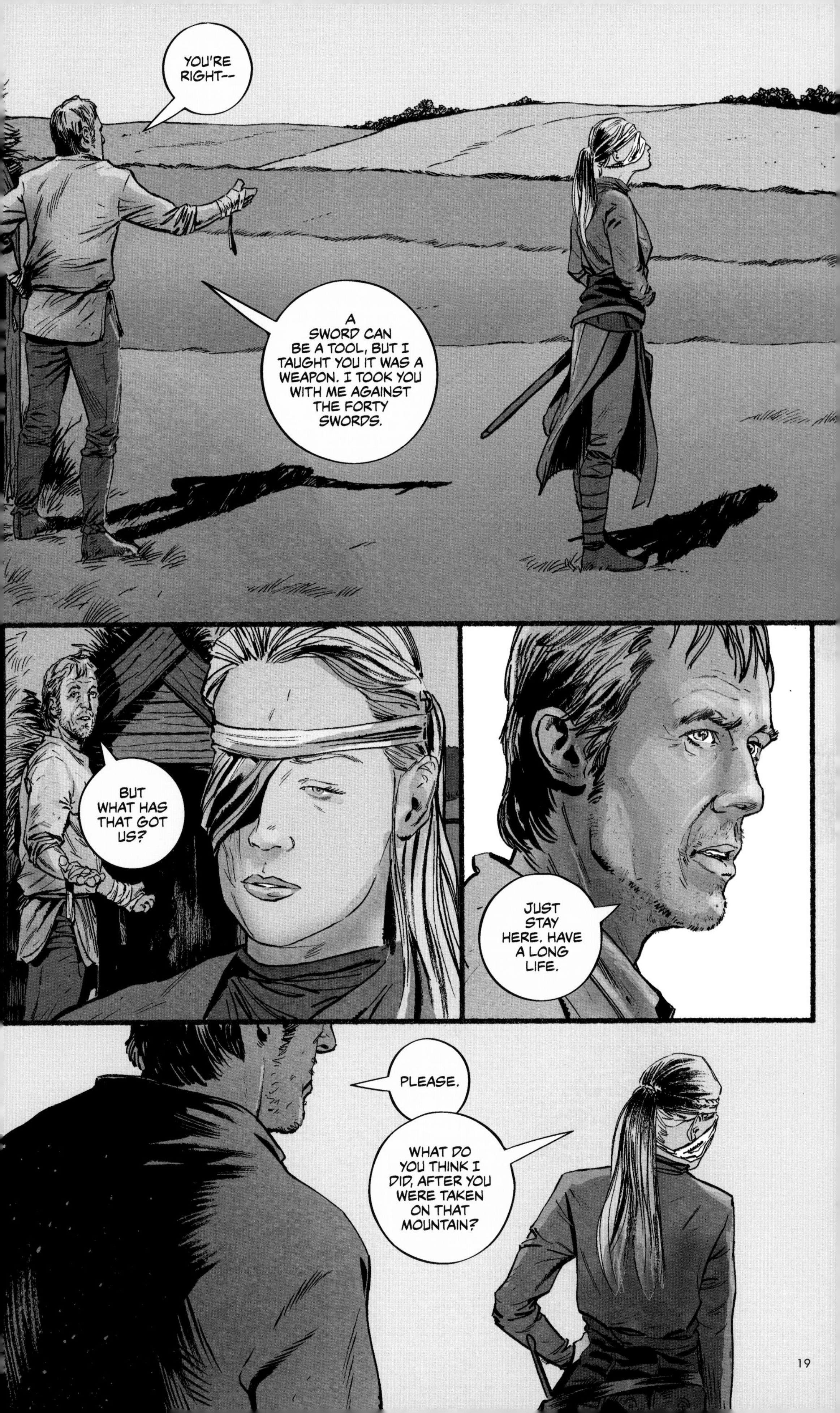
YOU'RE RIGHT--
A SWORD CAN BE A TOOL, BUT I TAUGHT YOU IT WAS A WEAPON. I TOOK YOU WITH ME AGAINST THE FORTY SWORDS.
BUT WHAT HAS THAT GOT US?
JUST STAY HERE. HAVE A LONG LIFE.
PLEASE.
WHAT DO YOU THINK I DID, AFTER YOU WERE TAKEN ON THAT MOUNTAIN?

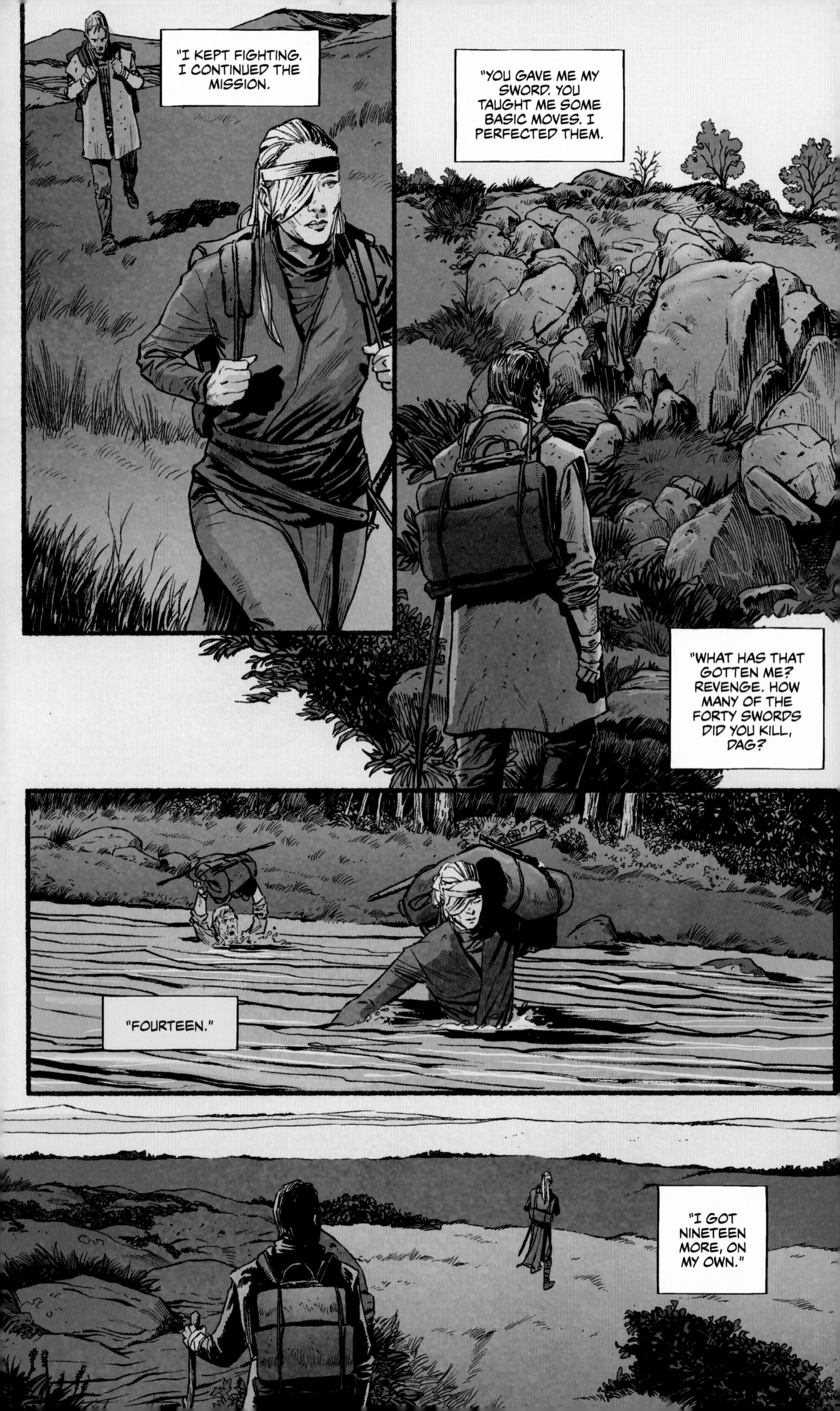
"I KEPT FIGHTING. I CONTINUED THE MISSION.
"YOU GAVE ME MY SWORD. YOU TAUGHT ME SOME BASIC MOVES. I PERFECTED THEM.
"WHAT HAS THAT GOTTEN ME? REVENGE. HOW MANY OF THE FORTY SWORDS DID YOU KILL, DAG?
"FOURTEEN."
"I GOT NINETEEN MORE, ON MY OWN."

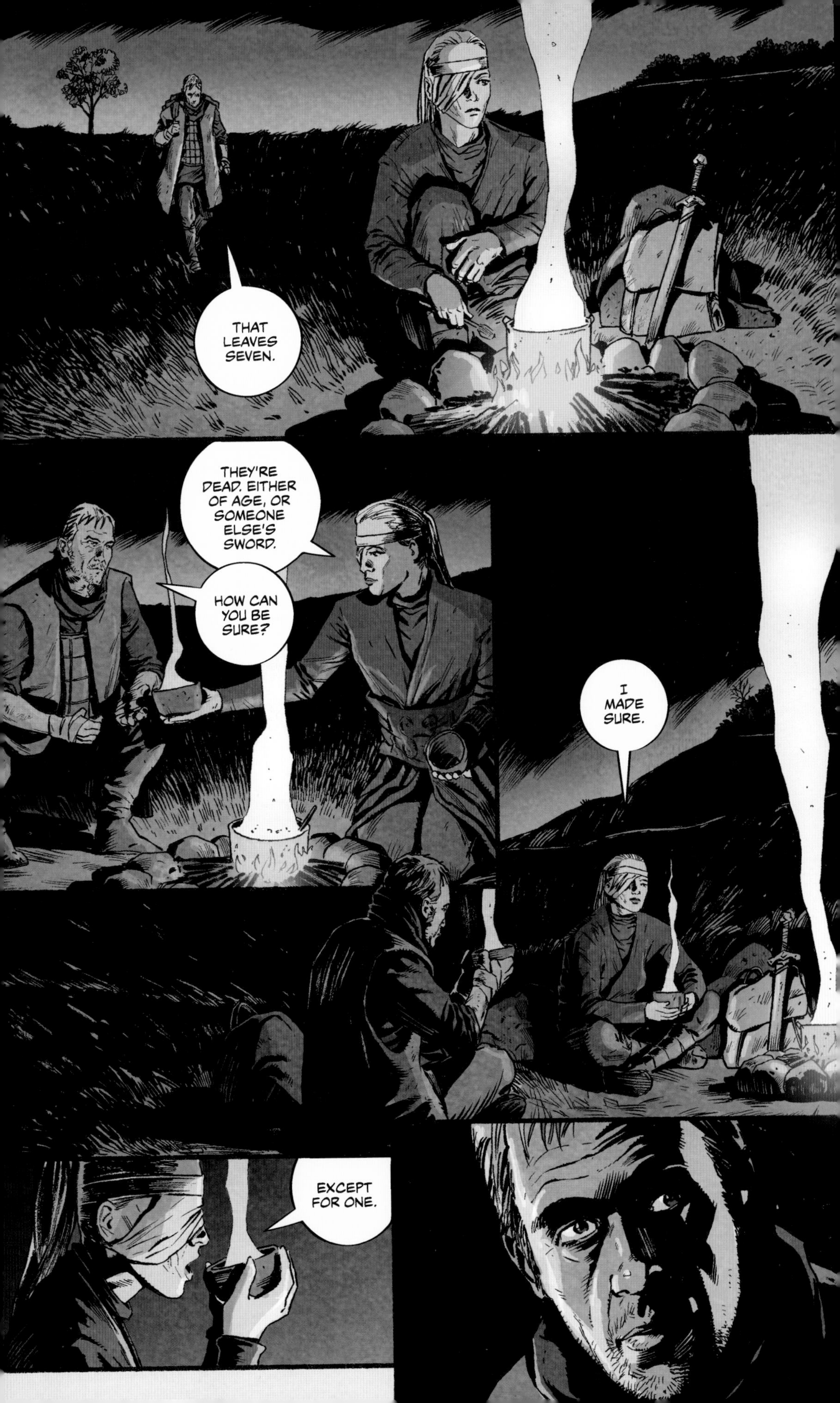
THAT LEAVES SEVEN.
THEY'RE DEAD. EITHER OF AGE, OR SOMEONE ELSE'S SWORD.
HOW CAN YOU BE SURE?
I MADE SURE.
EXCEPT FOR ONE.

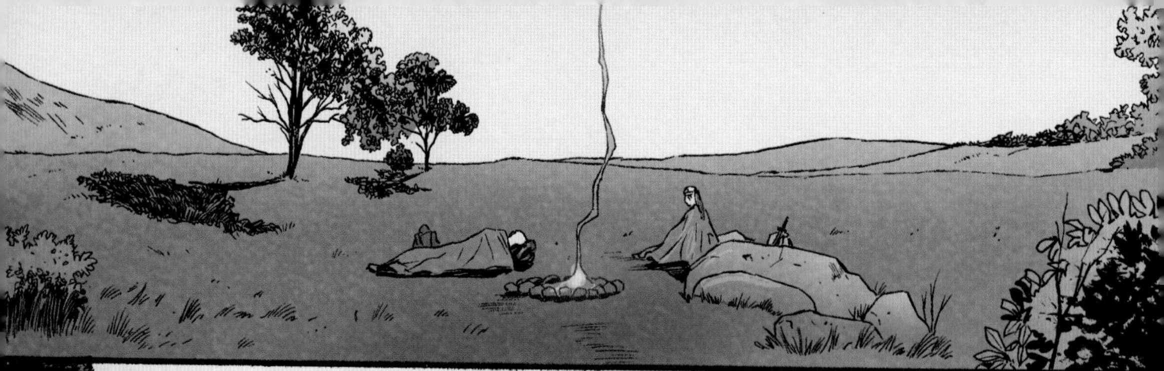

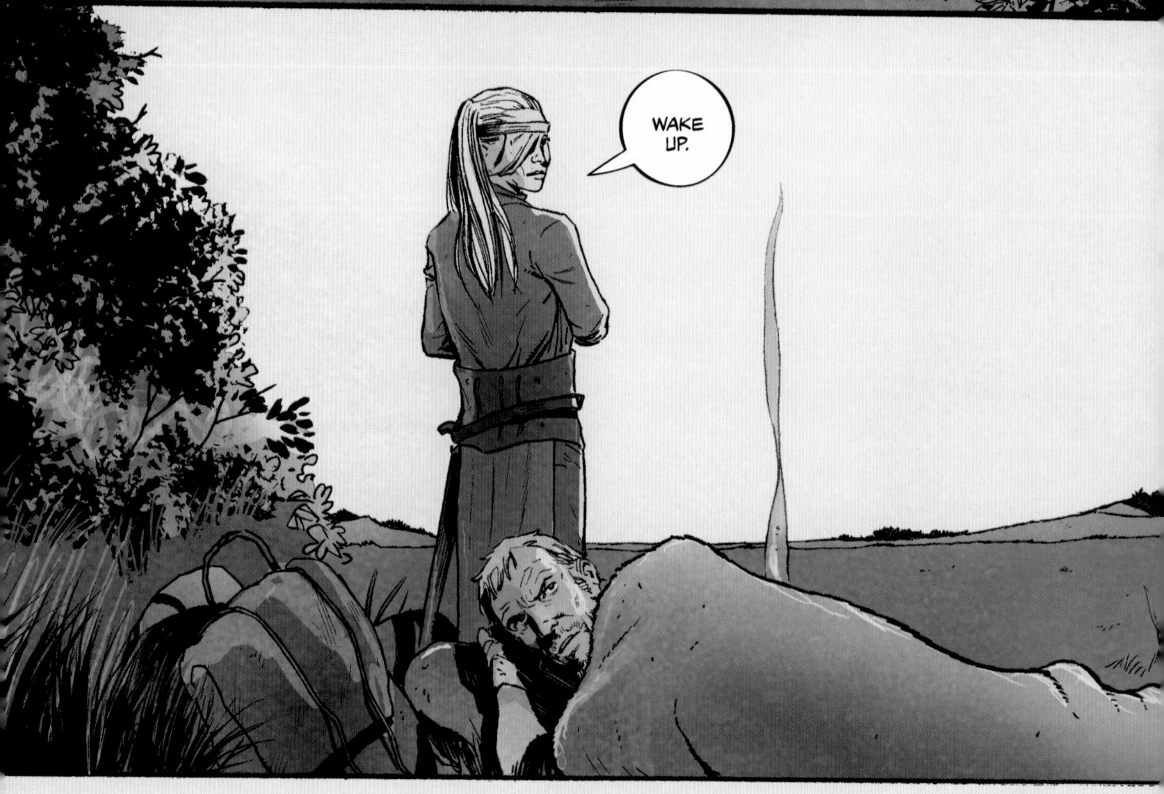
WAKE UP.

THE MOVING FINGER WRITES

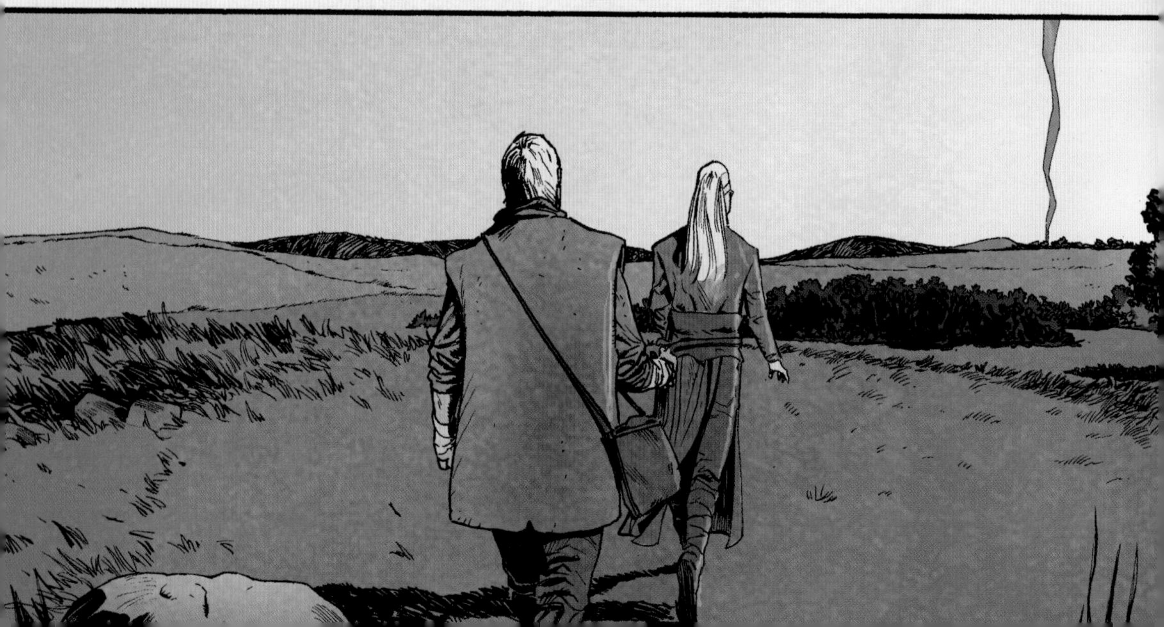

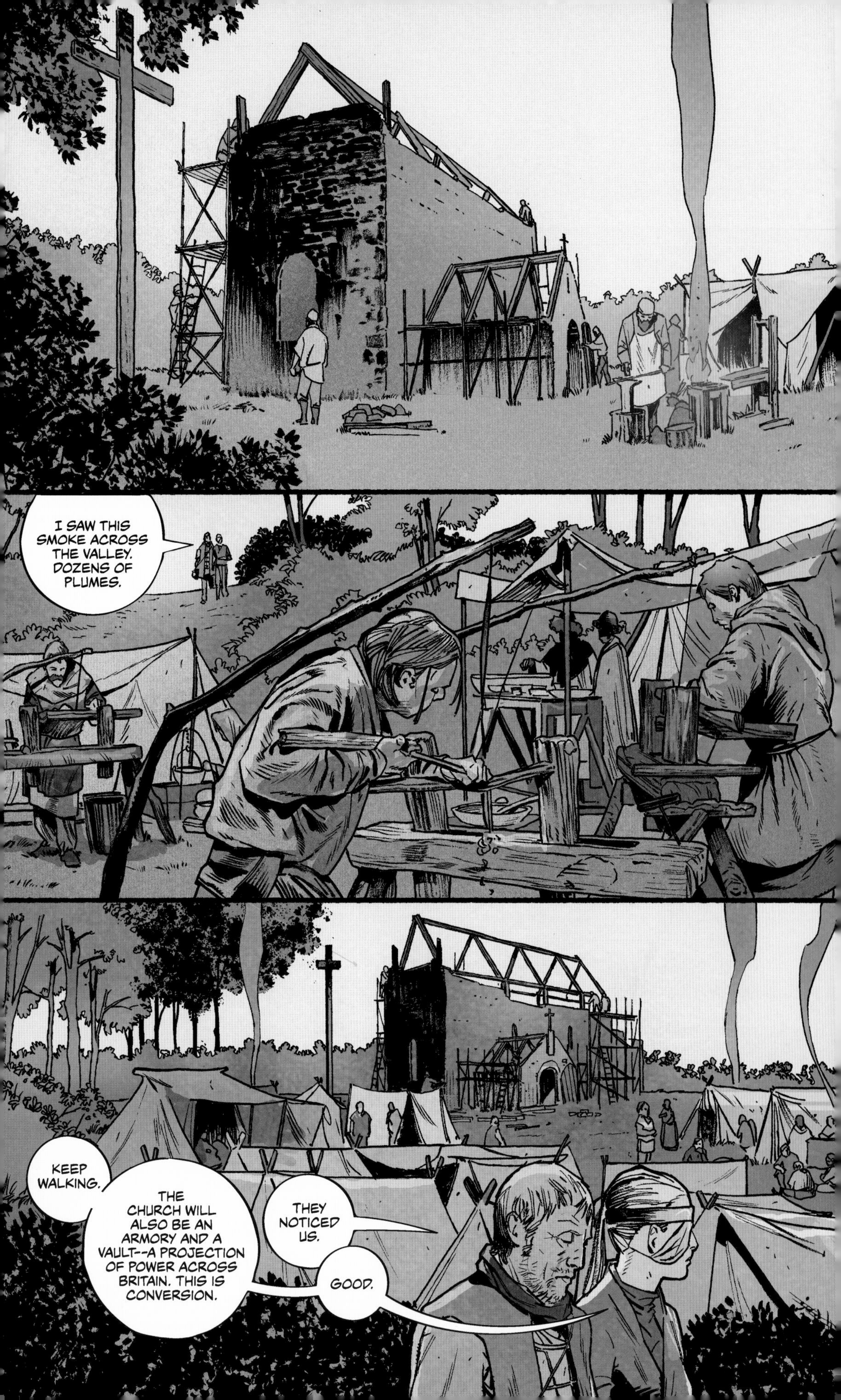
I SAW THIS SMOKE ACROSS THE VALLEY. DOZENS OF PLUMES.
KEEP WALKING.
THE CHURCH WILL ALSO BE AN ARMORY AND A VAULT--A PROJECTION OF POWER ACROSS BRITAIN. THIS IS CONVERSION.
THEY NOTICED US.
GOOD.

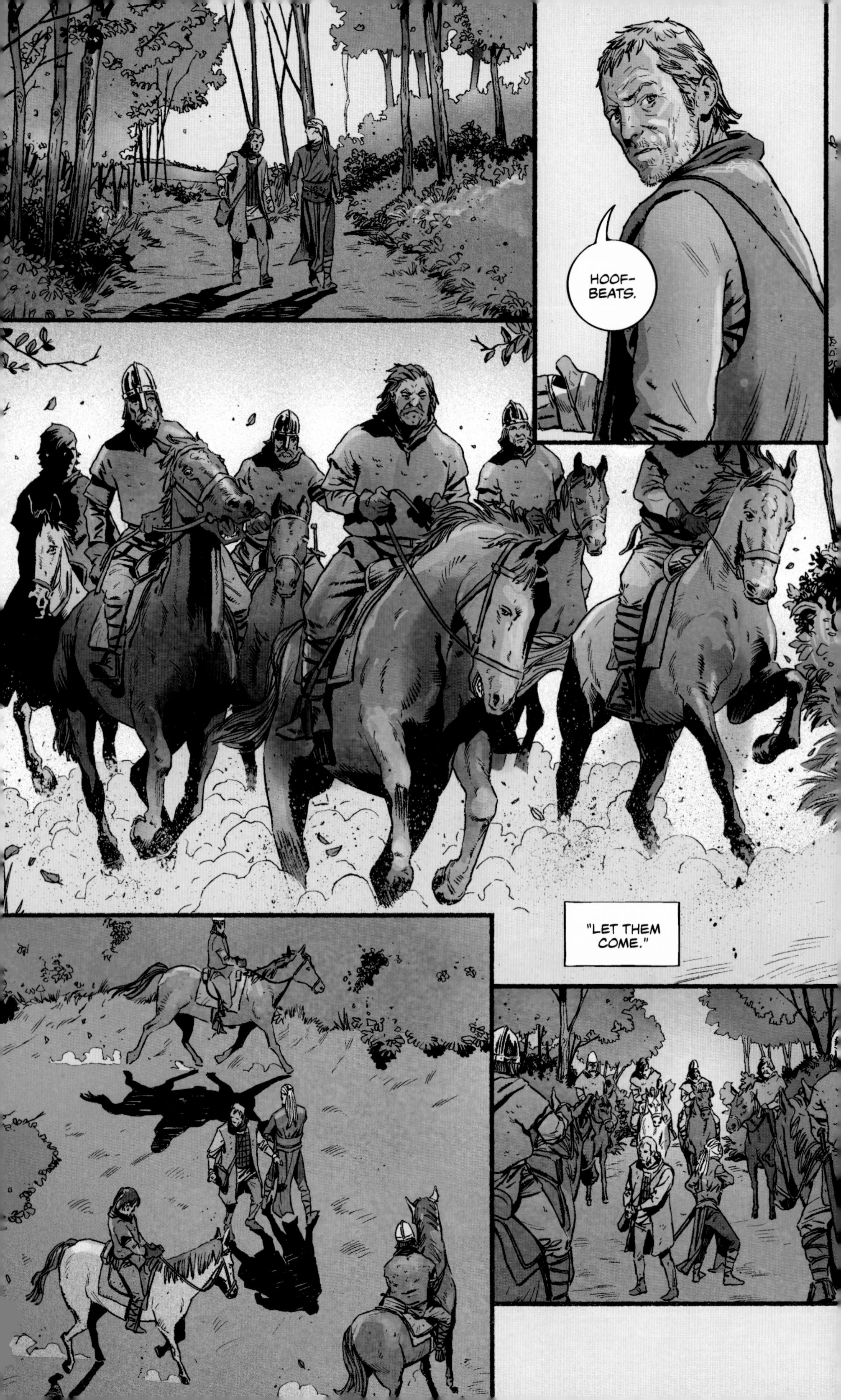
HOOF-
BEATS.
"LET THEM
COME."

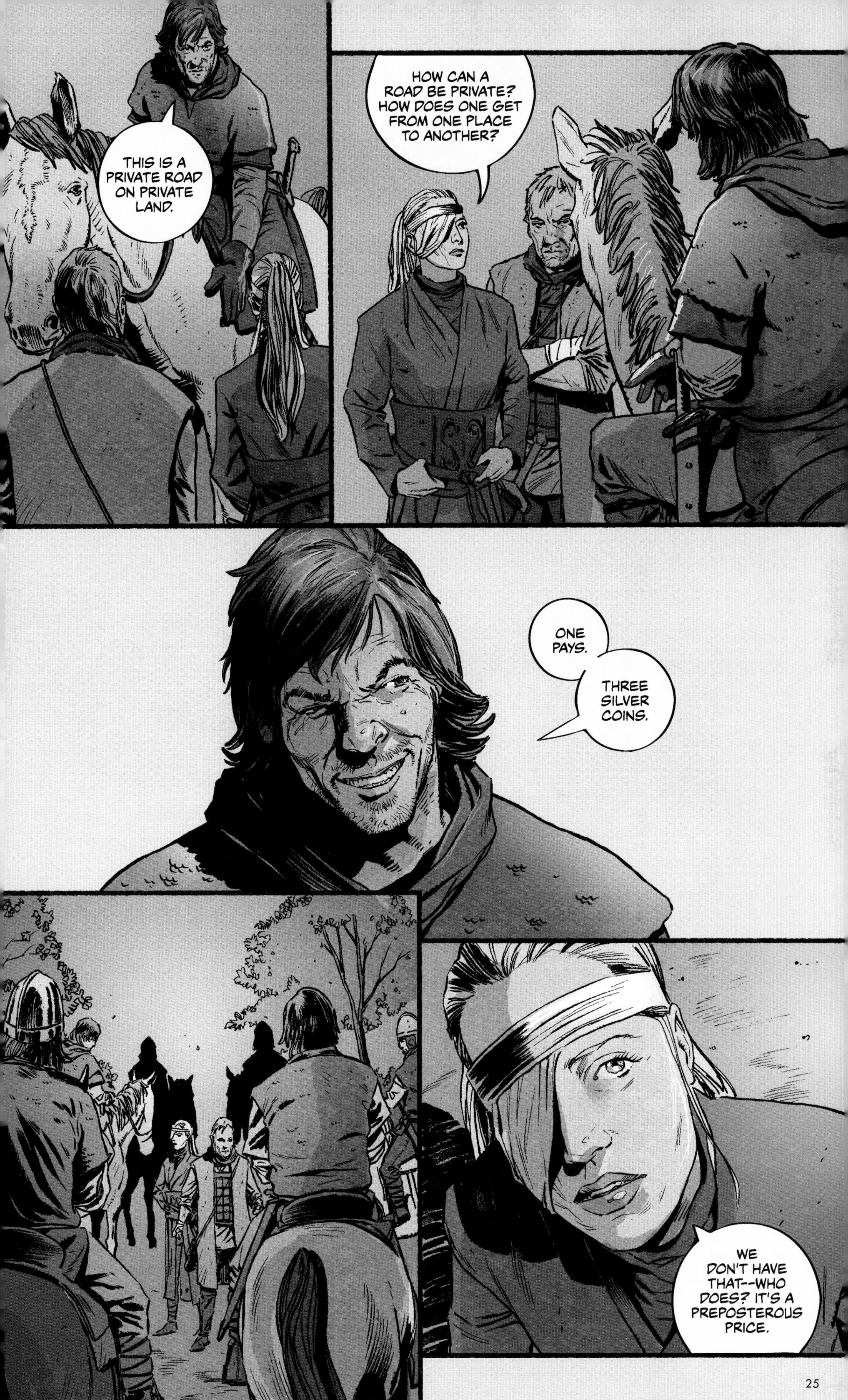
THIS IS A PRIVATE ROAD ON PRIVATE LAND.
HOW CAN A ROAD BE PRIVATE? HOW DOES ONE GET FROM ONE PLACE TO ANOTHER?
ONE PAYS.
THREE SILVER COINS.
WE DON'T HAVE THAT--WHO DOES? IT'S A PREPOSTEROUS PRICE.

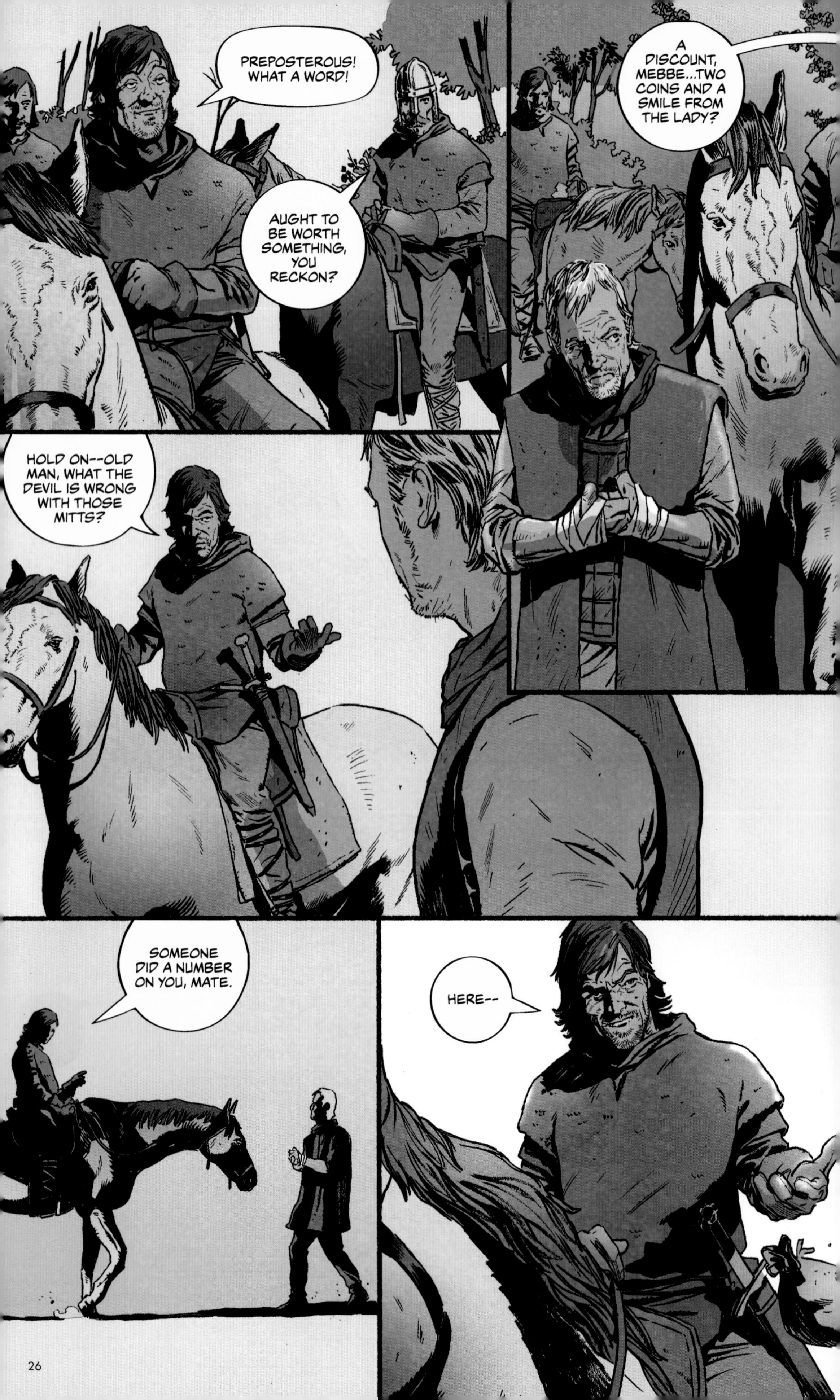
PREPOSTEROUS! WHAT A WORD!
AUGHT TO BE WORTH SOMETHING, YOU RECKON?
A DISCOUNT, MEBBE...TWO COINS AND A SMILE FROM THE LADY?
HOLD ON--OLD MAN, WHAT THE DEVIL IS WRONG WITH THOSE MITTS?
SOMEONE DID A NUMBER ON YOU, MATE.
HERE--

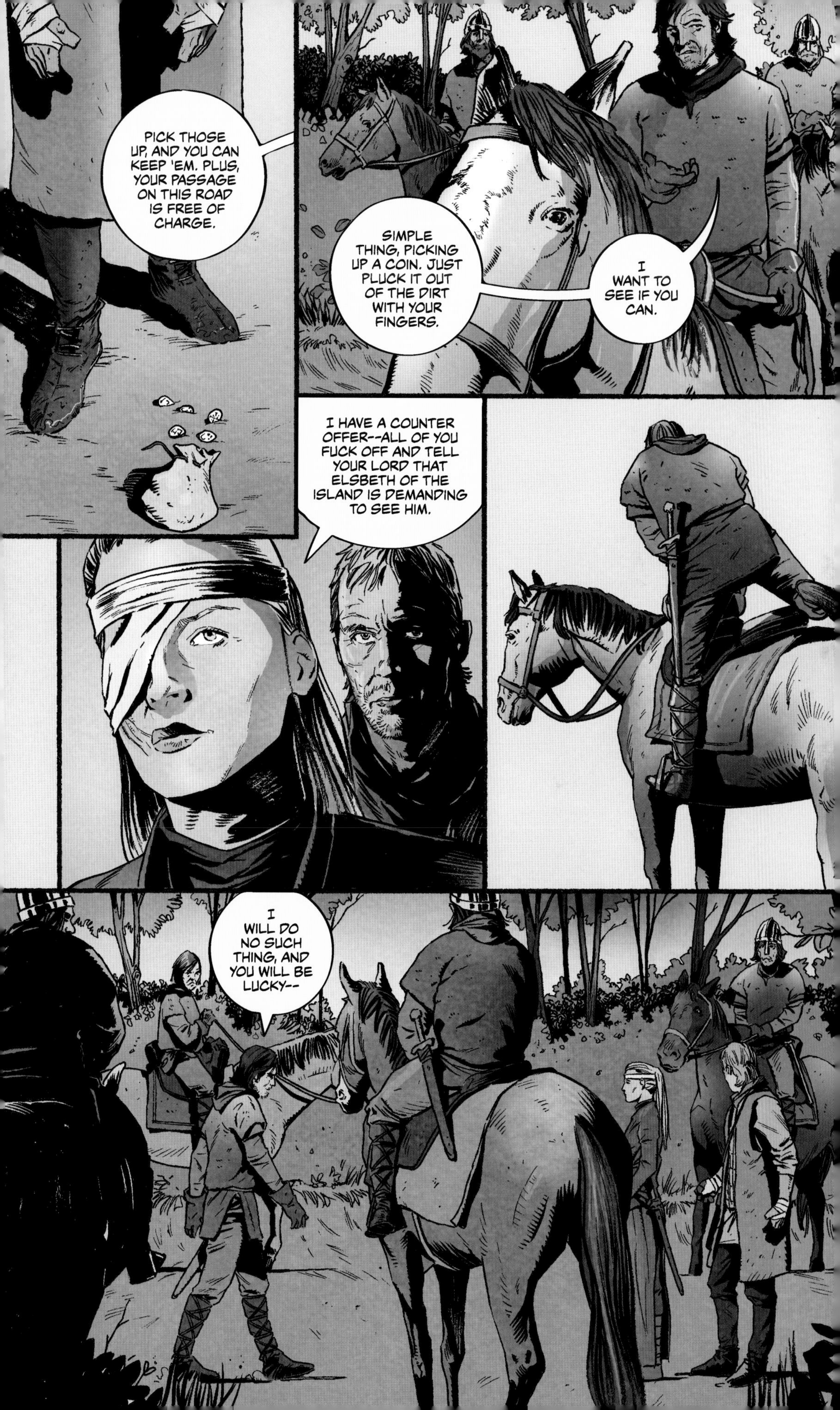
PICK THOSE UP, AND YOU CAN KEEP 'EM. PLUS, YOUR PASSAGE ON THIS ROAD IS FREE OF CHARGE.
SIMPLE THING, PICKING UP A COIN. JUST PLUCK IT OUT OF THE DIRT WITH YOUR FINGERS.
I WANT TO SEE IF YOU CAN.
I HAVE A COUNTER OFFER--ALL OF YOU FUCK OFF AND TELL YOUR LORD THAT ELSBETH OF THE ISLAND IS DEMANDING TO SEE HIM.
I WILL DO NO SUCH THING, AND YOU WILL BE LUCKY--

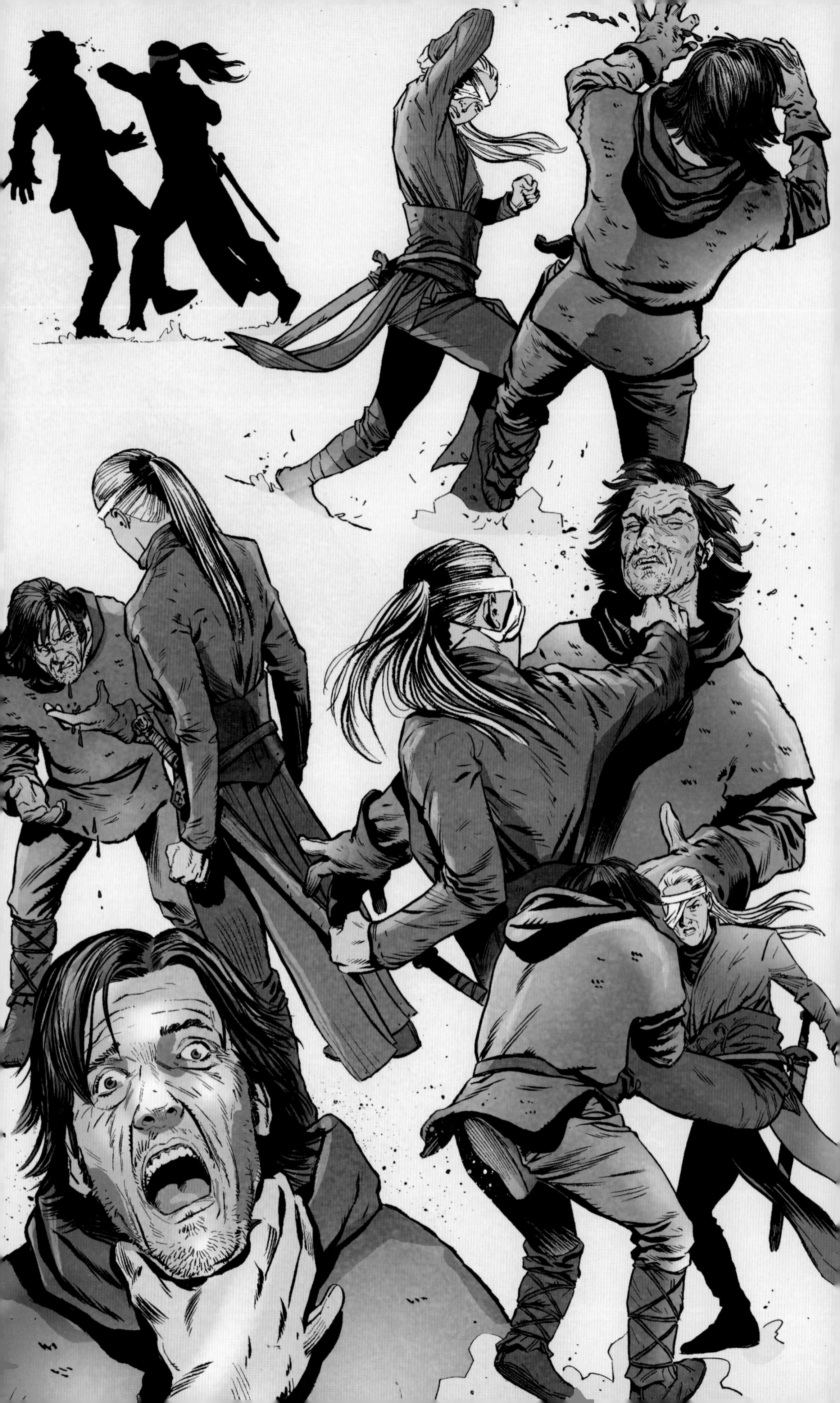

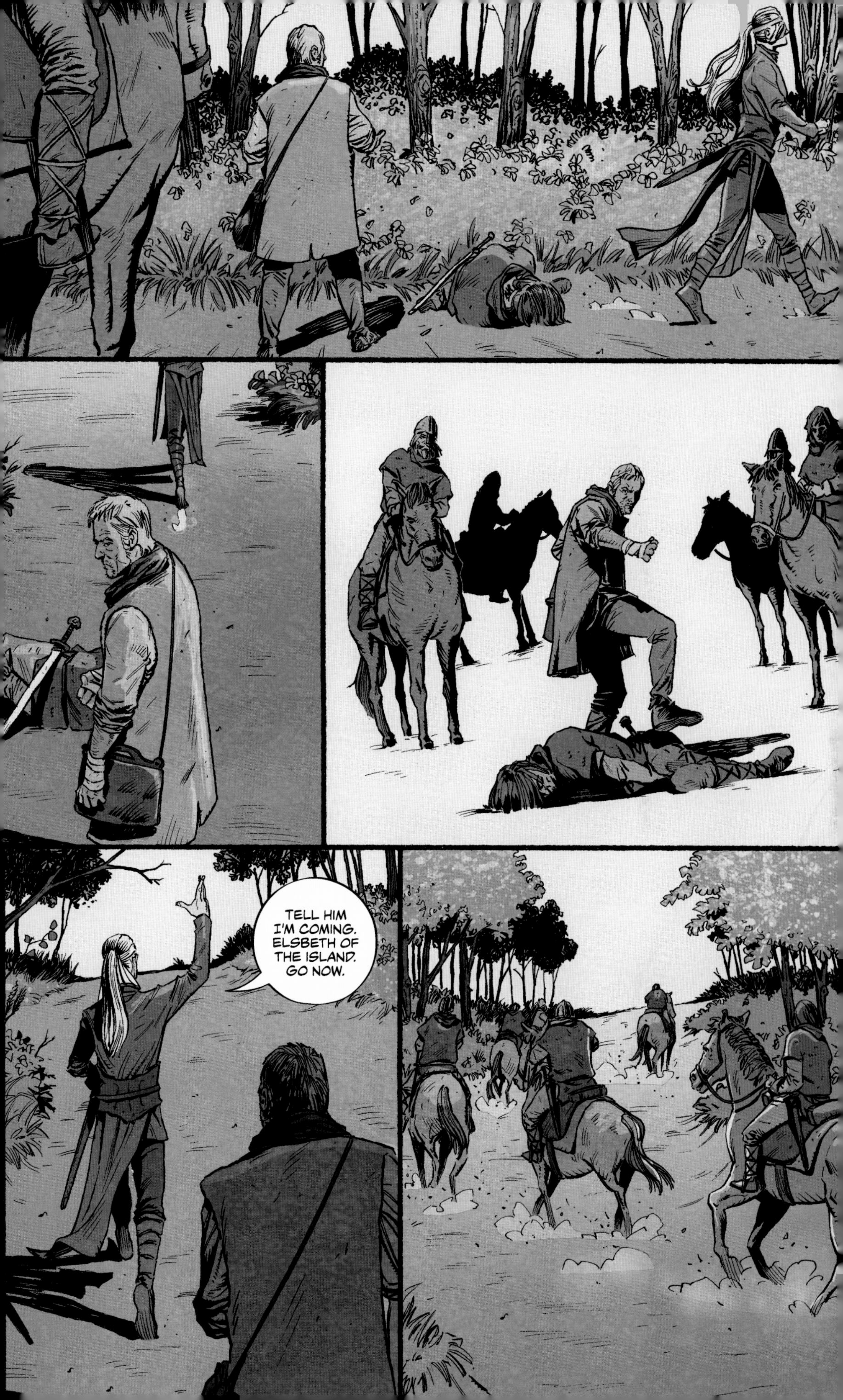
TELL HIM I'M COMING. ELSBETH OF THE ISLAND. GO NOW.

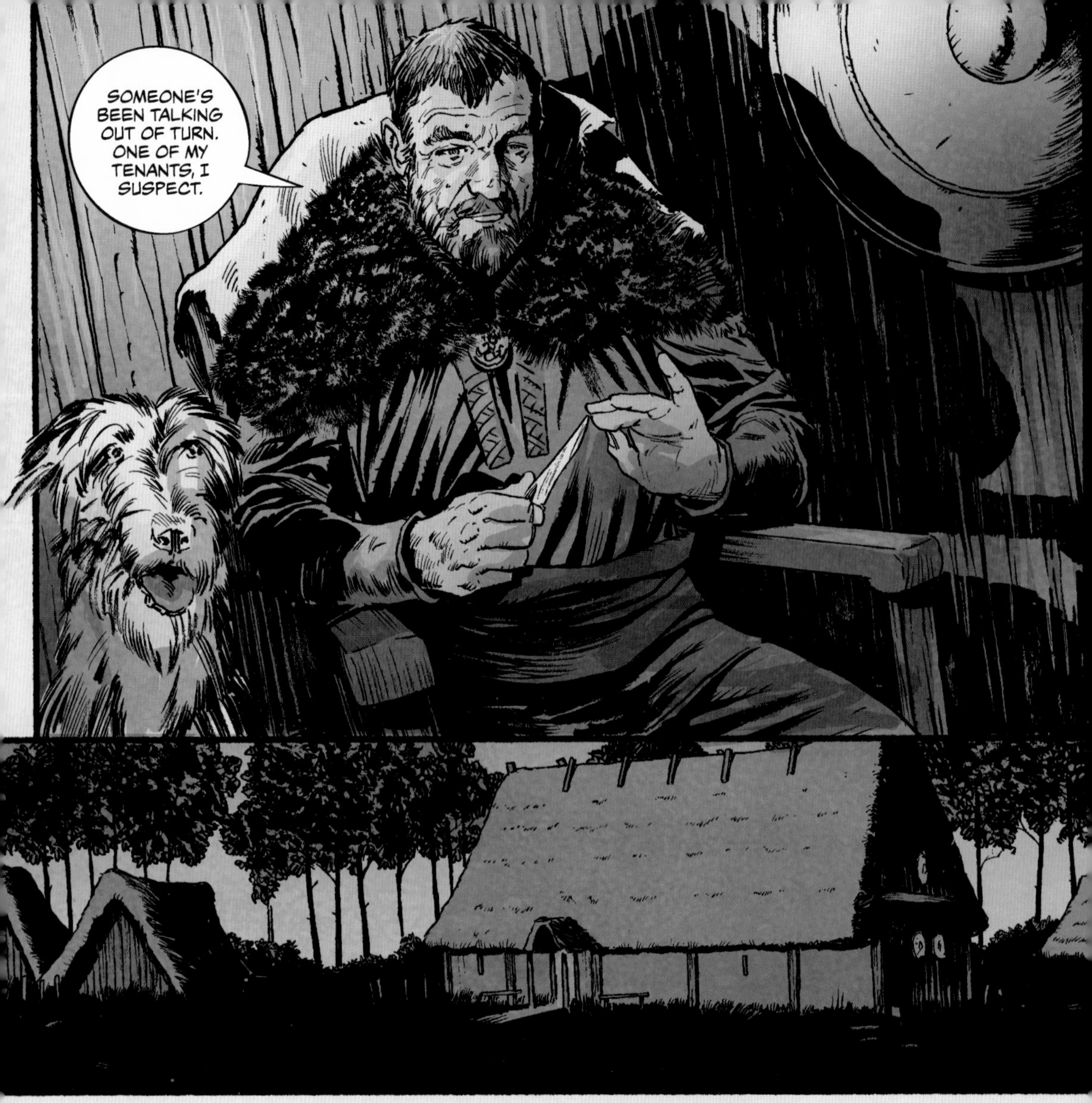
SOMEONE'S BEEN TALKING OUT OF TURN. ONE OF MY TENANTS, I SUSPECT.

THE HOUND OF THE VALLEY

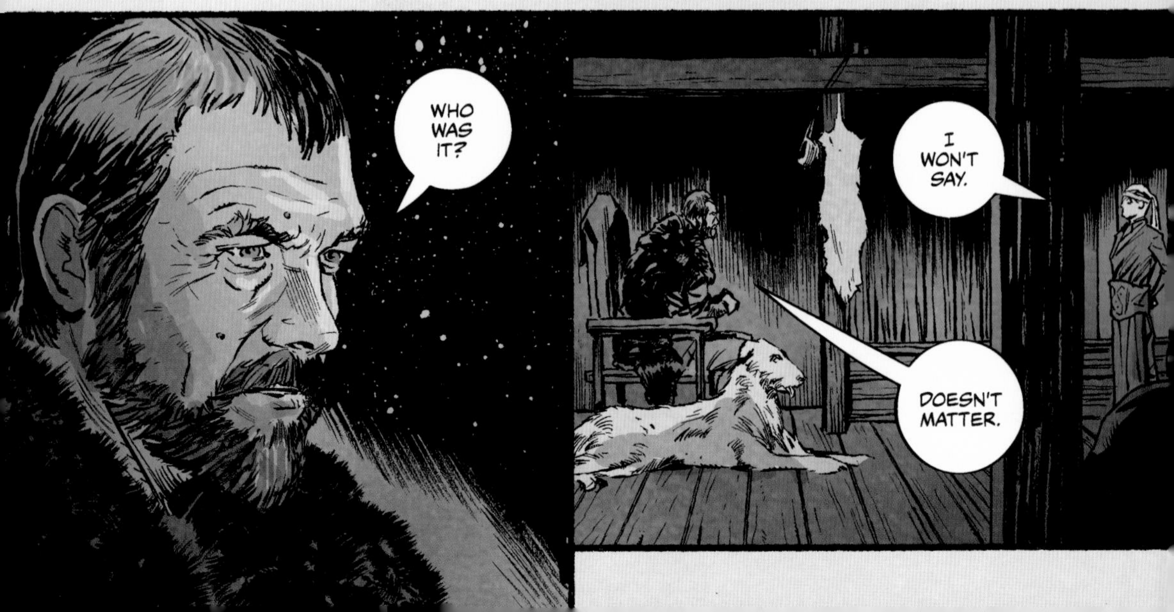
WHO WAS IT?
I WON'T SAY.
DOESN'T MATTER.

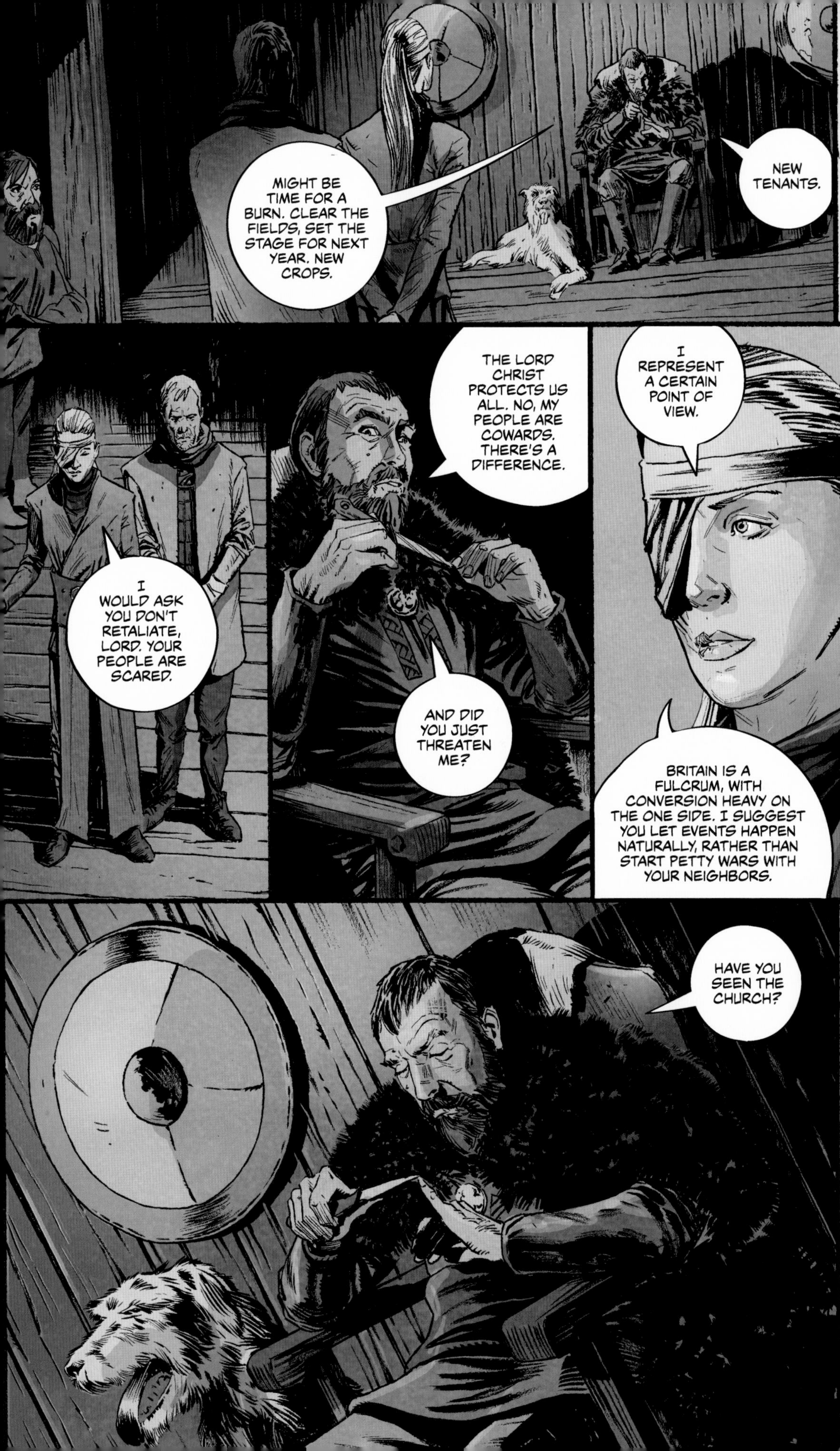

MIGHT BE TIME FOR A BURN. CLEAR THE FIELDS, SET THE STAGE FOR NEXT YEAR. NEW CROPS.
NEW TENANTS.
I WOULD ASK YOU DON'T RETALIATE, LORD. YOUR PEOPLE ARE SCARED.
THE LORD CHRIST PROTECTS US ALL. NO, MY PEOPLE ARE COWARDS. THERE'S A DIFFERENCE.
AND DID YOU JUST THREATEN ME?
I REPRESENT A CERTAIN POINT OF VIEW.
BRITAIN IS A FULCRUM, WITH CONVERSION HEAVY ON THE ONE SIDE. I SUGGEST YOU LET EVENTS HAPPEN NATURALLY, RATHER THAN START PETTY WARS WITH YOUR NEIGHBORS.
HAVE YOU SEEN THE CHURCH?

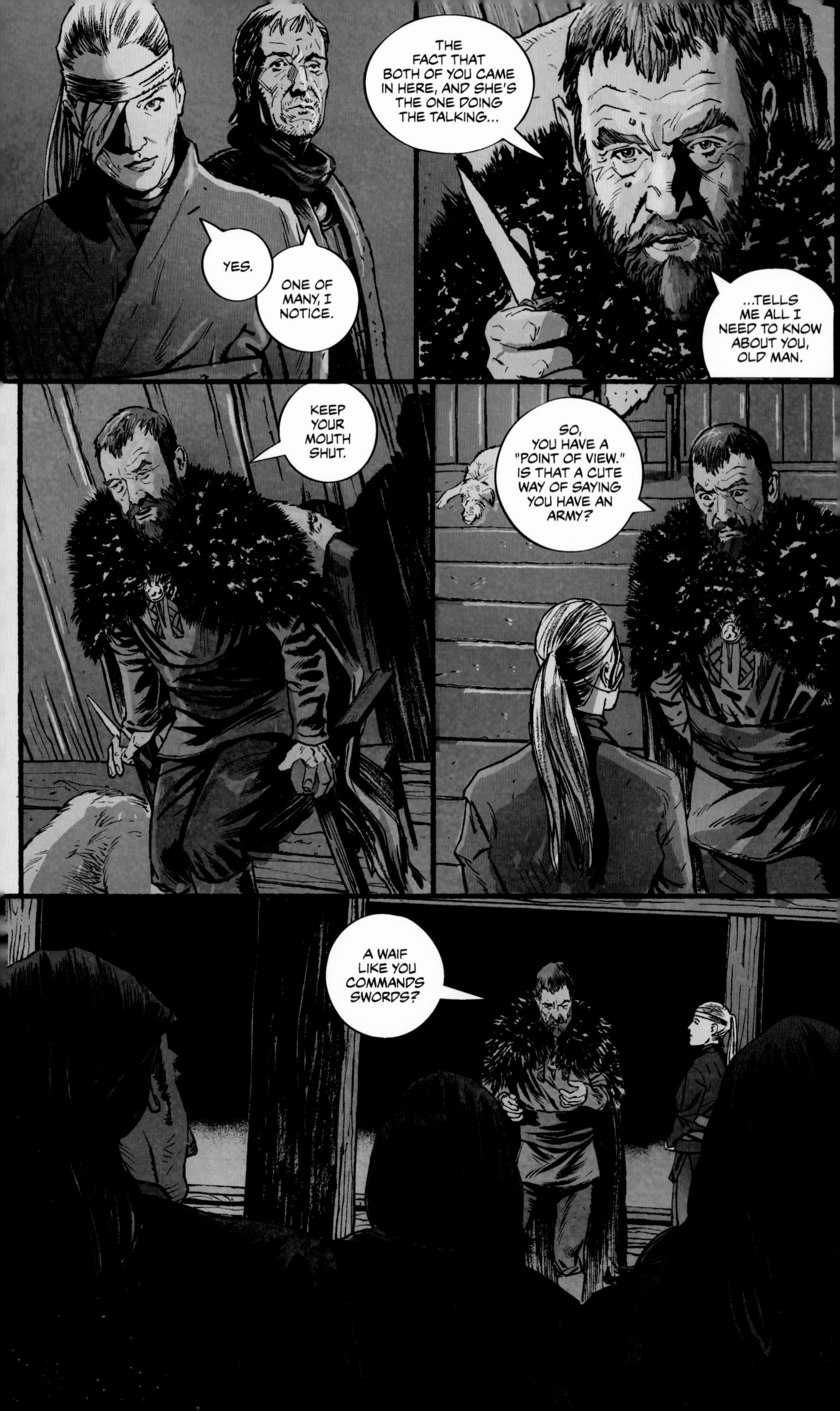
YES.
ONE OF MANY, I NOTICE.
THE FACT THAT BOTH OF YOU CAME IN HERE, AND SHE'S THE ONE DOING THE TALKING...
...TELLS ME ALL I NEED TO KNOW ABOUT YOU, OLD MAN.
KEEP YOUR MOUTH SHUT.
SO, YOU HAVE A "POINT OF VIEW." IS THAT A CUTE WAY OF SAYING YOU HAVE AN ARMY?
A WAIF LIKE YOU COMMANDS SWORDS?

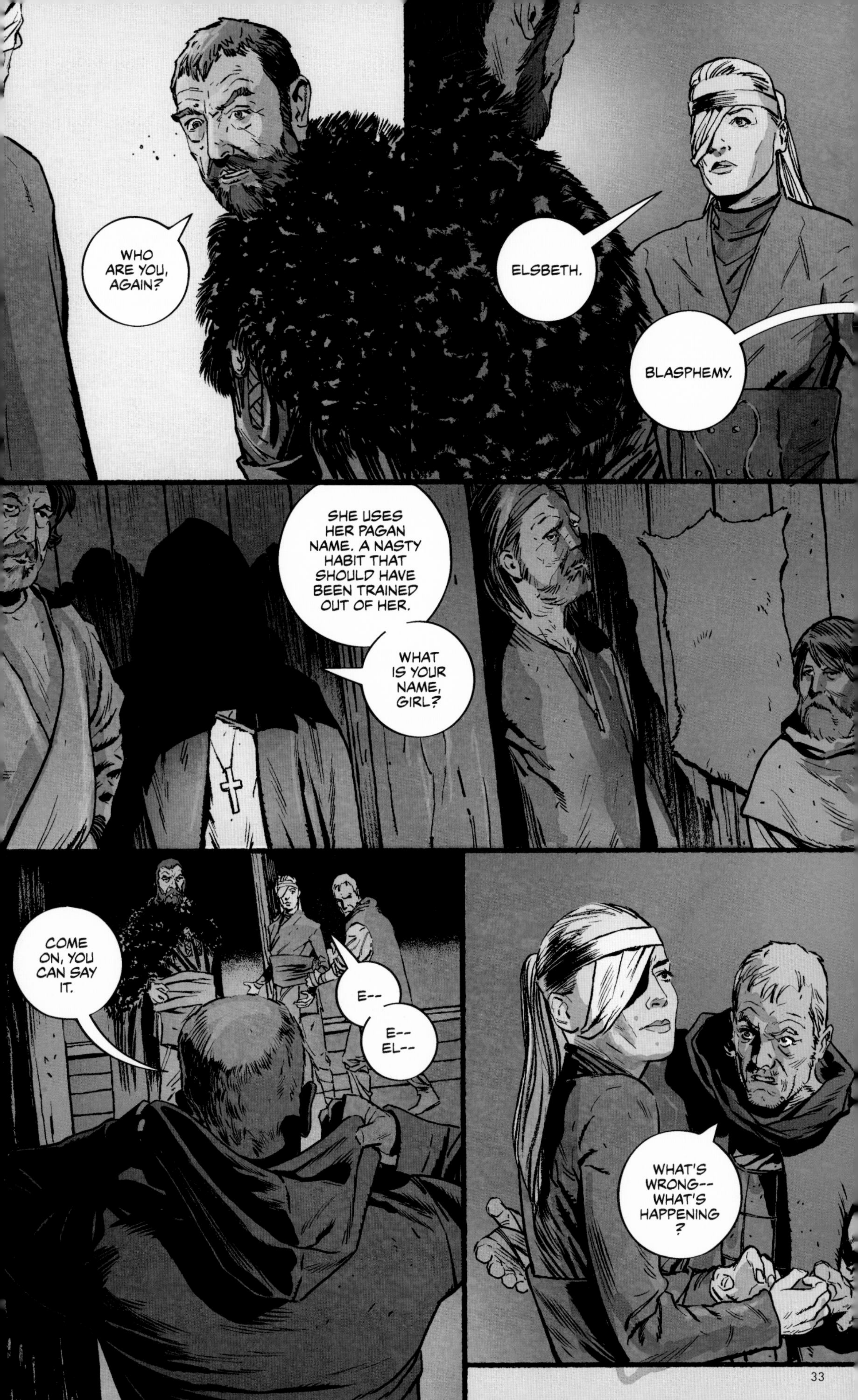
WHO ARE YOU, AGAIN?
ELSBETH.
BLASPHEMY.
SHE USES HER PAGAN NAME. A NASTY HABIT THAT SHOULD HAVE BEEN TRAINED OUT OF HER.
WHAT IS YOUR NAME, GIRL?
COME ON, YOU CAN SAY IT.
E--
E-- EL--
WHAT'S WRONG-- WHAT'S HAPPENING?

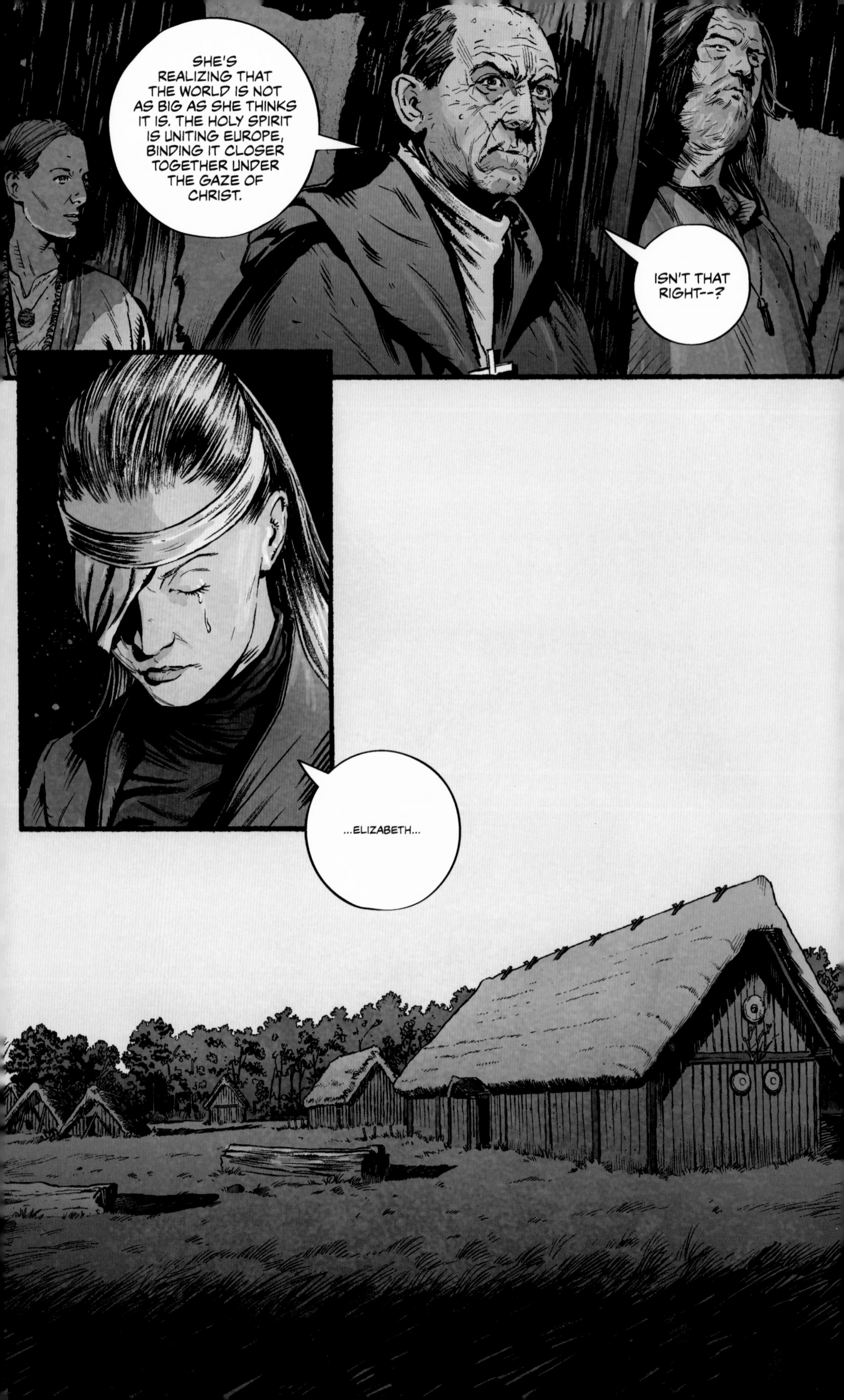
SHE'S REALIZING THAT THE WORLD IS NOT AS BIG AS SHE THINKS IT IS. THE HOLY SPIRIT IS UNITING EUROPE, BINDING IT CLOSER TOGETHER UNDER THE GAZE OF CHRIST.
ISN'T THAT RIGHT--?
...ELIZABETH...

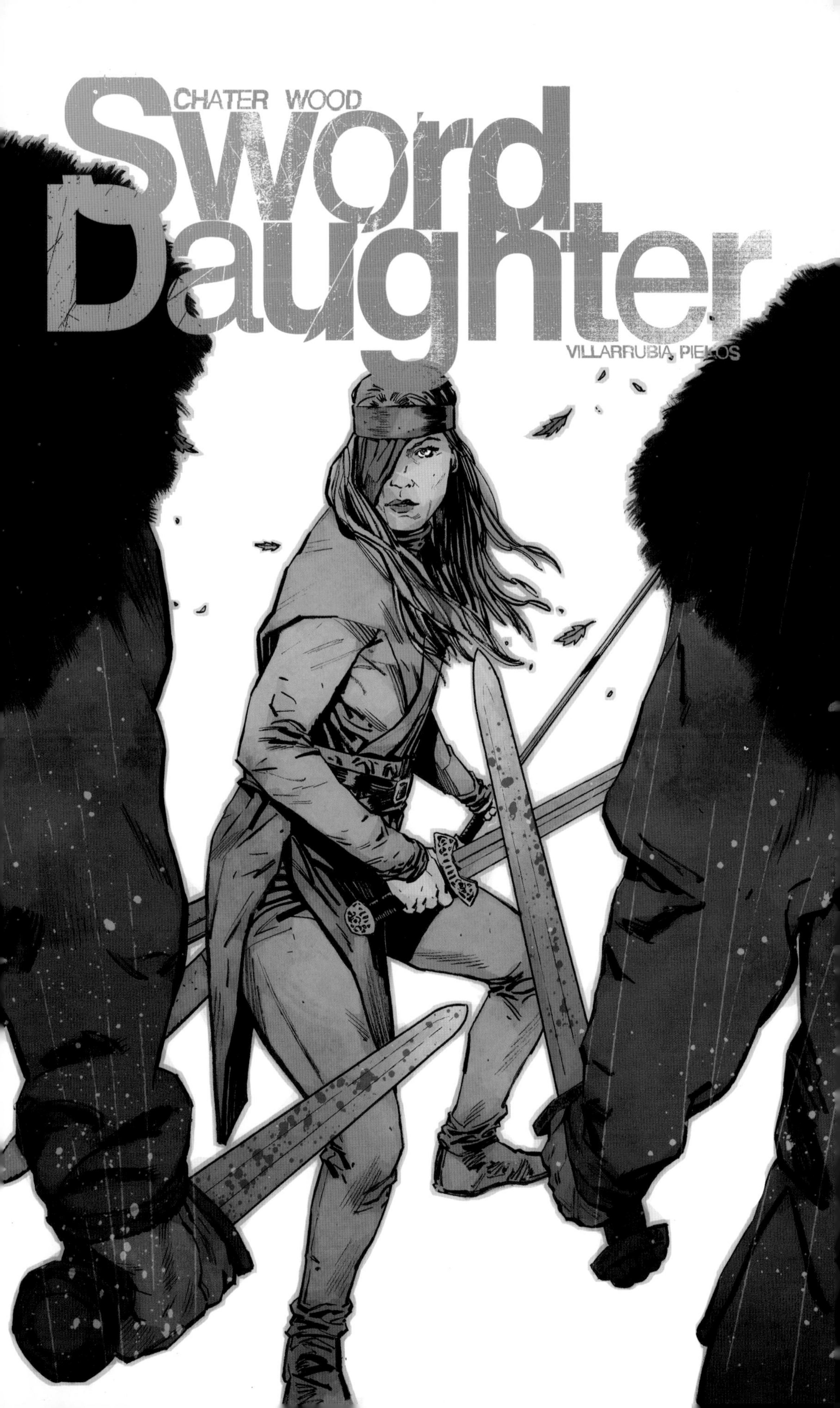
CHATER WOOD
Sword Daughter
VILLARRUBIA PIEKOS

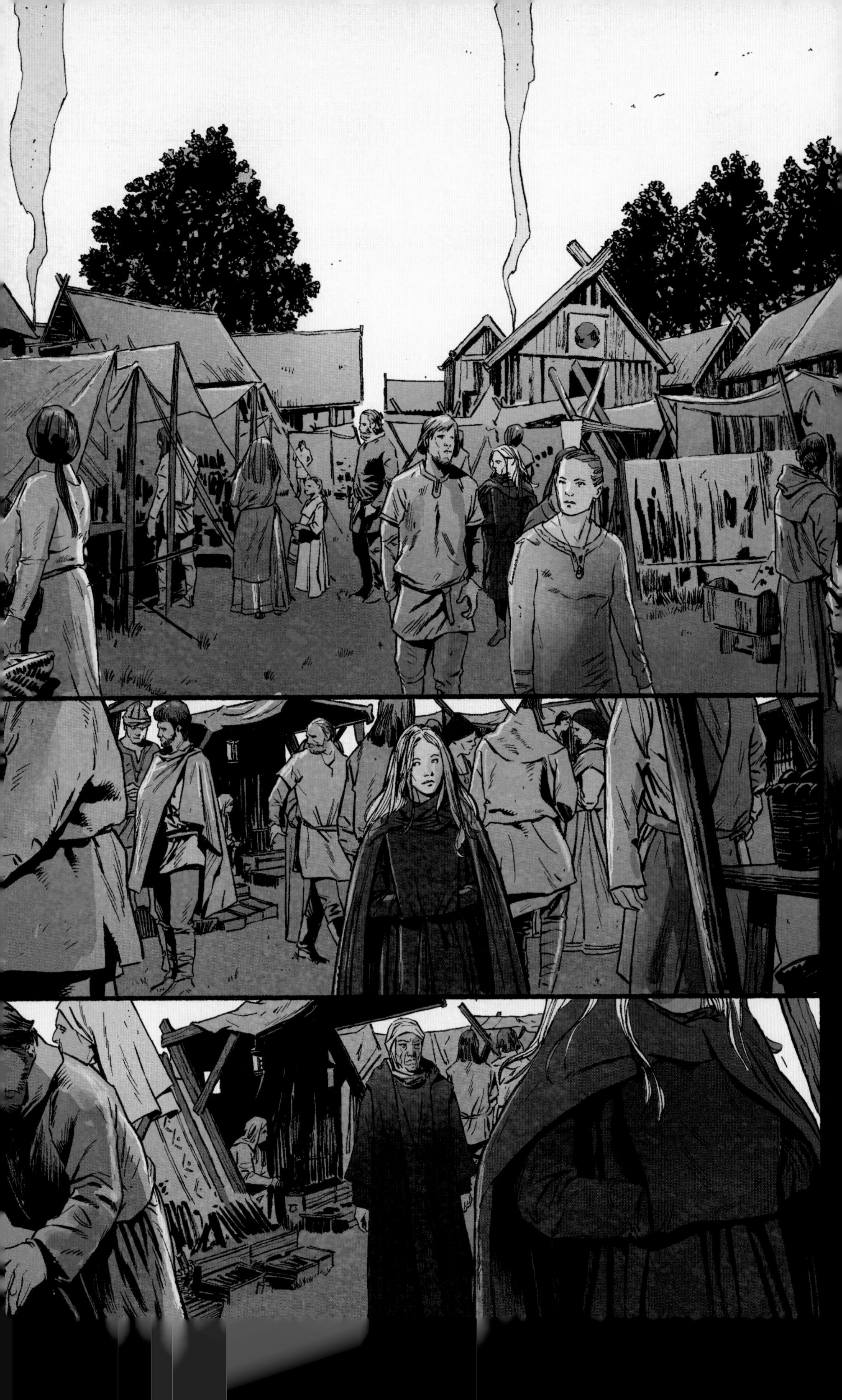

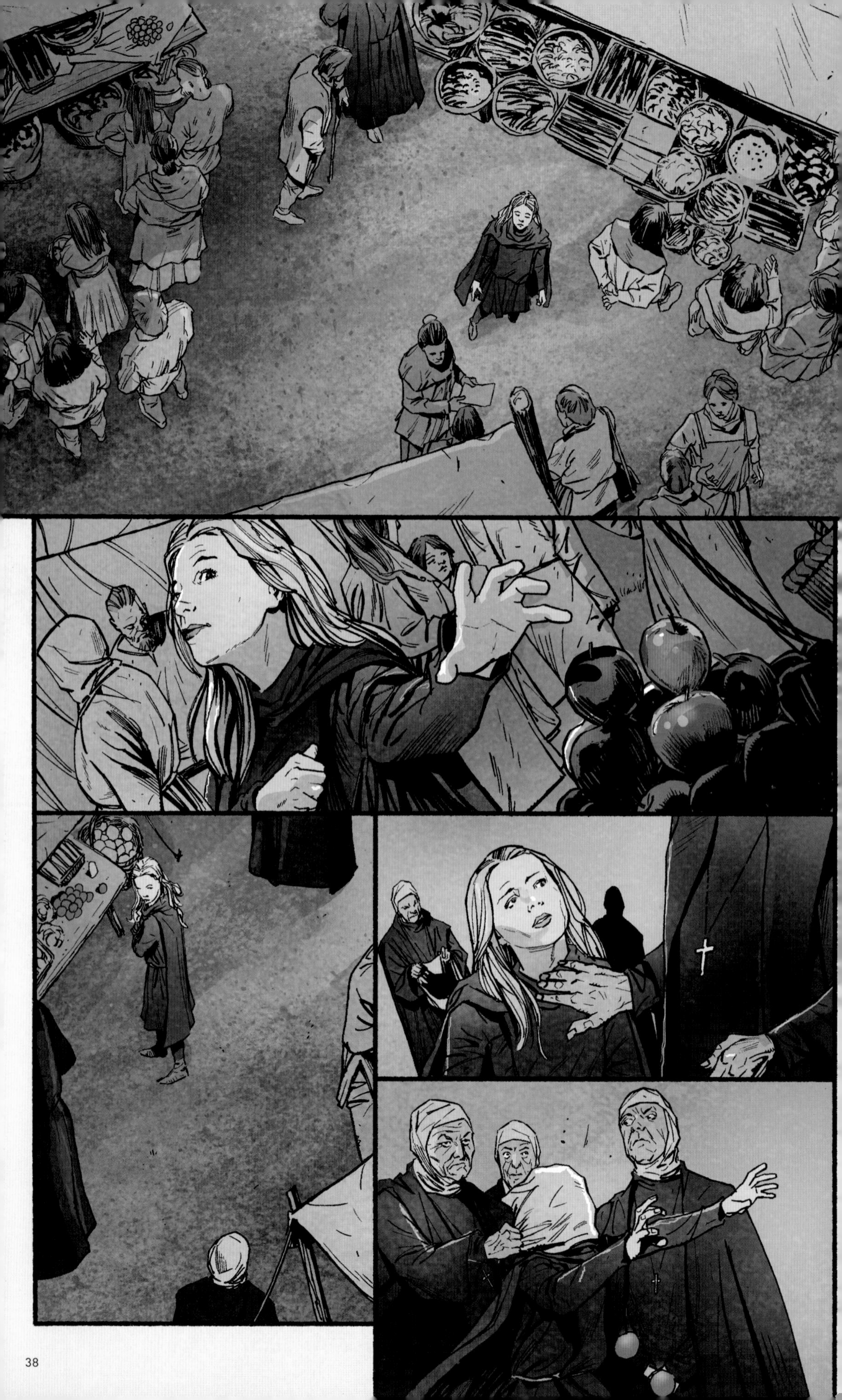

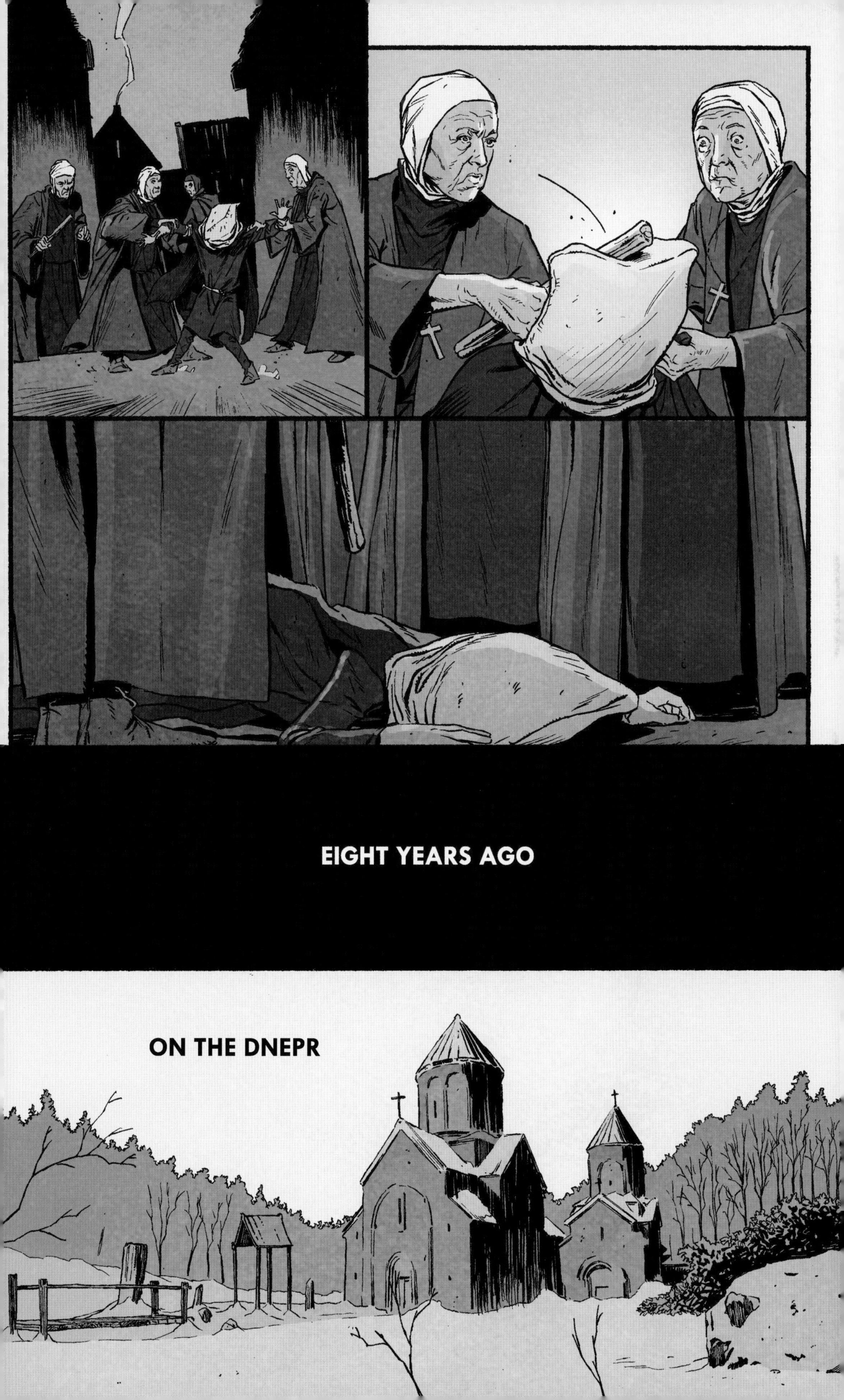
EIGHT YEARS AGO
ON THE DNEPR

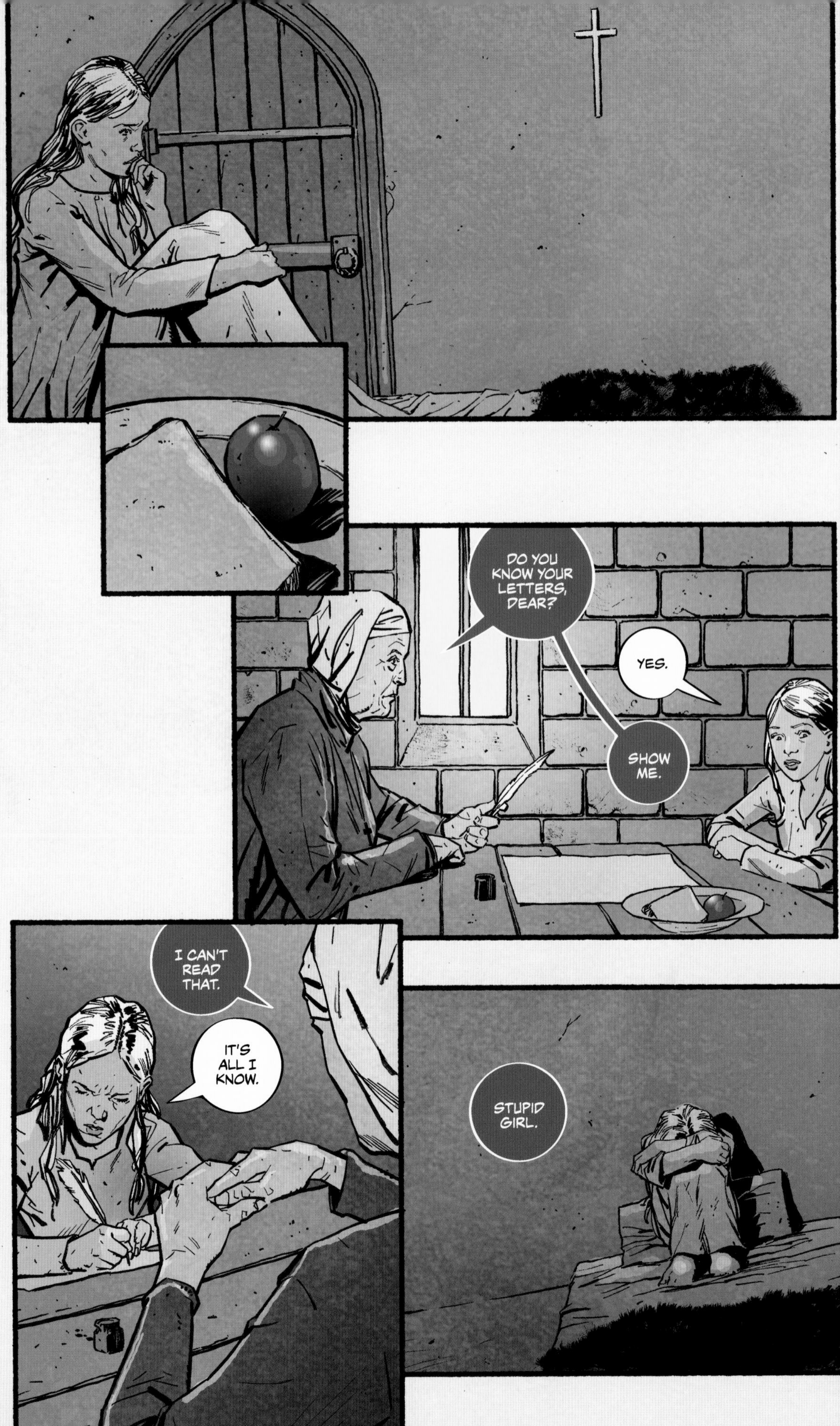
DO YOU KNOW YOUR LETTERS, DEAR?
YES.
SHOW ME.
I CAN'T READ THAT.
IT'S ALL I KNOW.
STUPID GIRL.

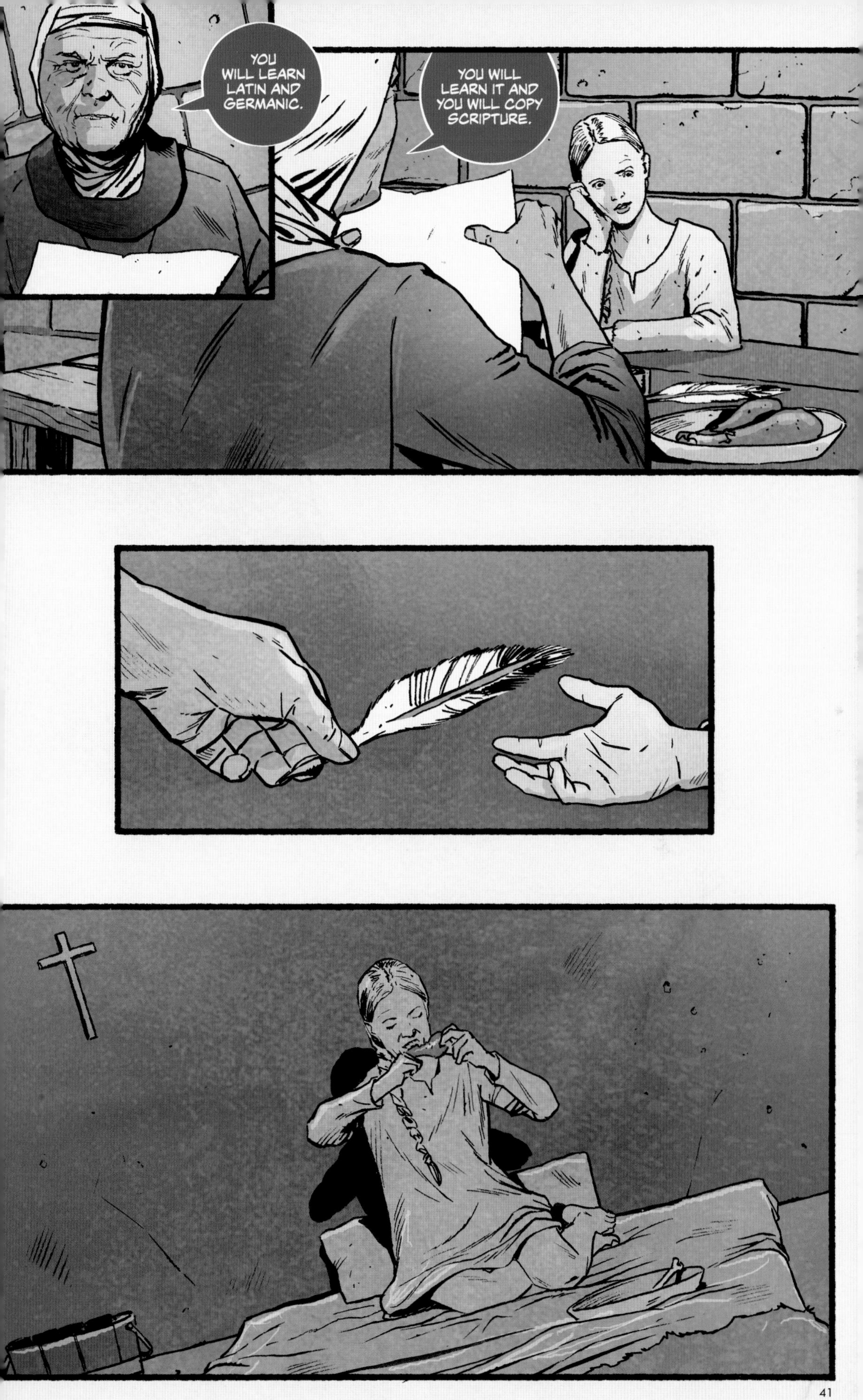
YOU WILL LEARN LATIN AND GERMANIC.
YOU WILL LEARN IT AND YOU WILL COPY SCRIPTURE.

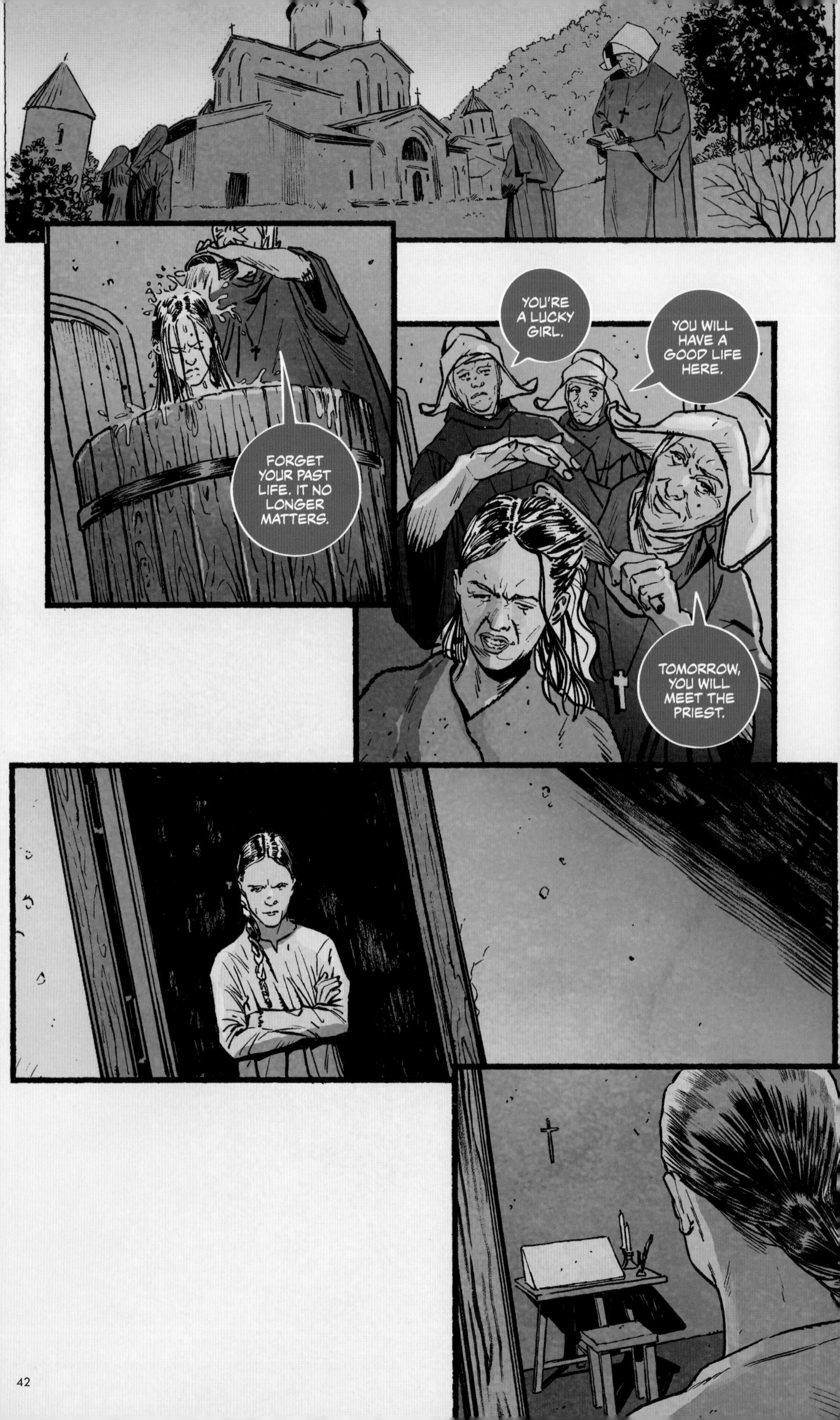
FORGET YOUR PAST LIFE. IT NO LONGER MATTERS.
YOU'RE A LUCKY GIRL.
YOU WILL HAVE A GOOD LIFE HERE.
TOMORROW, YOU WILL MEET THE PRIEST.

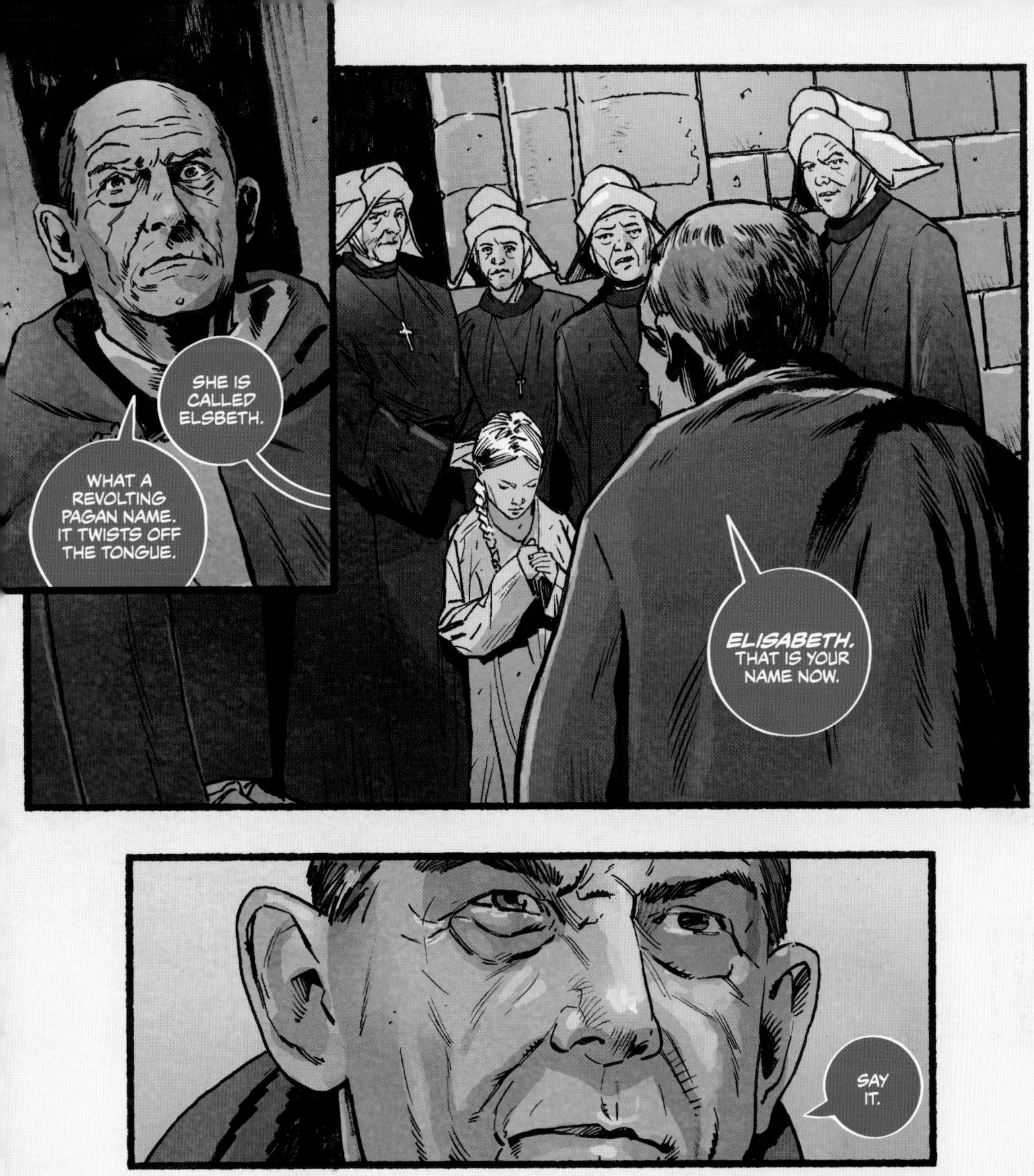
SHE IS CALLED ELSBETH.
WHAT A REVOLTING PAGAN NAME. IT TWISTS OFF THE TONGUE.
ELISABETH. THAT IS YOUR NAME NOW.
SAY IT.

SWORD DAUGHTER
A SPILLING OF BLOOD

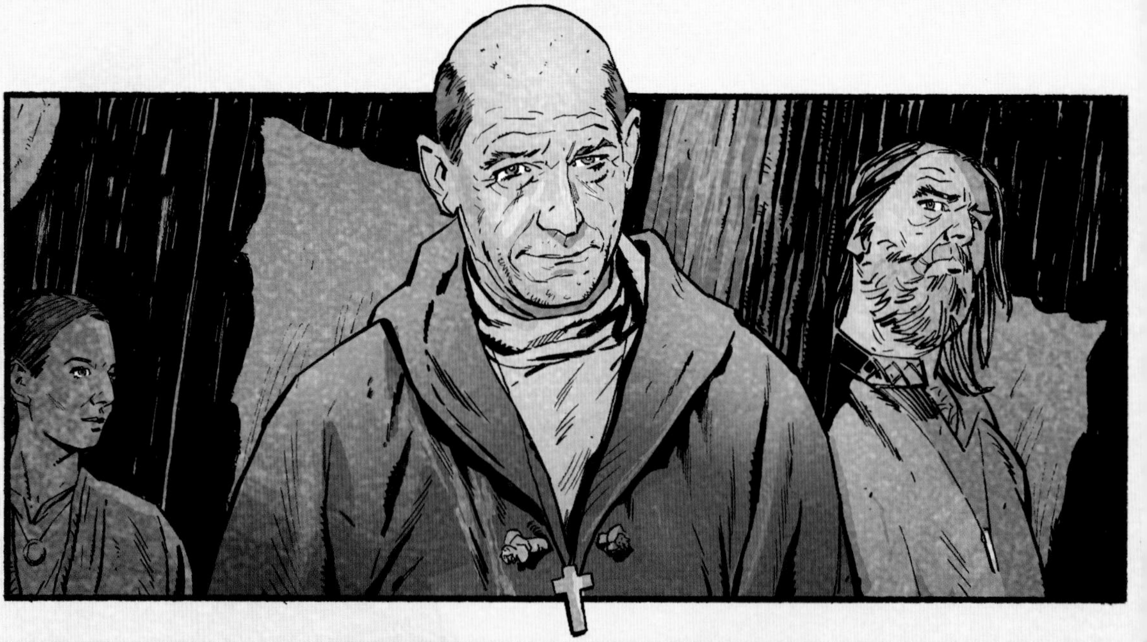

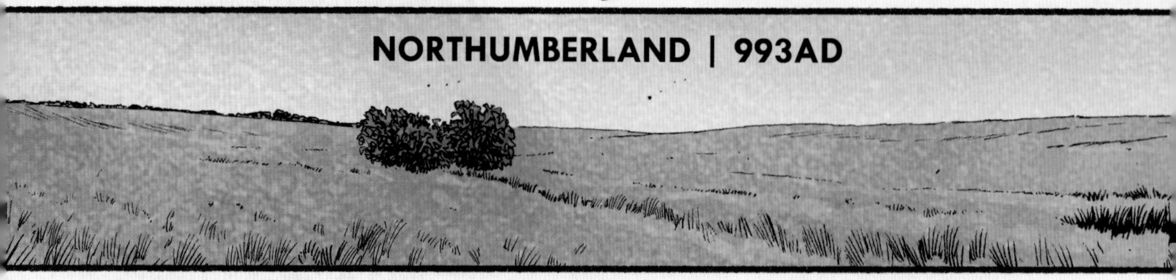
NORTHUMBERLAND | 993AD

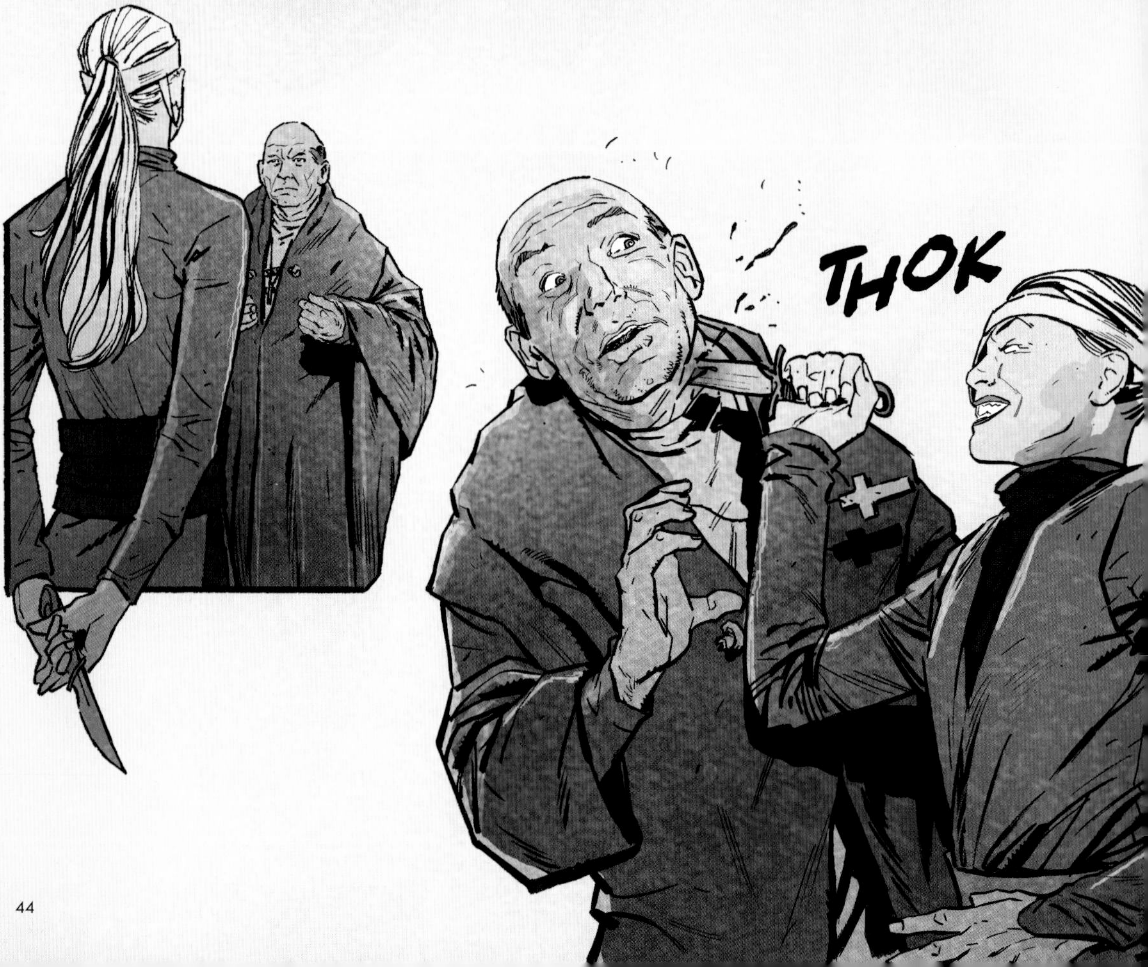
THOK

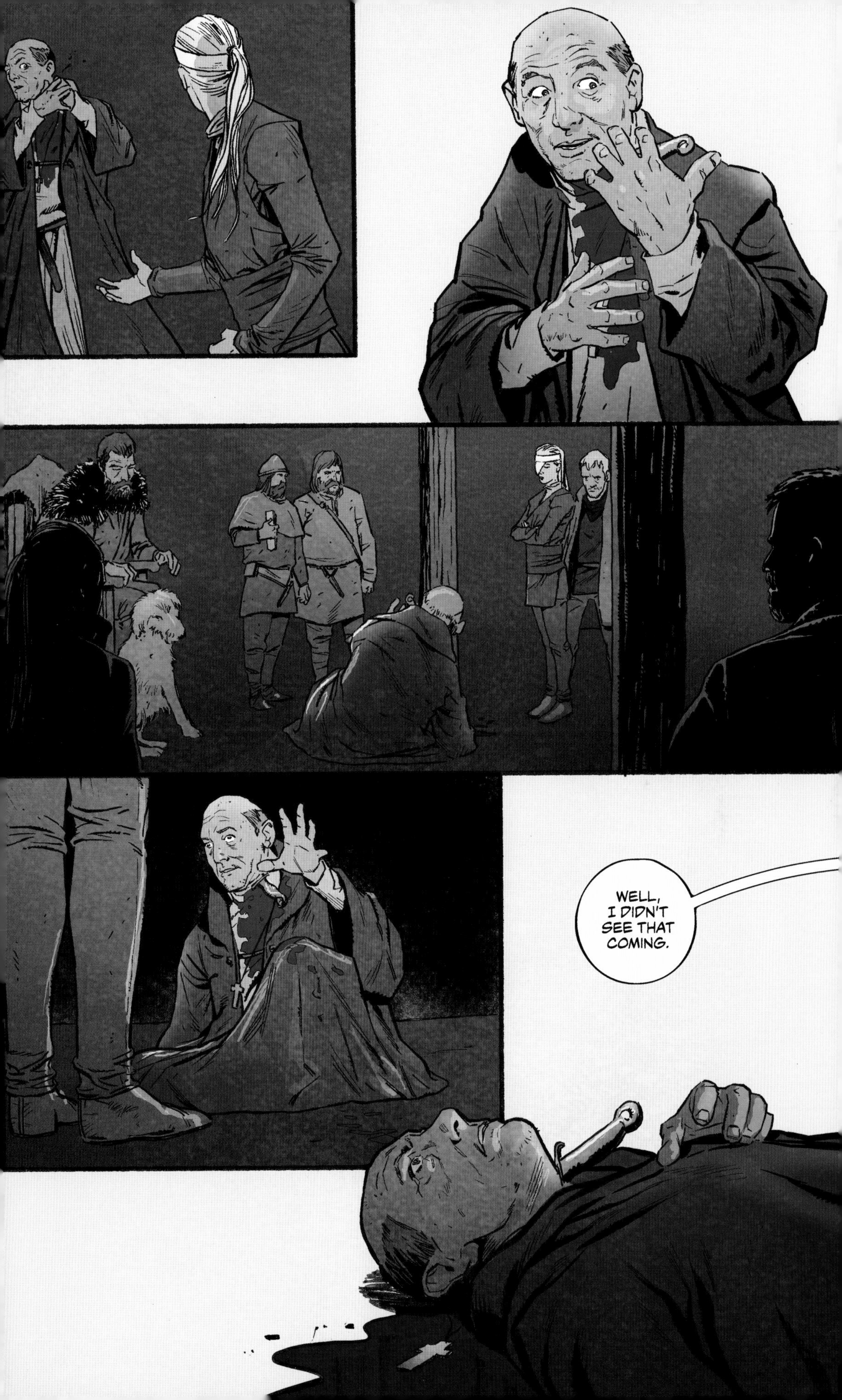
WELL, I DIDN'T SEE THAT COMING.

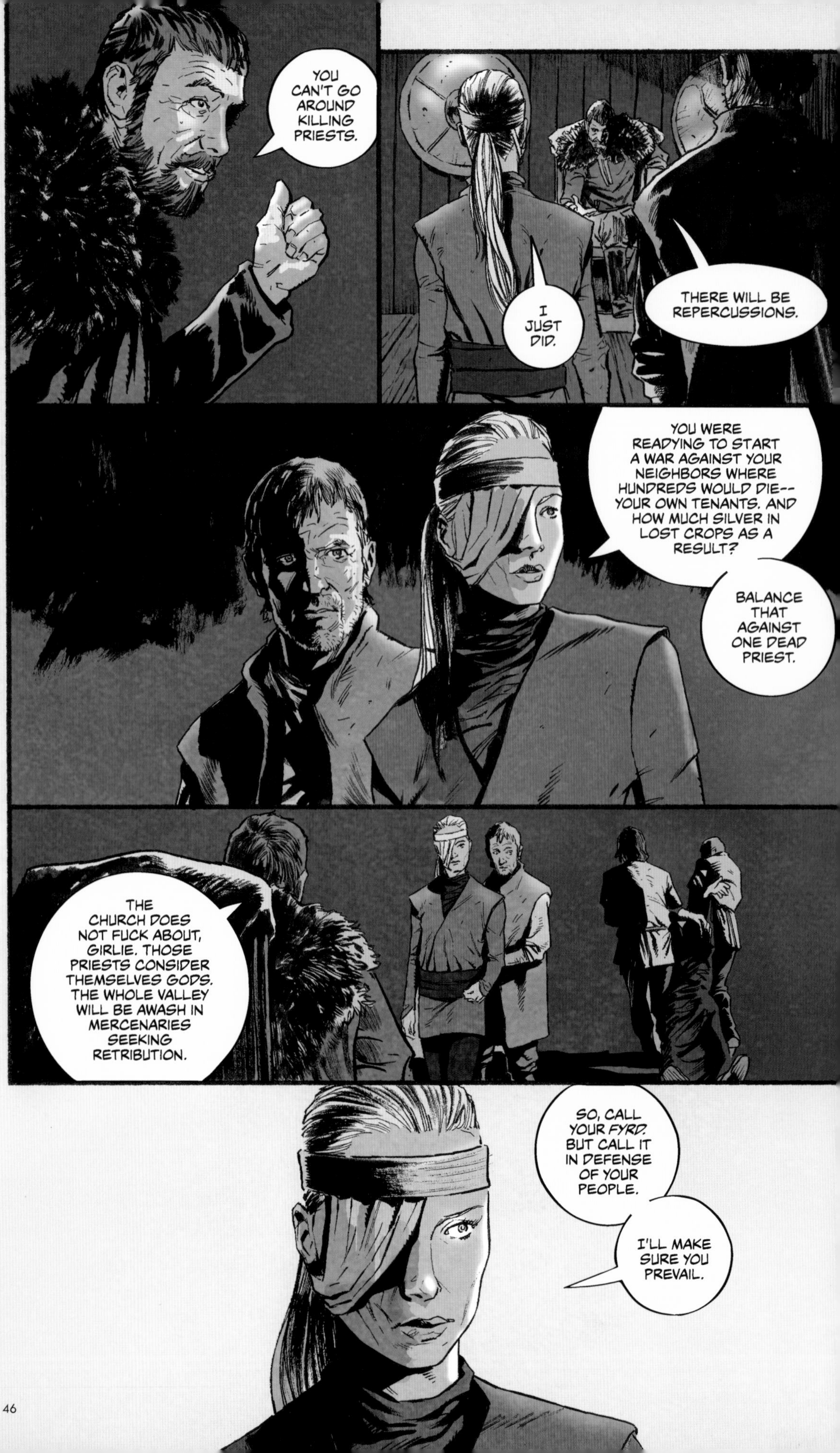
YOU CAN'T GO AROUND KILLING PRIESTS.
I JUST DID.
THERE WILL BE REPERCUSSIONS.
YOU WERE READYING TO START A WAR AGAINST YOUR NEIGHBORS WHERE HUNDREDS WOULD DIE-- YOUR OWN TENANTS. AND HOW MUCH SILVER IN LOST CROPS AS A RESULT?
BALANCE THAT AGAINST ONE DEAD PRIEST.
THE CHURCH DOES NOT FUCK ABOUT, GIRLIE. THOSE PRIESTS CONSIDER THEMSELVES GODS. THE WHOLE VALLEY WILL BE AWASH IN MERCENARIES SEEKING RETRIBUTION.
SO, CALL YOUR *FYRD*. BUT CALL IT IN DEFENSE OF YOUR PEOPLE.
I'LL MAKE SURE YOU PREVAIL.

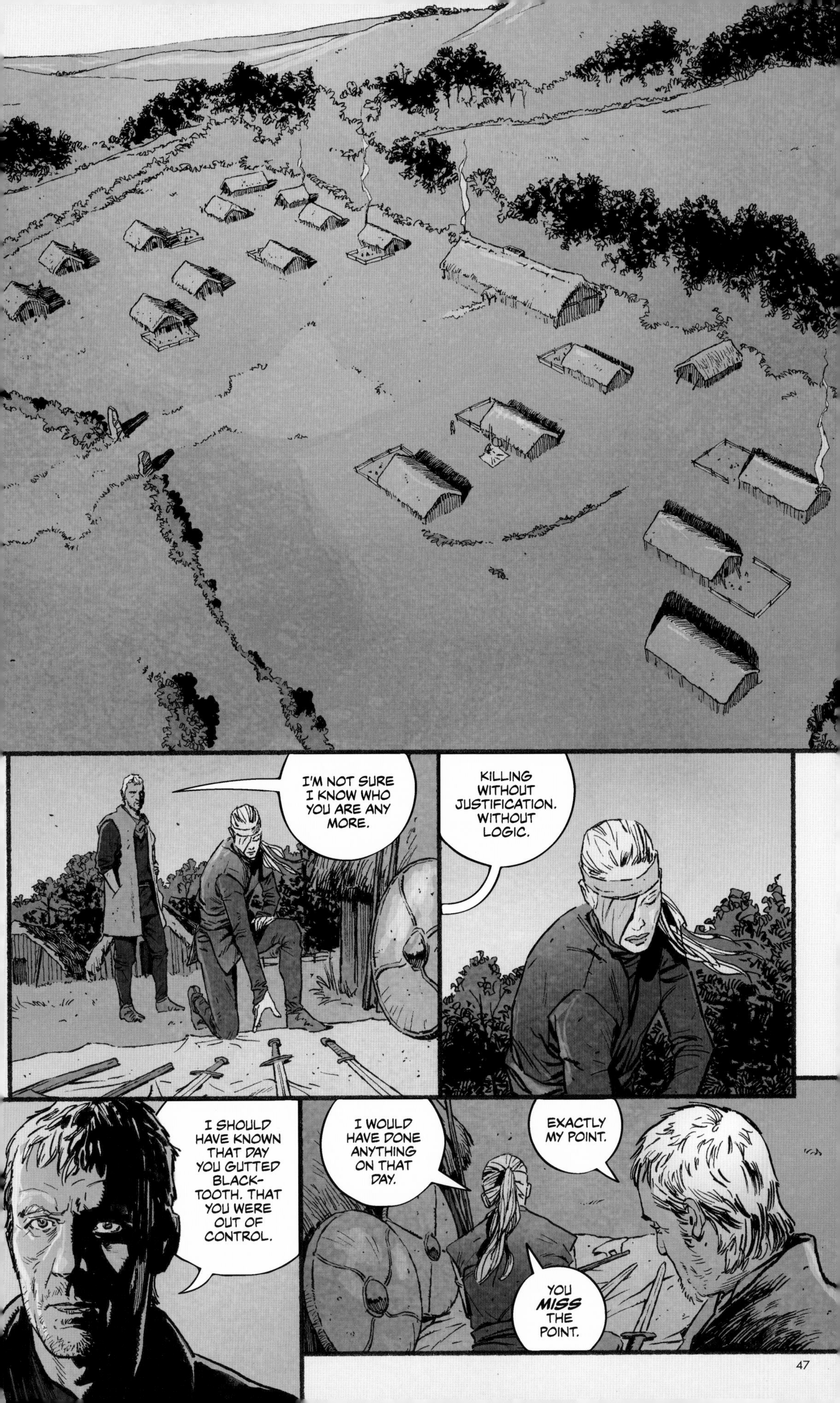
I'M NOT SURE I KNOW WHO YOU ARE ANY MORE.
KILLING WITHOUT JUSTIFICATION. WITHOUT LOGIC.
I SHOULD HAVE KNOWN THAT DAY YOU GUTTED BLACK-TOOTH. THAT YOU WERE OUT OF CONTROL.
I WOULD HAVE DONE ANYTHING ON THAT DAY.
EXACTLY MY POINT.
YOU ***MISS*** THE POINT.

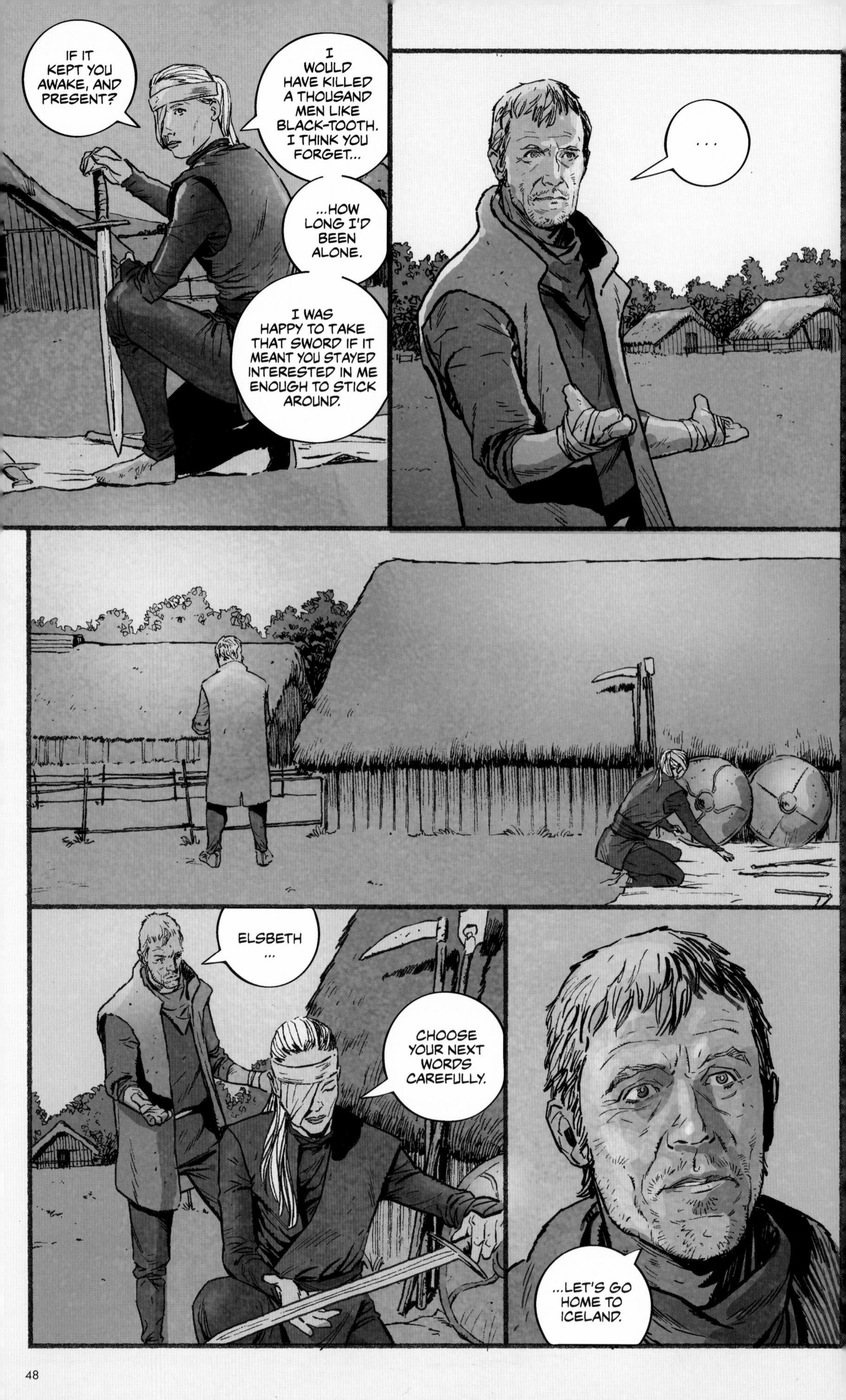
IF IT KEPT YOU AWAKE, AND PRESENT?
I WOULD HAVE KILLED A THOUSAND MEN LIKE BLACK-TOOTH. I THINK YOU FORGET...
...HOW LONG I'D BEEN ALONE.
I WAS HAPPY TO TAKE THAT SWORD IF IT MEANT YOU STAYED INTERESTED IN ME ENOUGH TO STICK AROUND.
...
ELSBETH ...
CHOOSE YOUR NEXT WORDS CAREFULLY.
...LET'S GO HOME TO ICELAND.

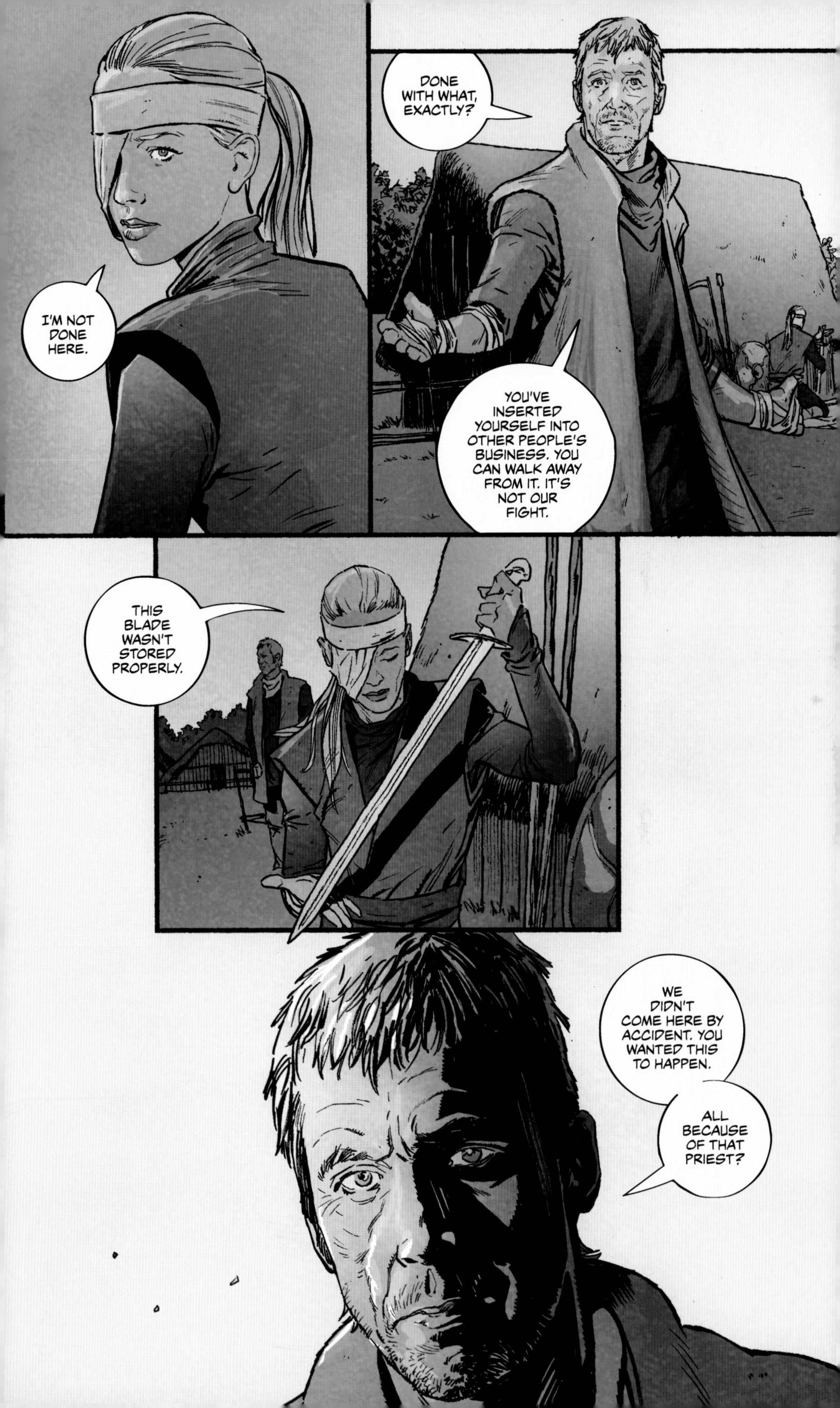
I'M NOT DONE HERE.
DONE WITH WHAT, EXACTLY?
YOU'VE INSERTED YOURSELF INTO OTHER PEOPLE'S BUSINESS. YOU CAN WALK AWAY FROM IT. IT'S NOT OUR FIGHT.
THIS BLADE WASN'T STORED PROPERLY.
WE DIDN'T COME HERE BY ACCIDENT. YOU WANTED THIS TO HAPPEN.
ALL BECAUSE OF THAT PRIEST?

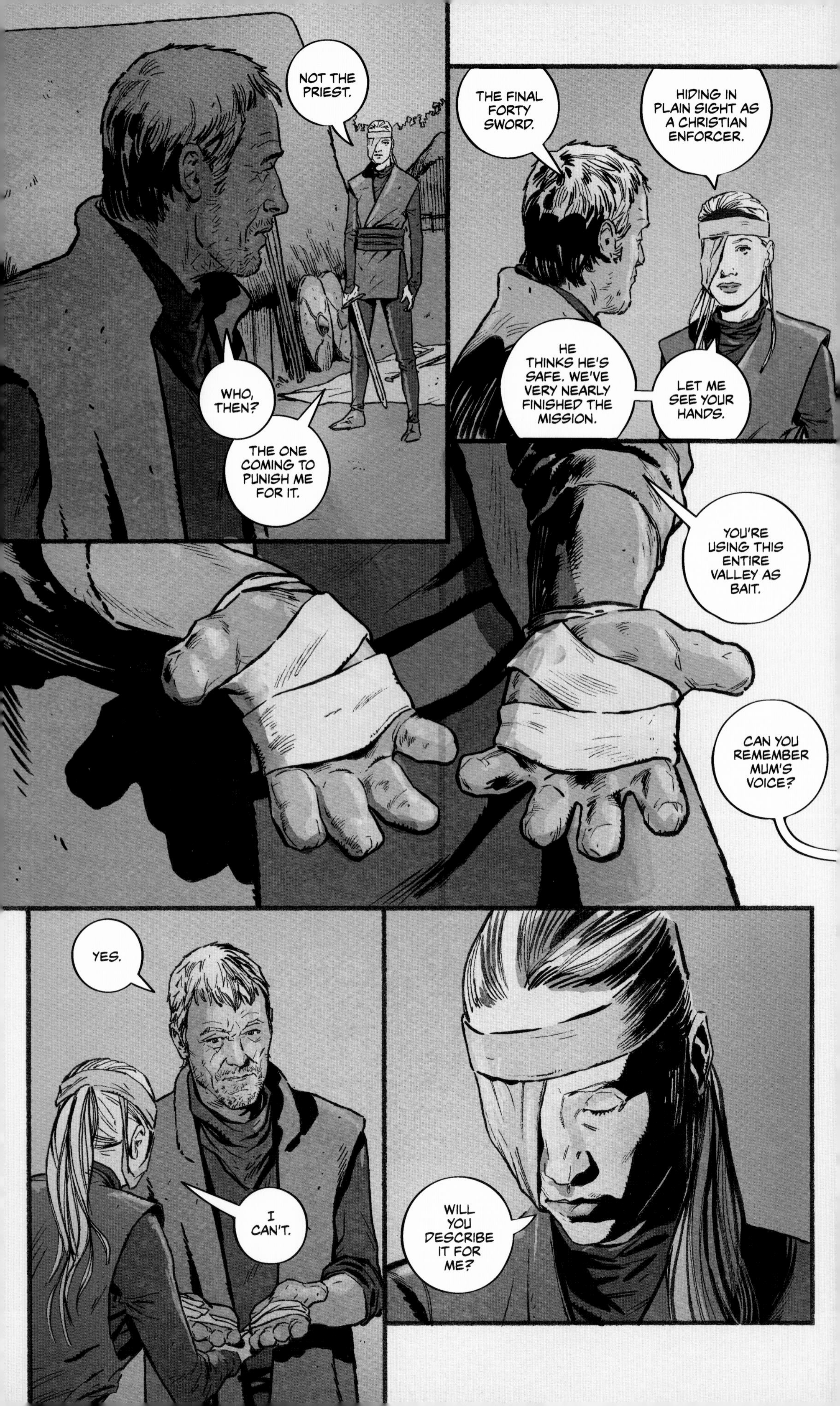
NOT THE PRIEST.
WHO, THEN?
THE ONE COMING TO PUNISH ME FOR IT.
THE FINAL FORTY SWORD.
HIDING IN PLAIN SIGHT AS A CHRISTIAN ENFORCER.
HE THINKS HE'S SAFE. WE'VE VERY NEARLY FINISHED THE MISSION.
LET ME SEE YOUR HANDS.
YOU'RE USING THIS ENTIRE VALLEY AS BAIT.
CAN YOU REMEMBER MUM'S VOICE?
YES.
I CAN'T.
WILL YOU DESCRIBE IT FOR ME?

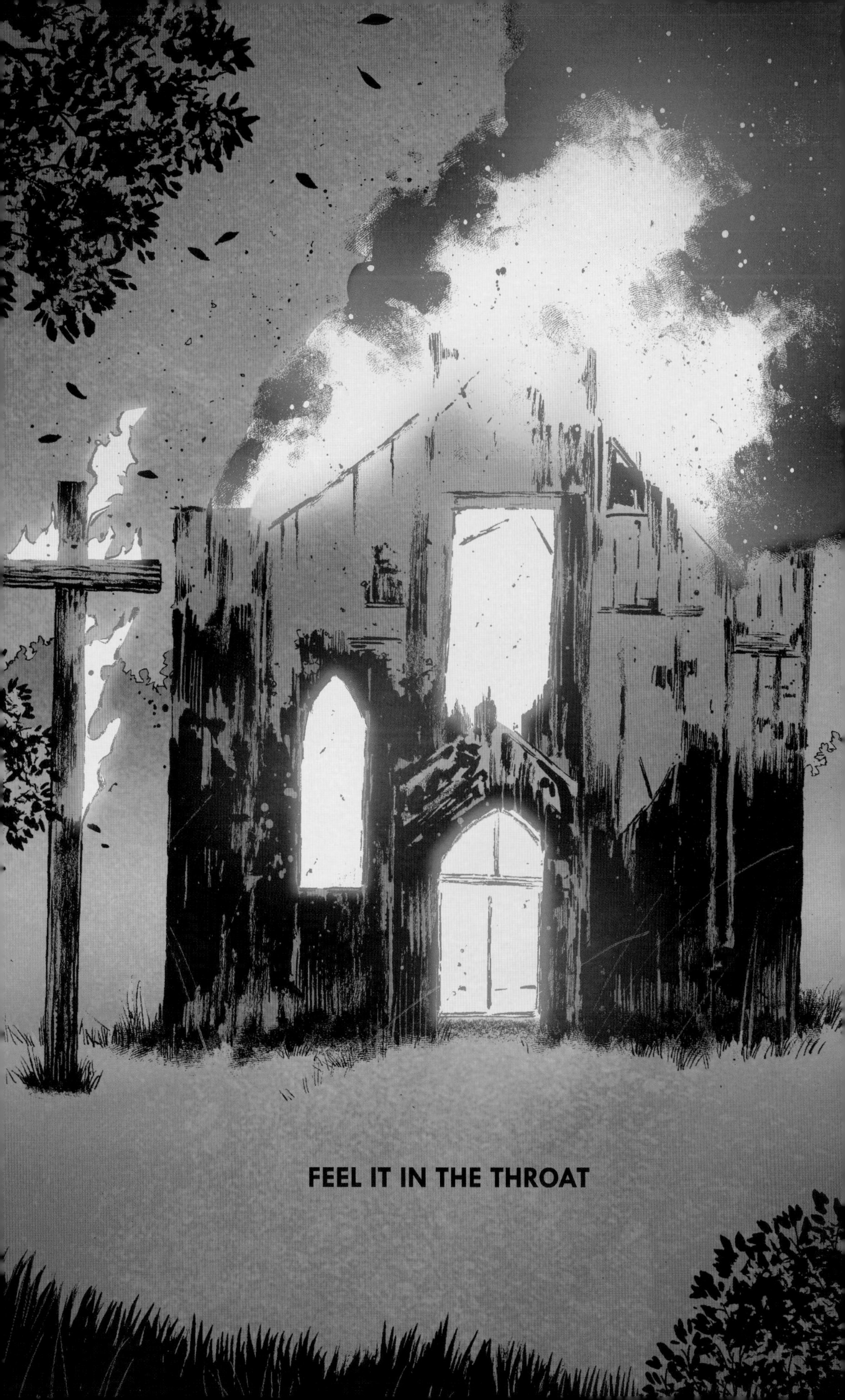
FEEL IT IN THE THROAT

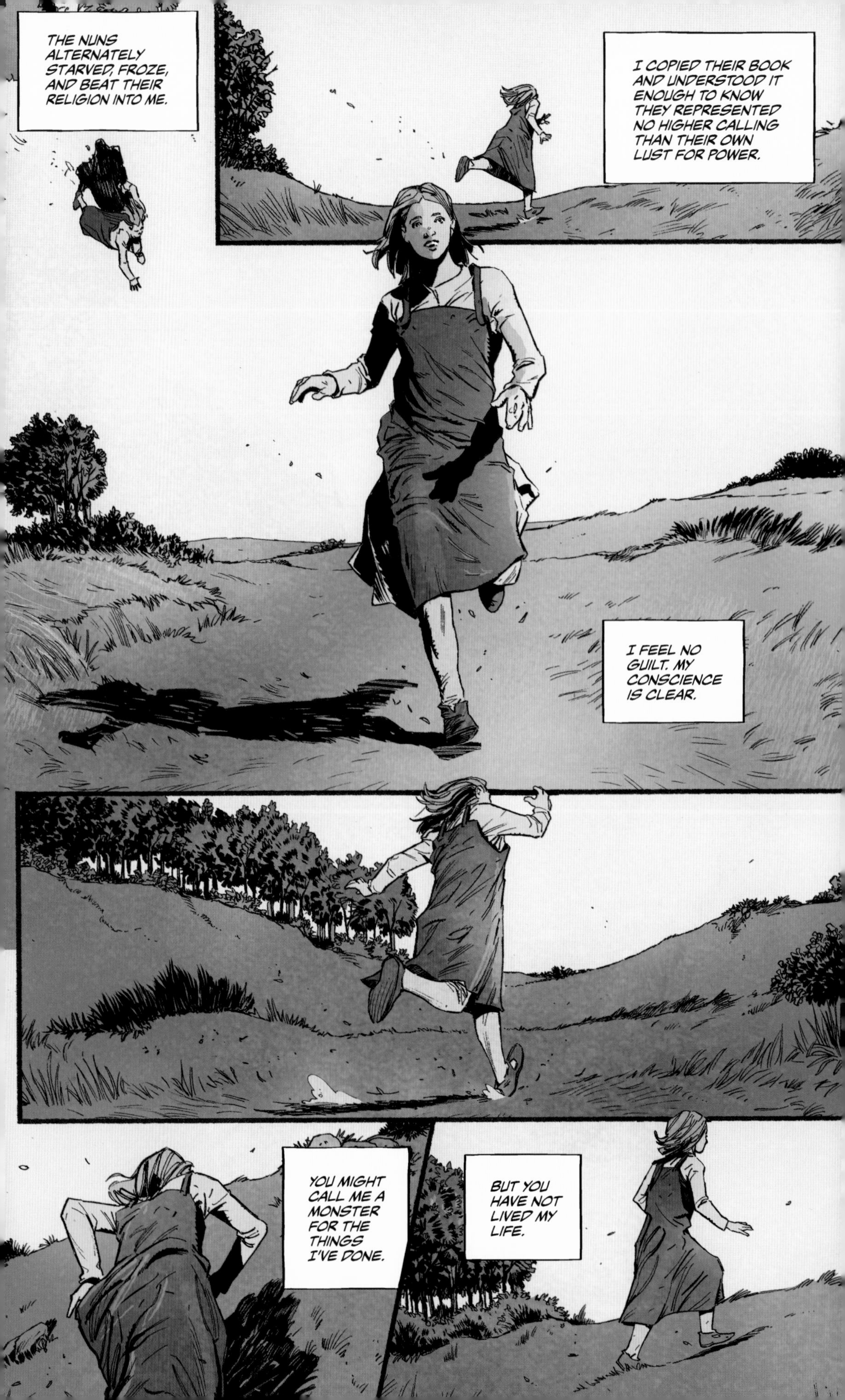
THE NUNS ALTERNATELY STARVED, FROZE, AND BEAT THEIR RELIGION INTO ME.
I COPIED THEIR BOOK AND UNDERSTOOD IT ENOUGH TO KNOW THEY REPRESENTED NO HIGHER CALLING THAN THEIR OWN LUST FOR POWER.
I FEEL NO GUILT. MY CONSCIENCE IS CLEAR.
YOU MIGHT CALL ME A MONSTER FOR THE THINGS I'VE DONE.
BUT YOU HAVE NOT LIVED MY LIFE.

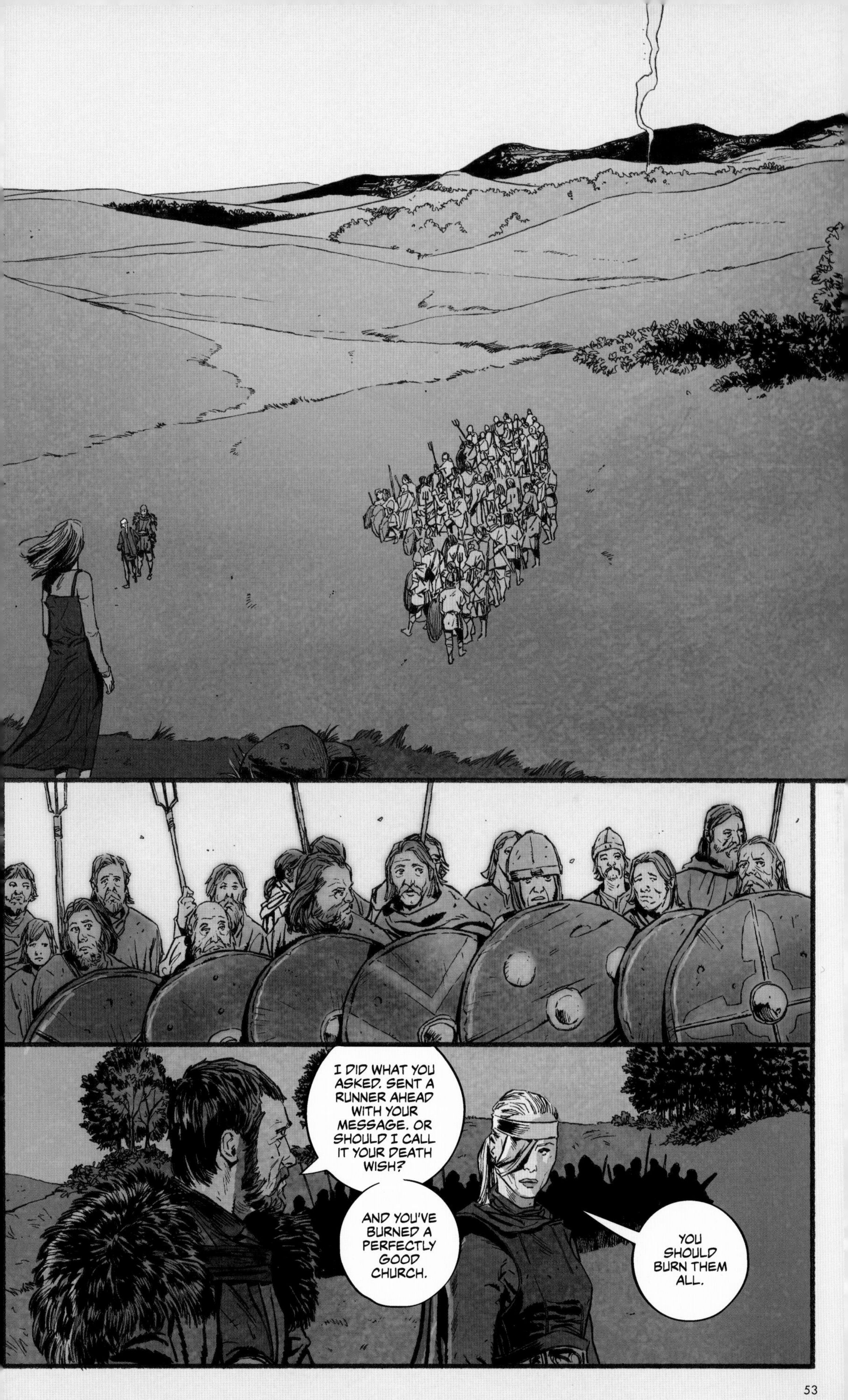
I DID WHAT YOU ASKED. SENT A RUNNER AHEAD WITH YOUR MESSAGE. OR SHOULD I CALL IT YOUR DEATH WISH?
AND YOU'VE BURNED A PERFECTLY GOOD CHURCH.
YOU SHOULD BURN THEM ALL.

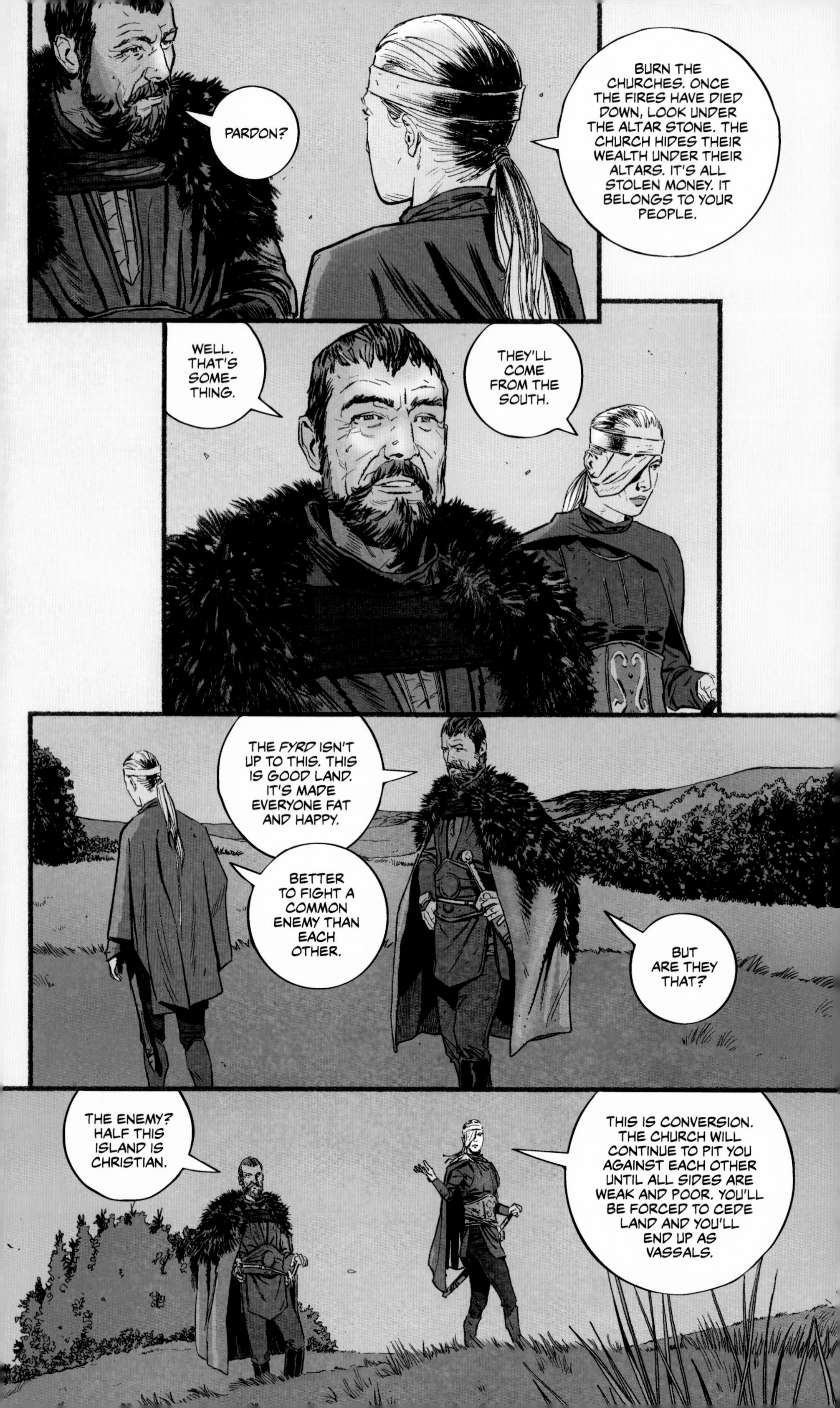

PARDON?
BURN THE CHURCHES. ONCE THE FIRES HAVE DIED DOWN, LOOK UNDER THE ALTAR STONE. THE CHURCH HIDES THEIR WEALTH UNDER THEIR ALTARS. IT'S ALL STOLEN MONEY. IT BELONGS TO YOUR PEOPLE.
WELL. THAT'S SOME-THING.
THEY'LL COME FROM THE SOUTH.
THE *FYRD* ISN'T UP TO THIS. THIS IS GOOD LAND. IT'S MADE EVERYONE FAT AND HAPPY.
BETTER TO FIGHT A COMMON ENEMY THAN EACH OTHER.
BUT ARE THEY THAT?
THE ENEMY? HALF THIS ISLAND IS CHRISTIAN.
THIS IS CONVERSION. THE CHURCH WILL CONTINUE TO PIT YOU AGAINST EACH OTHER UNTIL ALL SIDES ARE WEAK AND POOR. YOU'LL BE FORCED TO CEDE LAND AND YOU'LL END UP AS VASSALS.

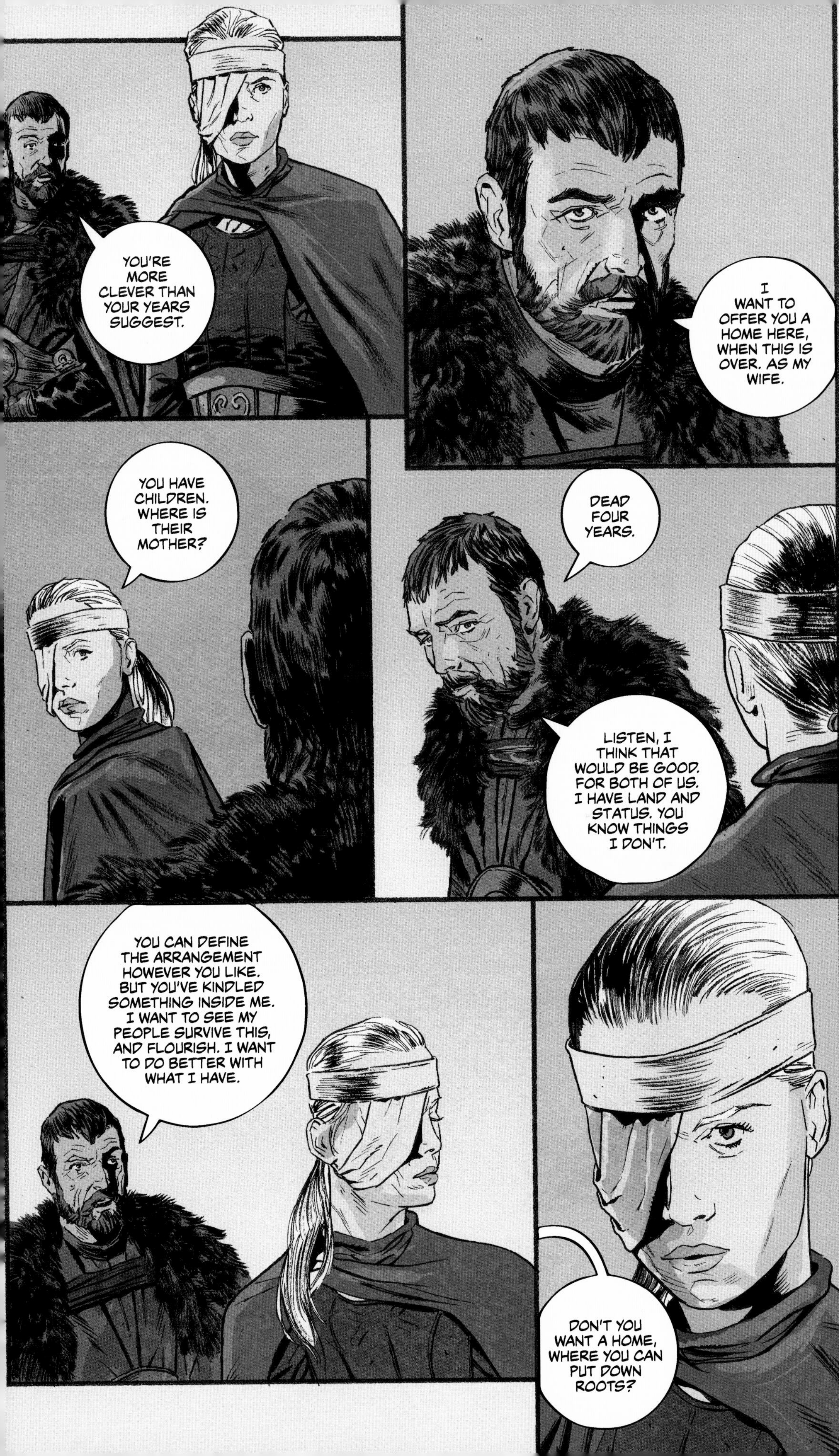
YOU'RE MORE CLEVER THAN YOUR YEARS SUGGEST.
I WANT TO OFFER YOU A HOME HERE, WHEN THIS IS OVER. AS MY WIFE.
YOU HAVE CHILDREN. WHERE IS THEIR MOTHER?
DEAD FOUR YEARS.
LISTEN, I THINK THAT WOULD BE GOOD. FOR BOTH OF US. I HAVE LAND AND STATUS. YOU KNOW THINGS I DON'T.
YOU CAN DEFINE THE ARRANGEMENT HOWEVER YOU LIKE. BUT YOU'VE KINDLED SOMETHING INSIDE ME. I WANT TO SEE MY PEOPLE SURVIVE THIS, AND FLOURISH. I WANT TO DO BETTER WITH WHAT I HAVE.
DON'T YOU WANT A HOME, WHERE YOU CAN PUT DOWN ROOTS?

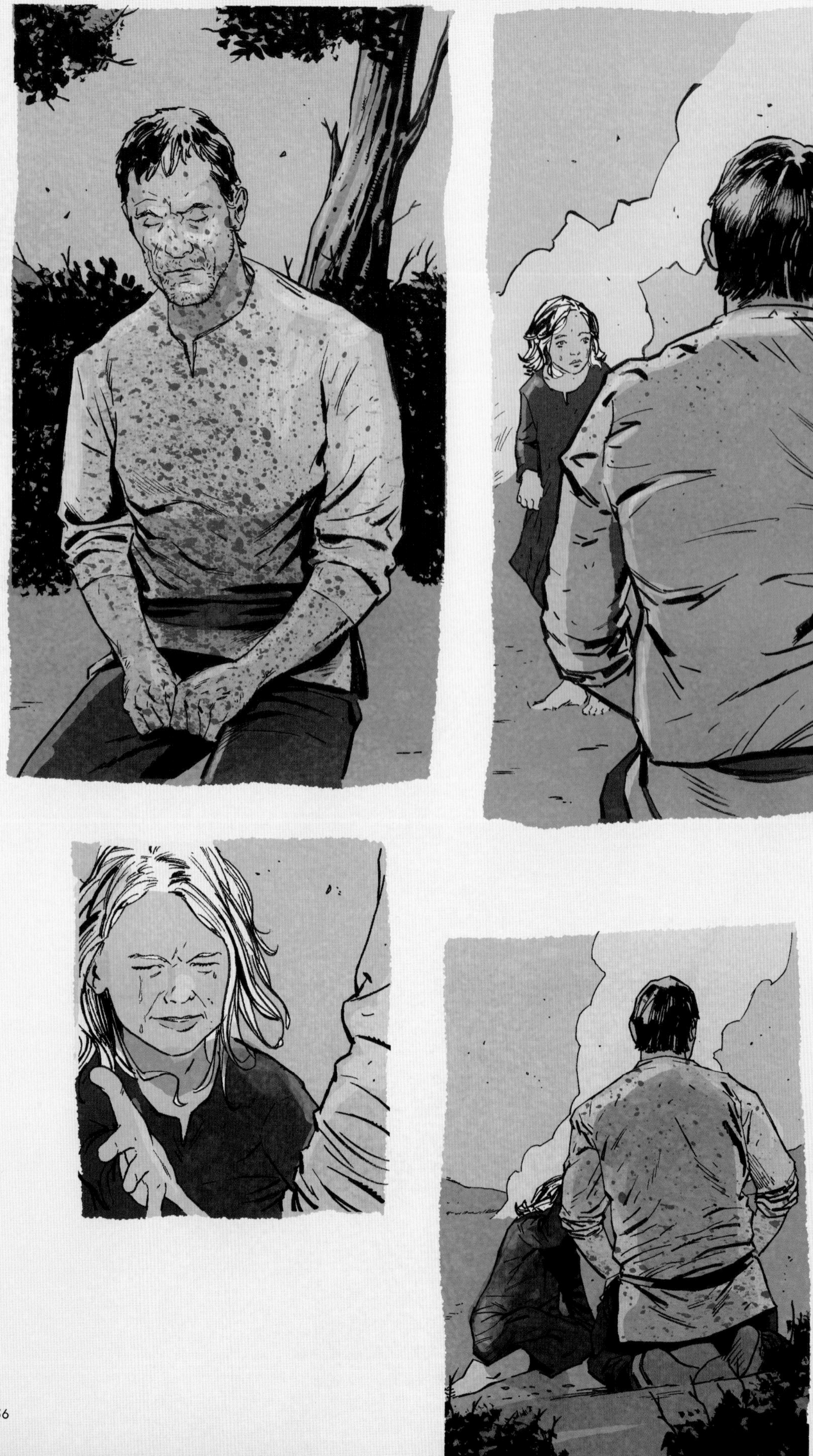

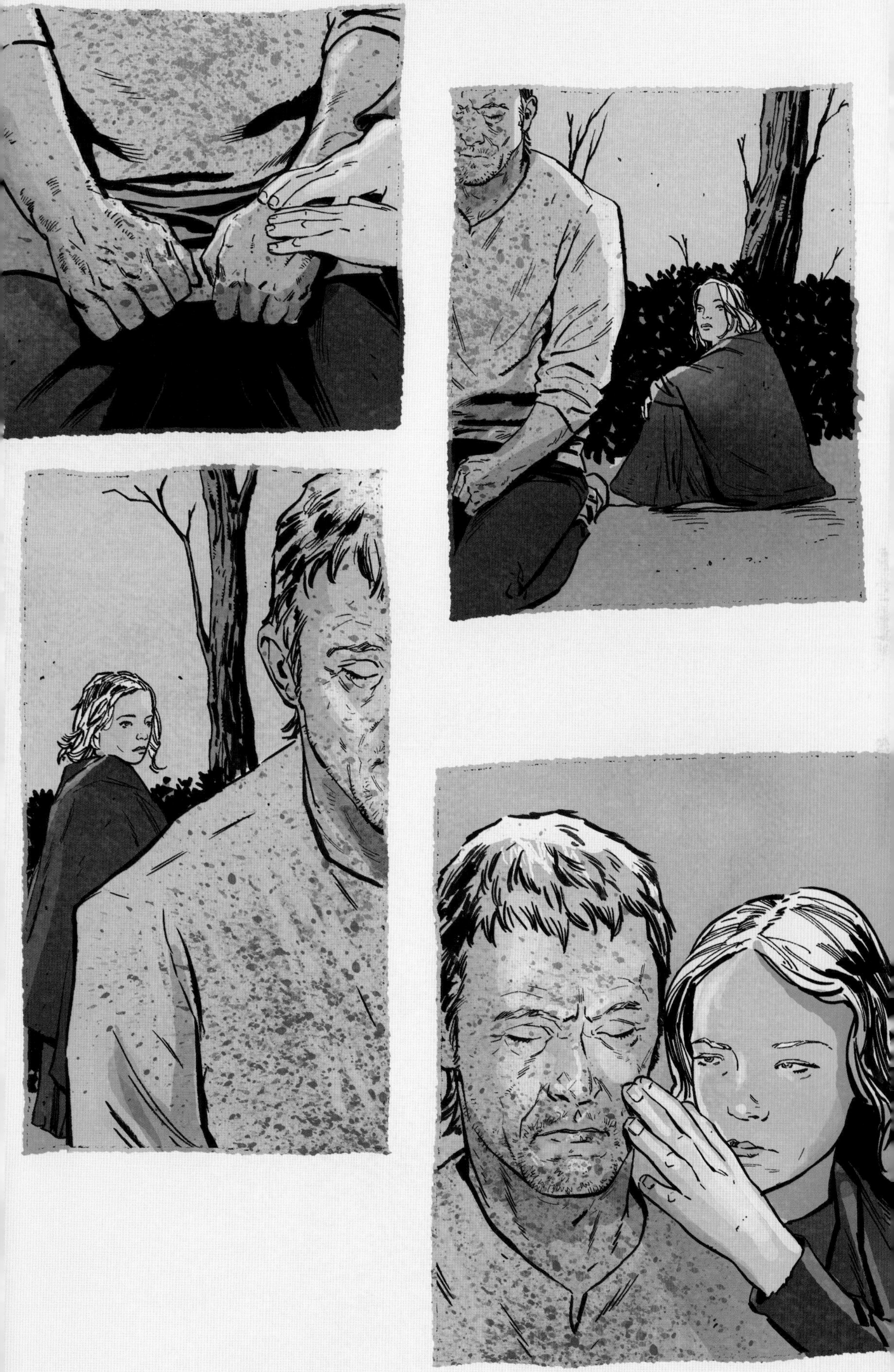

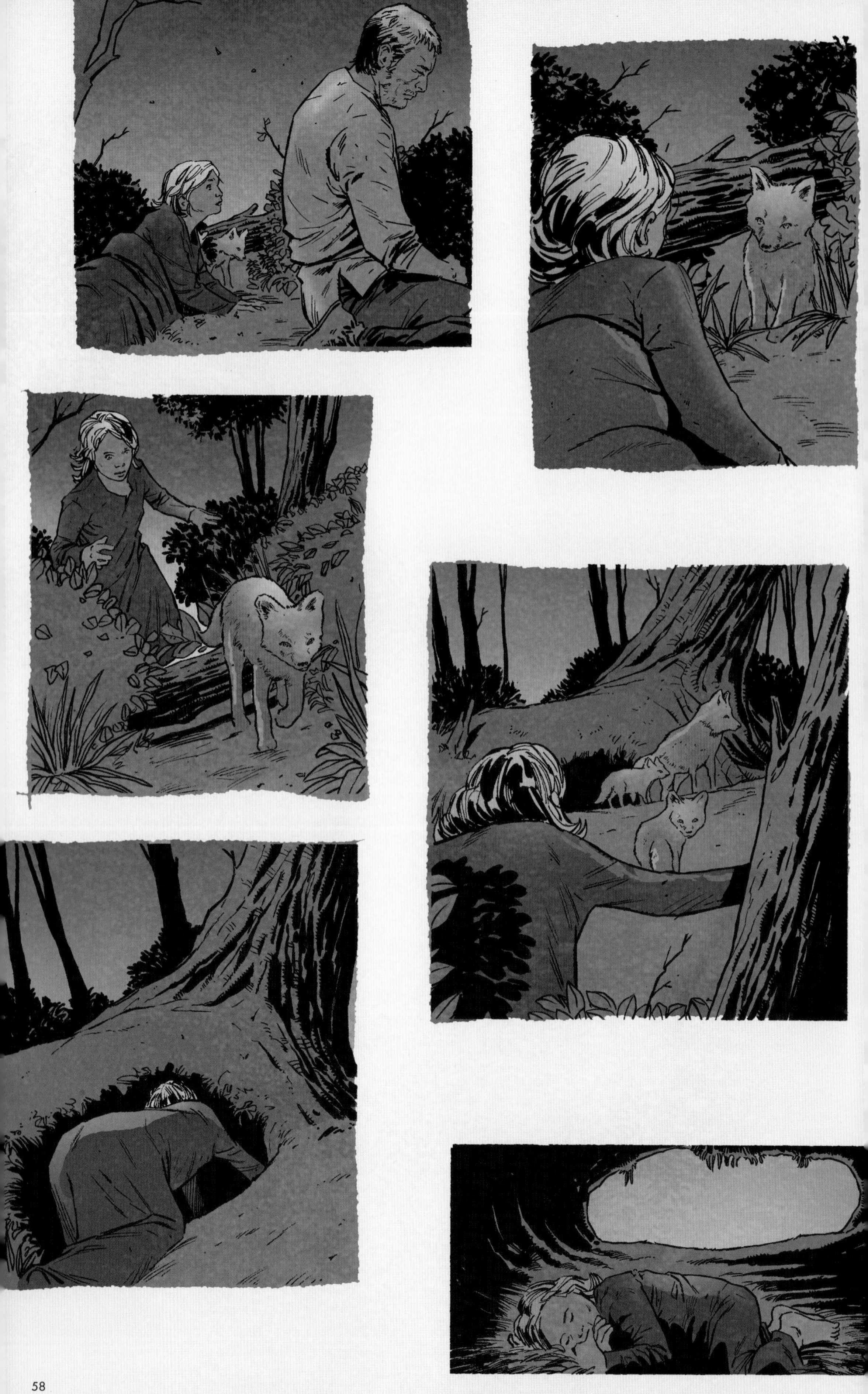

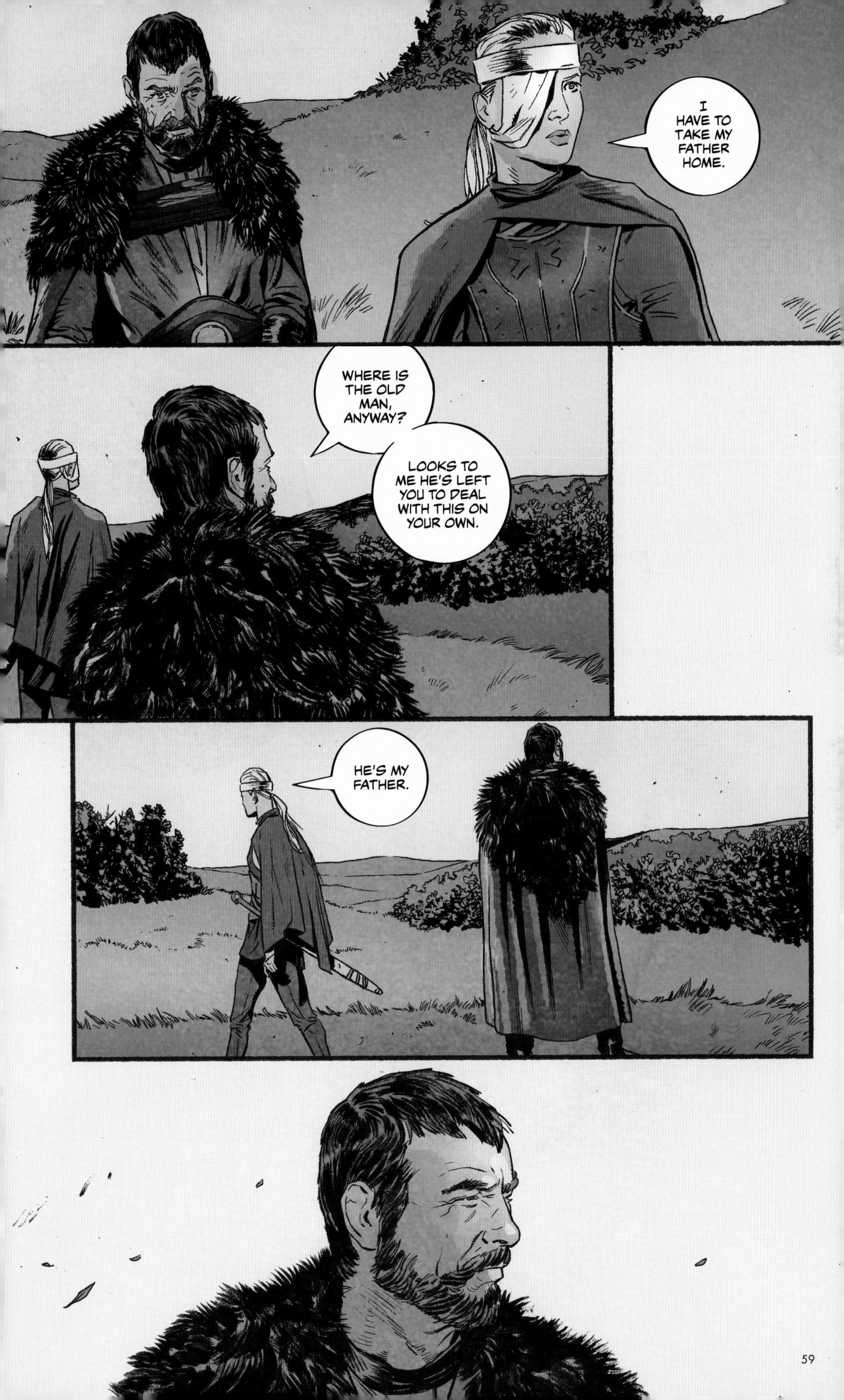
I HAVE TO TAKE MY FATHER HOME.
WHERE IS THE OLD MAN, ANYWAY?
LOOKS TO ME HE'S LEFT YOU TO DEAL WITH THIS ON YOUR OWN.
HE'S MY FATHER.

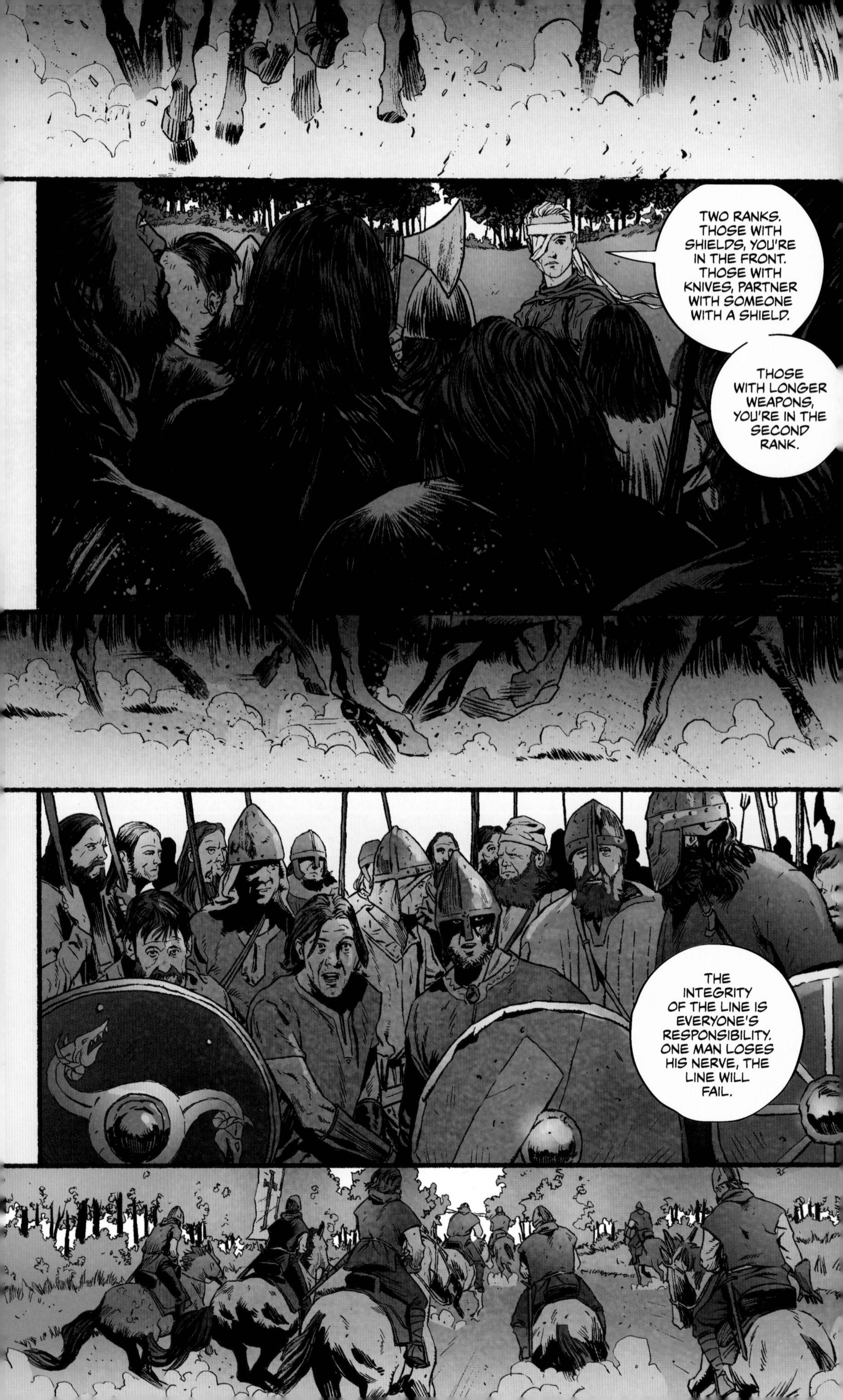
TWO RANKS. THOSE WITH SHIELDS, YOU'RE IN THE FRONT. THOSE WITH KNIVES, PARTNER WITH SOMEONE WITH A SHIELD.
THOSE WITH LONGER WEAPONS, YOU'RE IN THE SECOND RANK.
THE INTEGRITY OF THE LINE IS EVERYONE'S RESPONSIBILITY. ONE MAN LOSES HIS NERVE, THE LINE WILL FAIL.

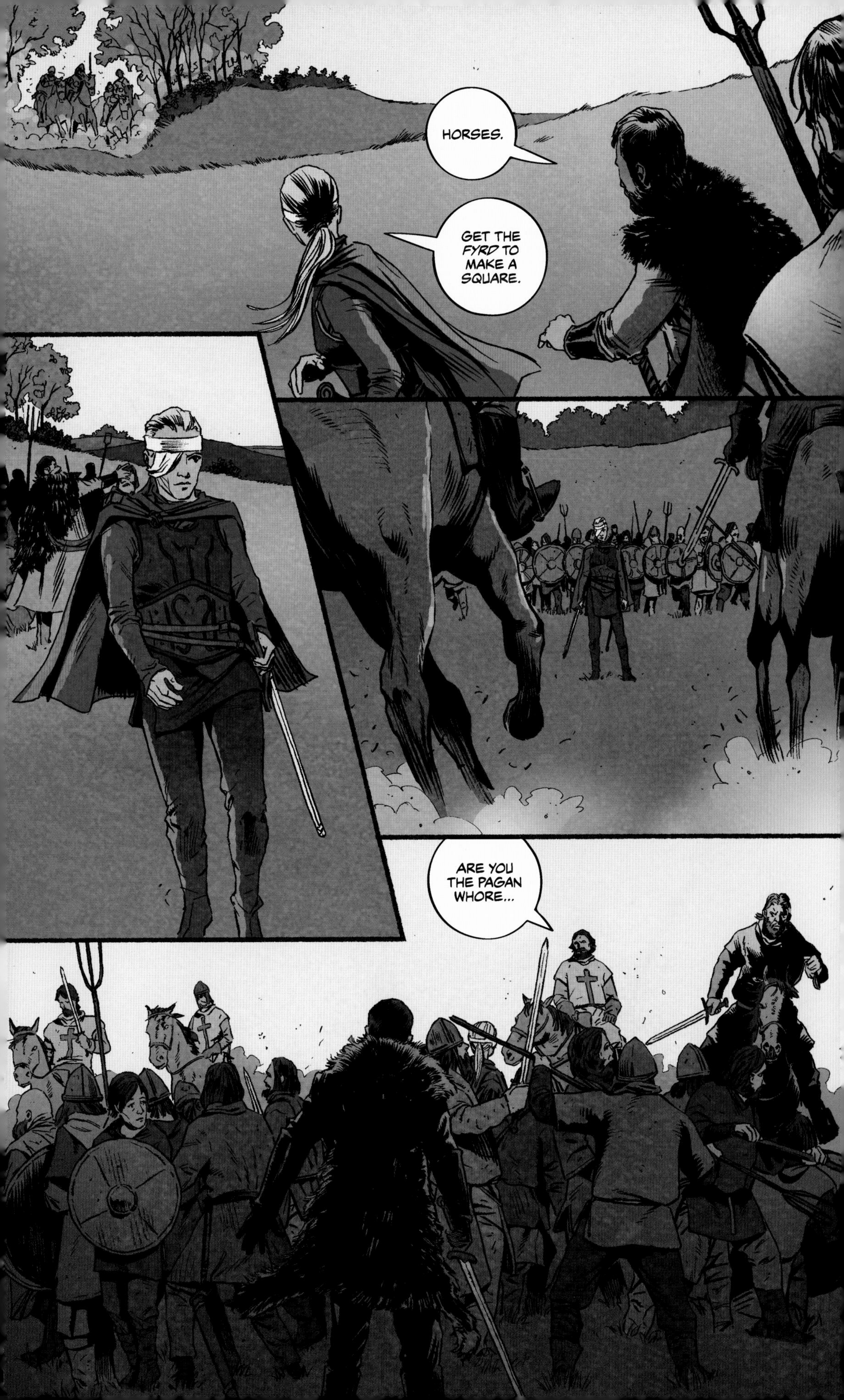
HORSES.
GET THE FYRD TO MAKE A SQUARE.
ARE YOU THE PAGAN WHORE...

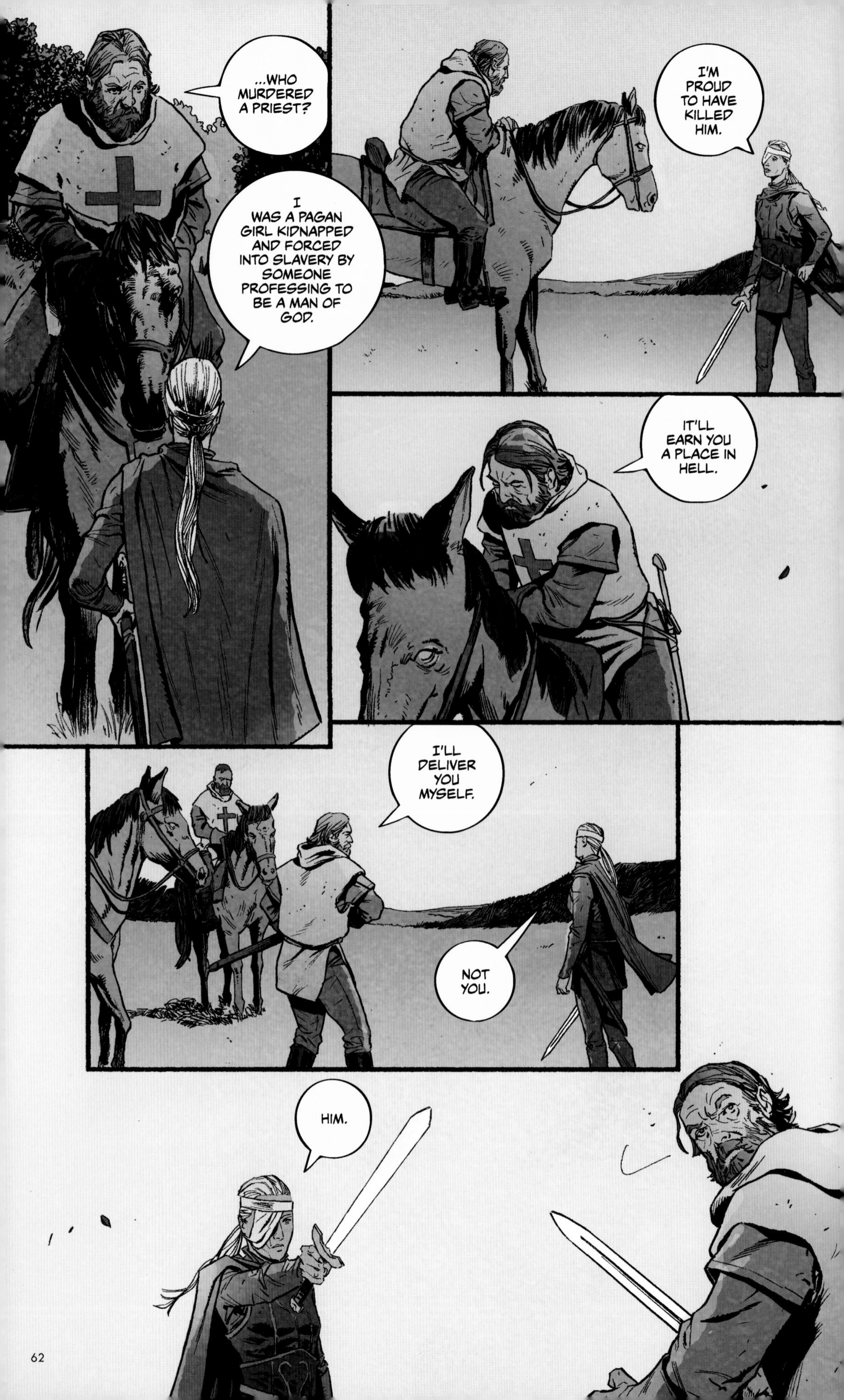
...WHO MURDERED A PRIEST?
I WAS A PAGAN GIRL KIDNAPPED AND FORCED INTO SLAVERY BY SOMEONE PROFESSING TO BE A MAN OF GOD.
I'M PROUD TO HAVE KILLED HIM.
IT'LL EARN YOU A PLACE IN HELL.
I'LL DELIVER YOU MYSELF.
NOT YOU.
HIM.

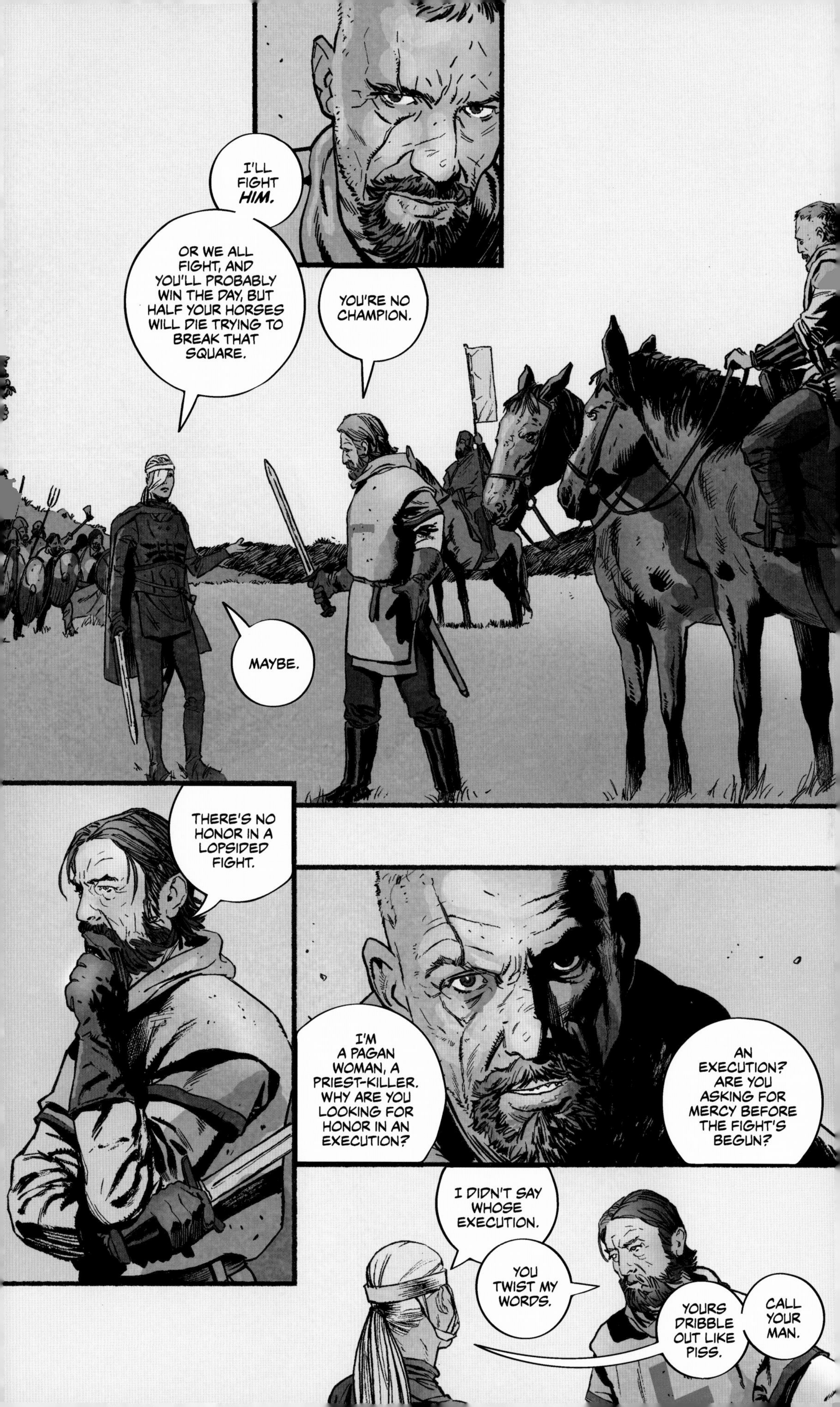
I'LL FIGHT *HIM.*
OR WE ALL FIGHT, AND YOU'LL PROBABLY WIN THE DAY, BUT HALF YOUR HORSES WILL DIE TRYING TO BREAK THAT SQUARE.
YOU'RE NO CHAMPION.
MAYBE.
THERE'S NO HONOR IN A LOPSIDED FIGHT.
I'M A PAGAN WOMAN, A PRIEST-KILLER. WHY ARE YOU LOOKING FOR HONOR IN AN EXECUTION?
AN EXECUTION? ARE YOU ASKING FOR MERCY BEFORE THE FIGHT'S BEGUN?
I DIDN'T SAY WHOSE EXECUTION.
YOU TWIST MY WORDS.
YOURS DRIBBLE OUT LIKE PISS.
CALL YOUR MAN.

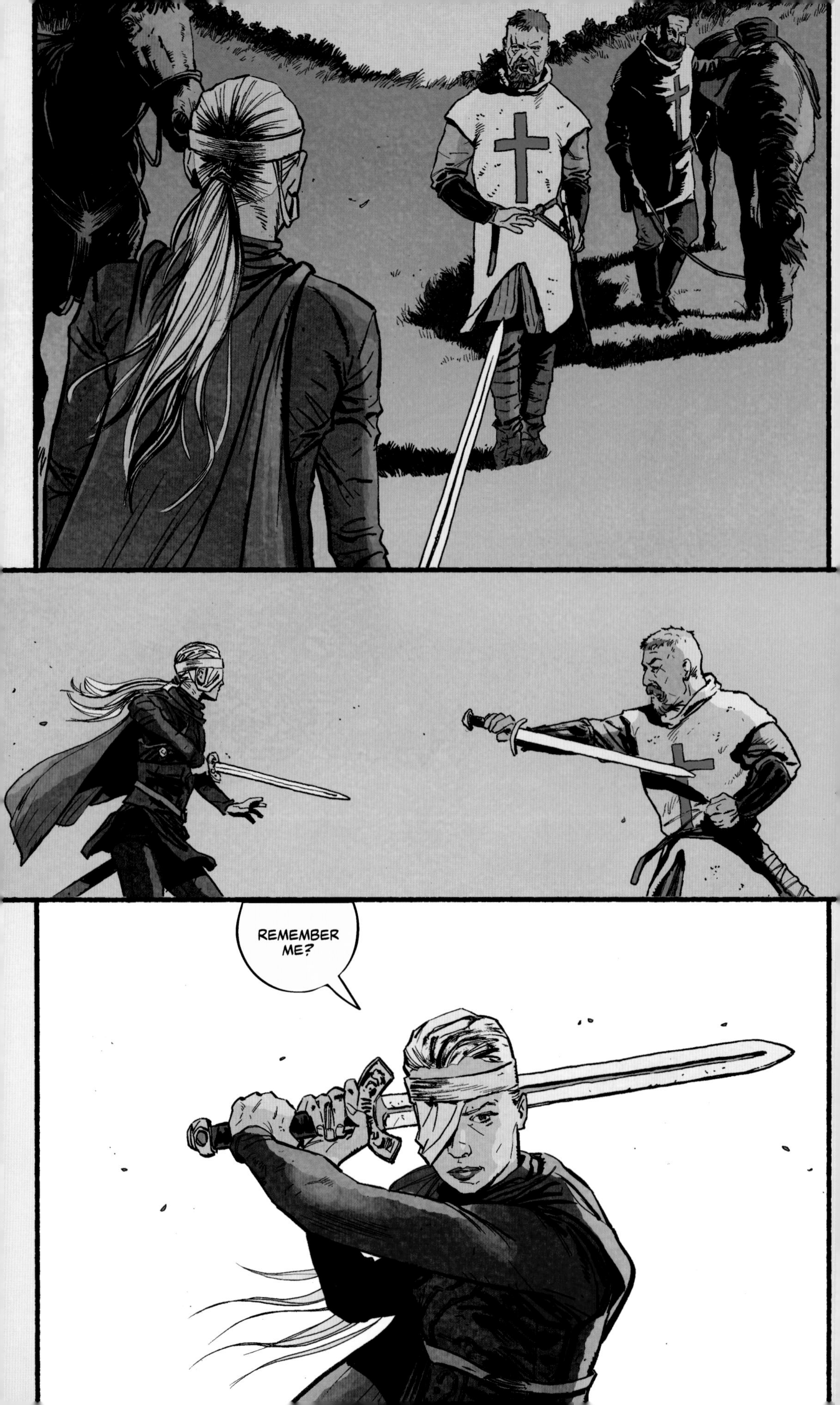
REMEMBER ME?

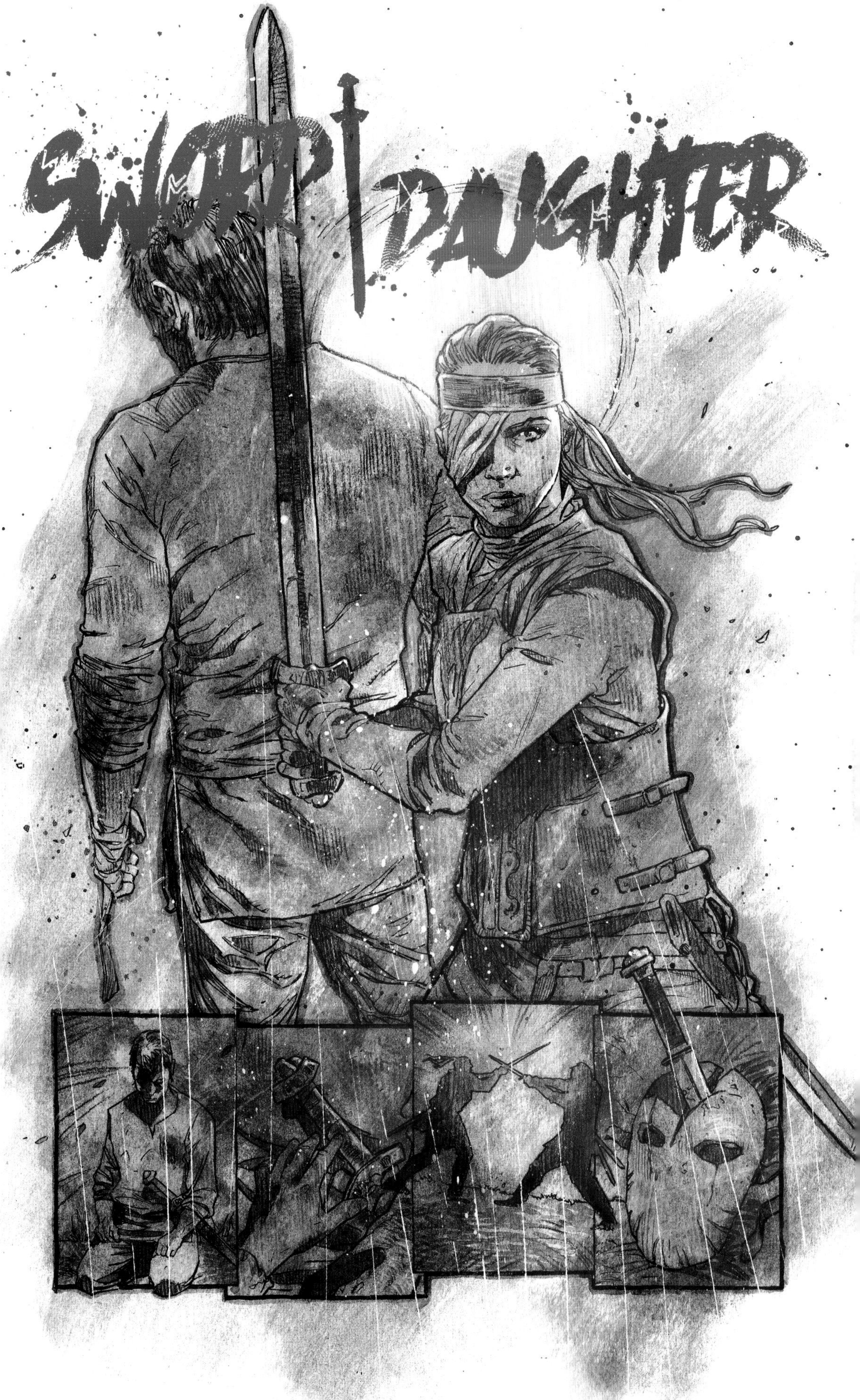
SWORD DAUGHTER

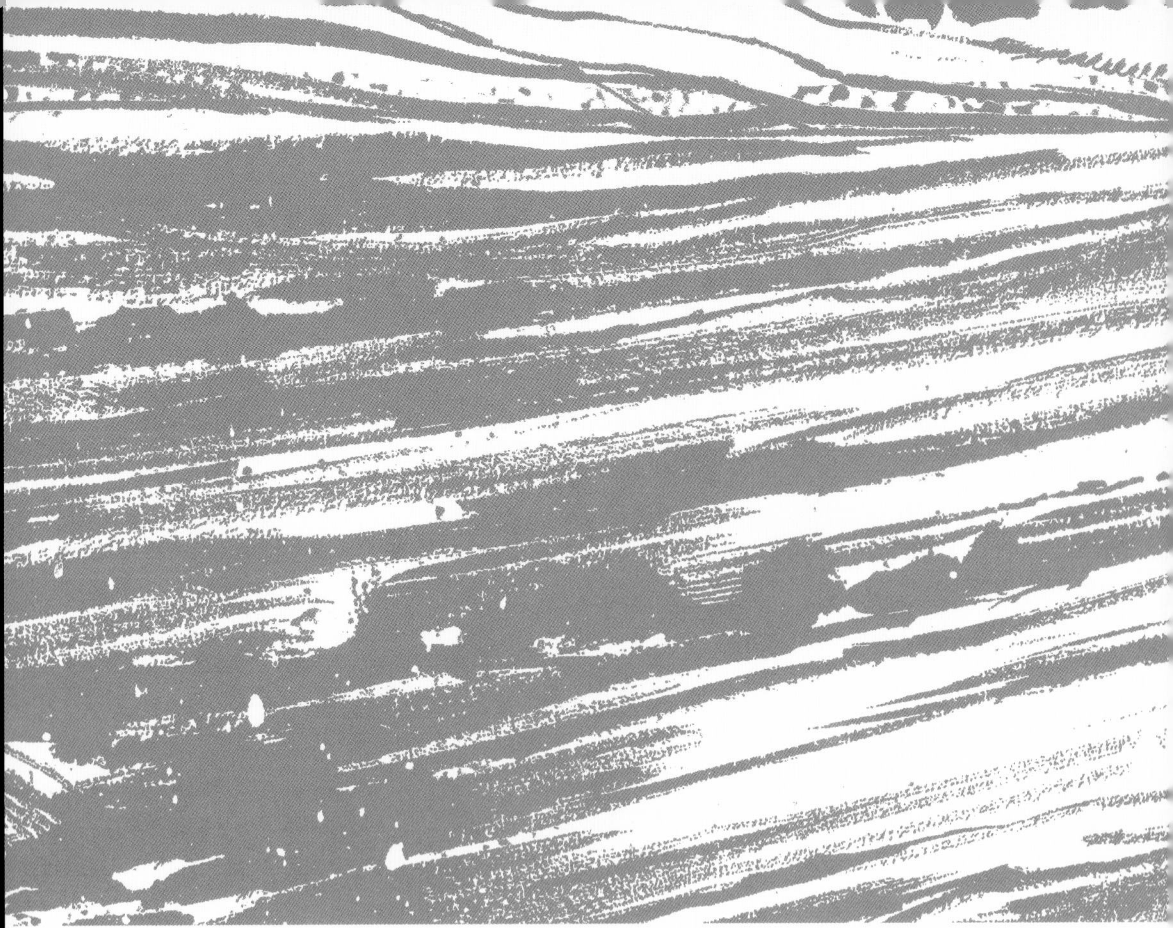

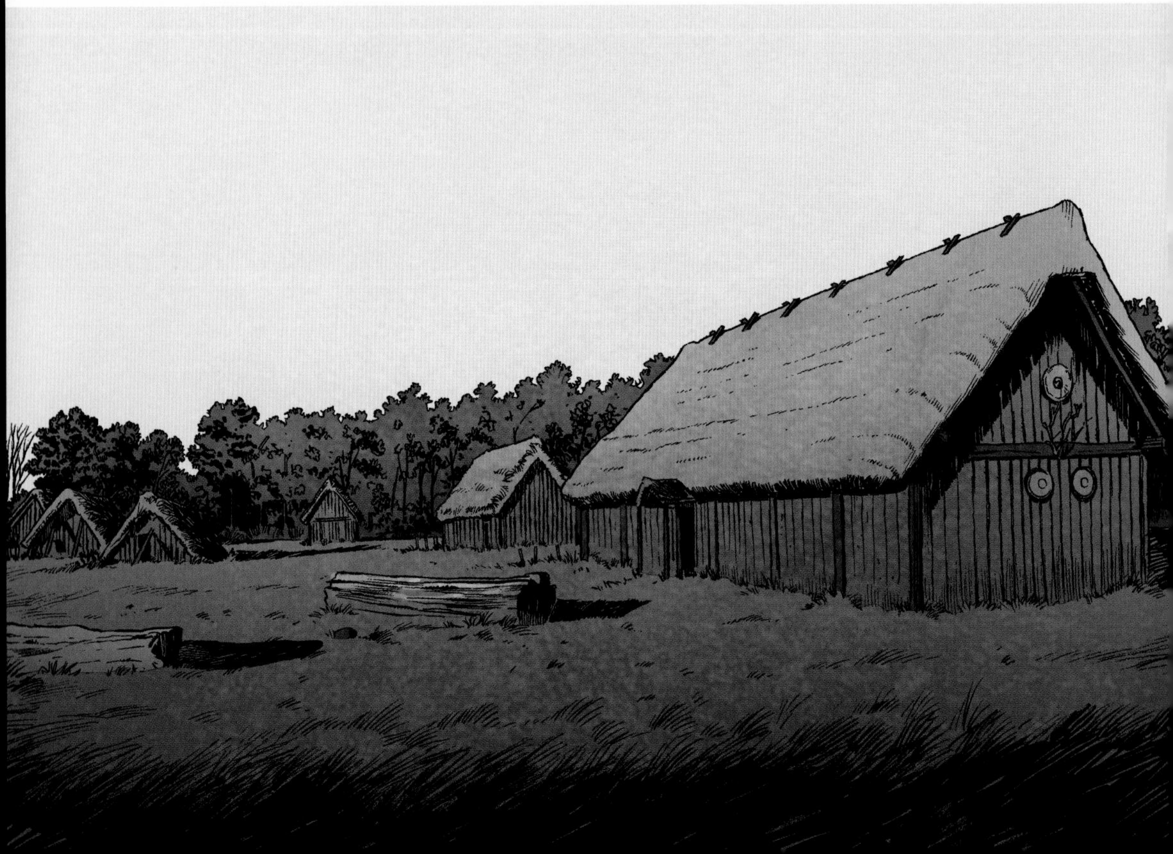

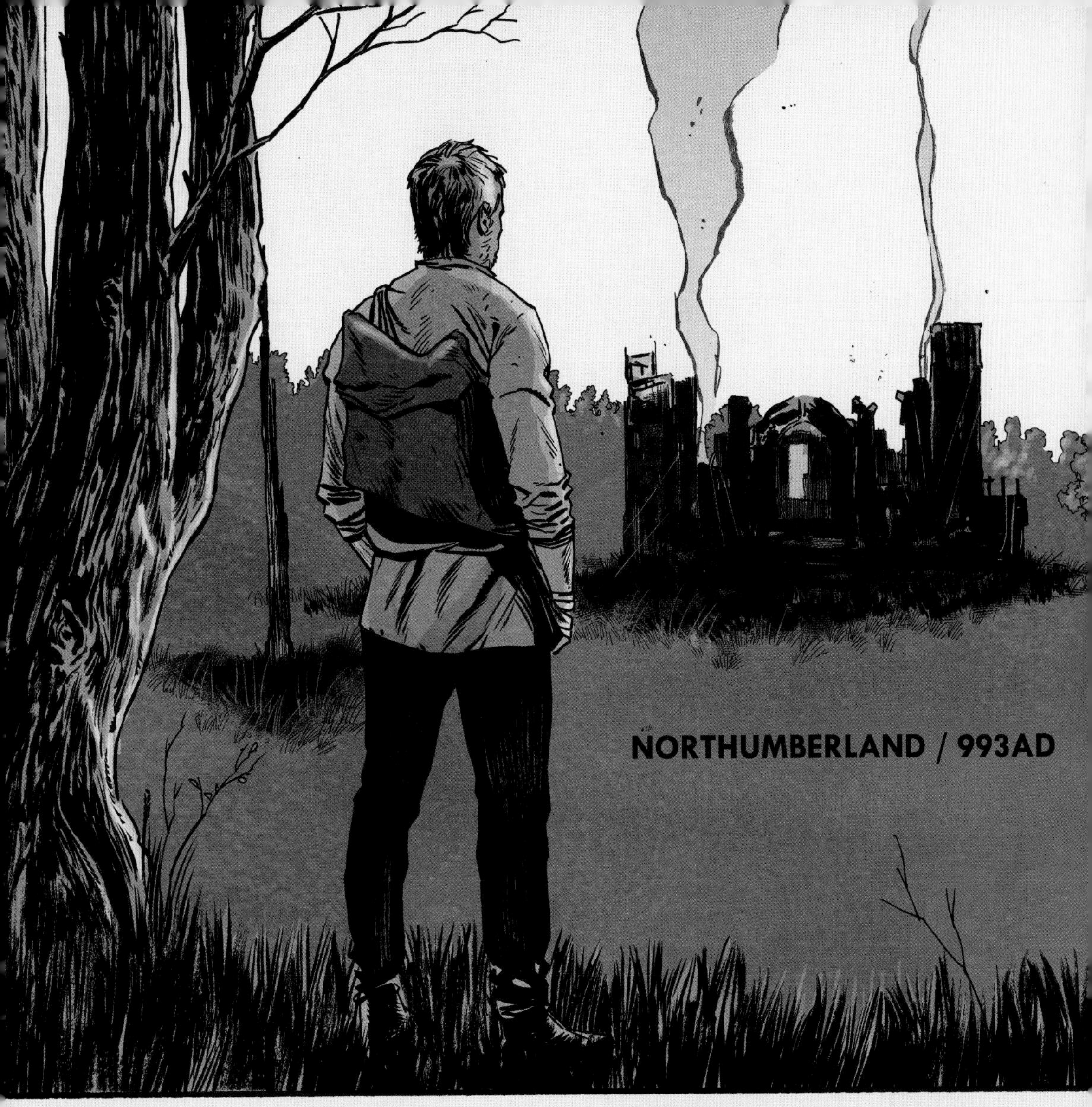
NORTHUMBERLAND / 993AD

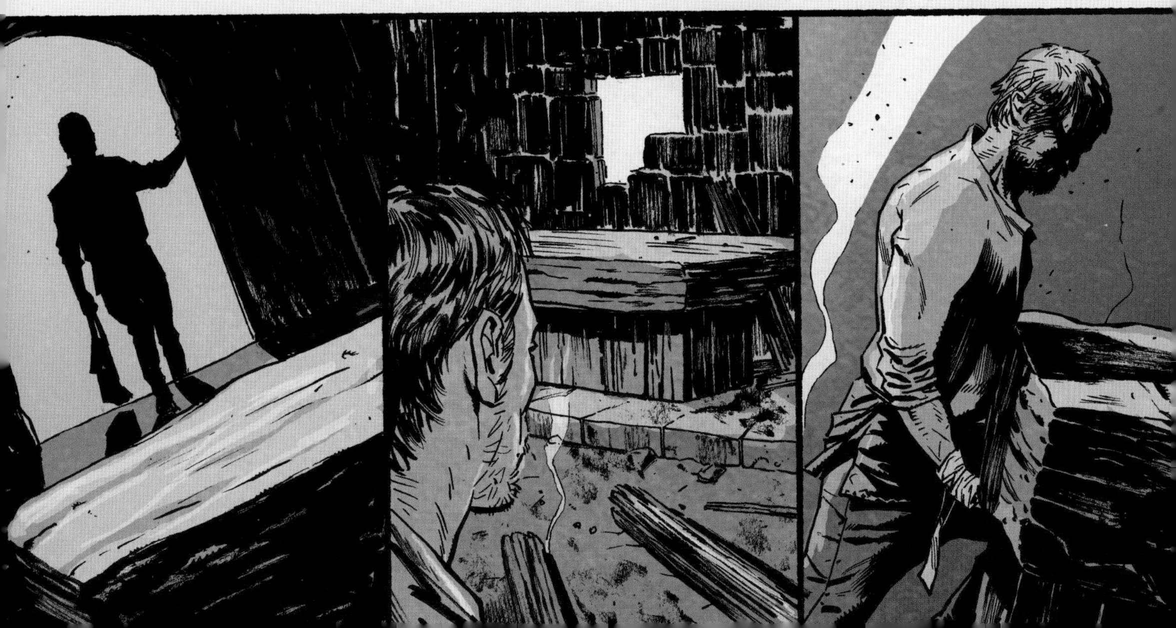

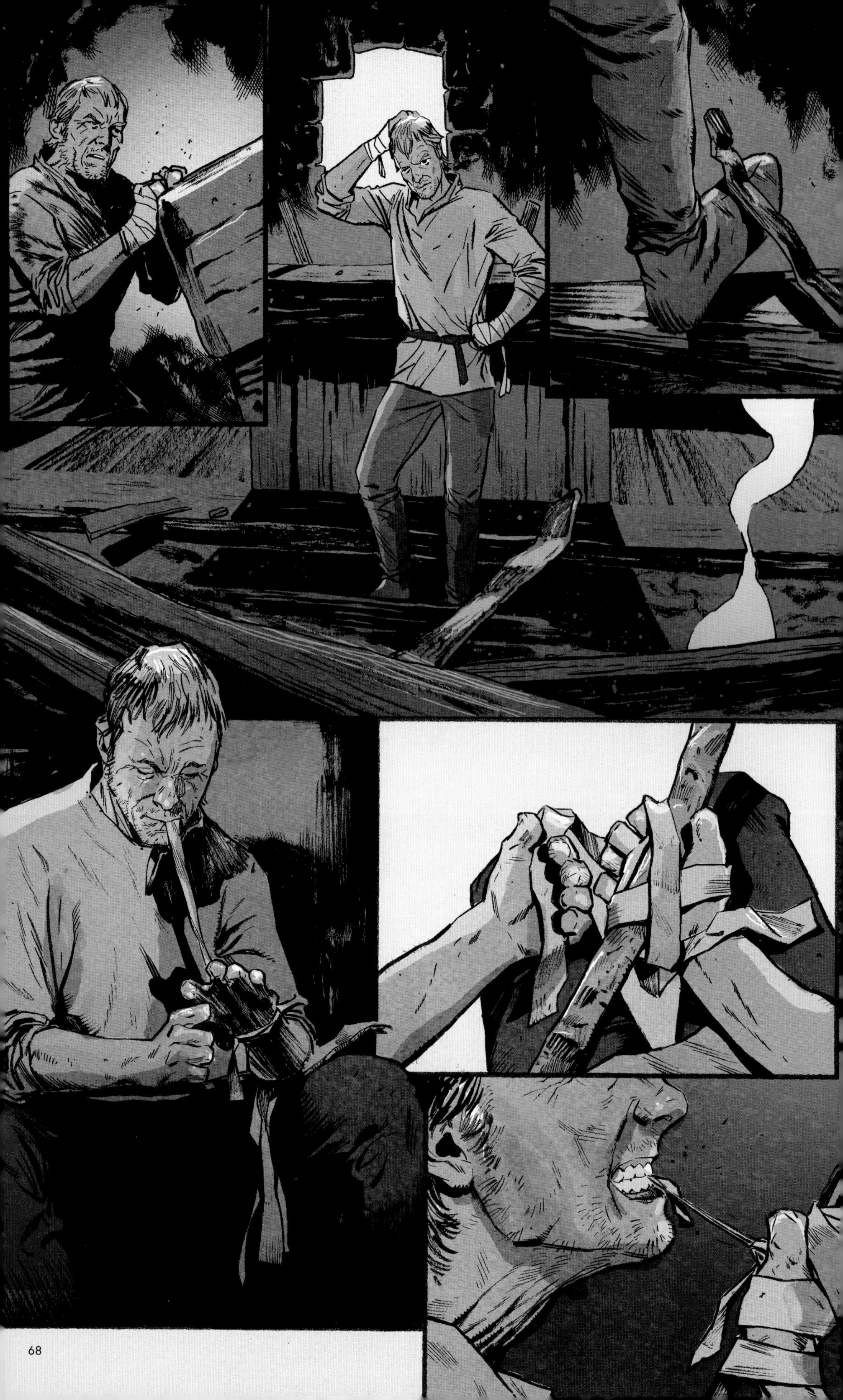

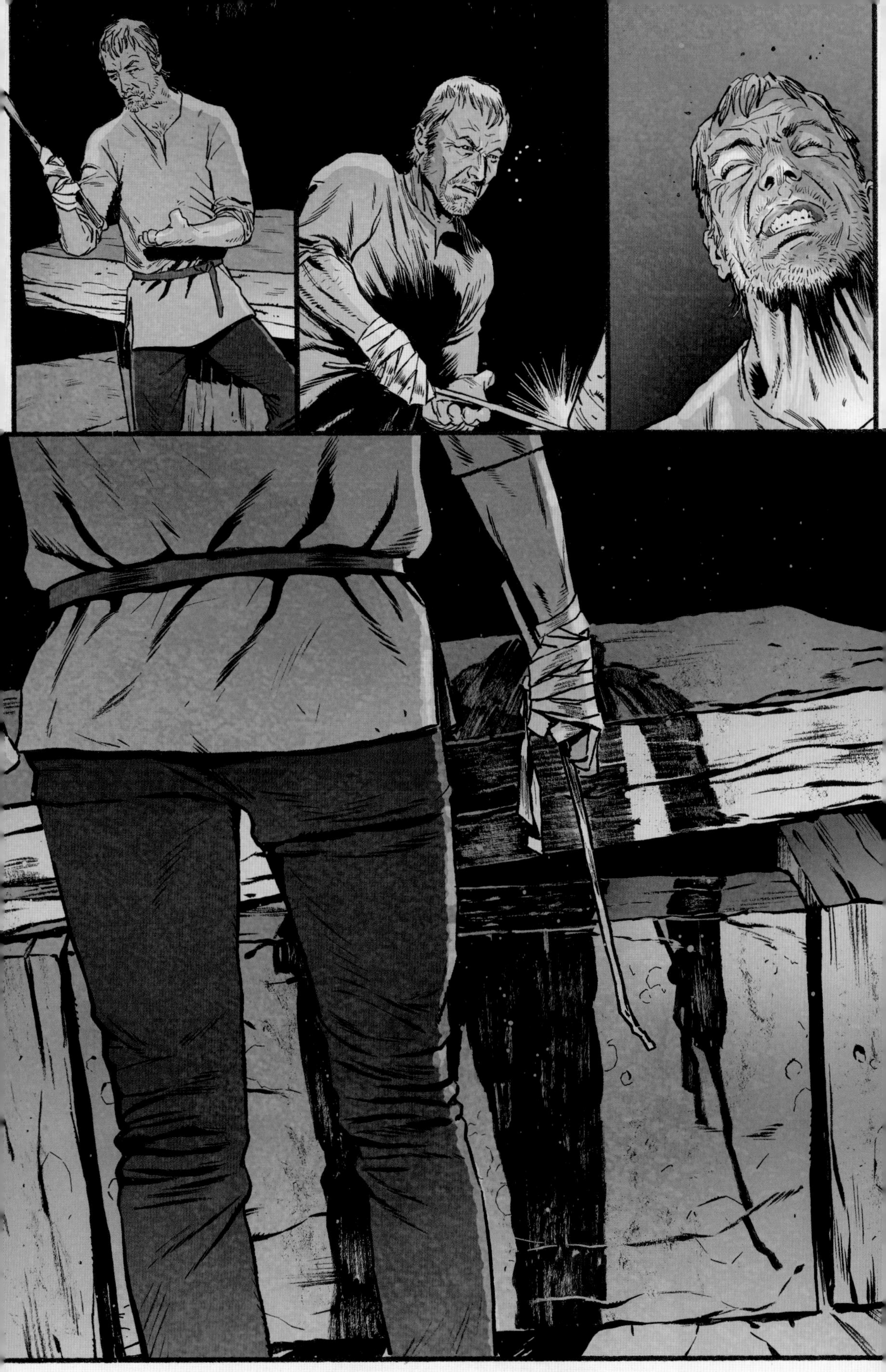

SWORD DAUGHTER

SHATTERED AGAINST STEEL

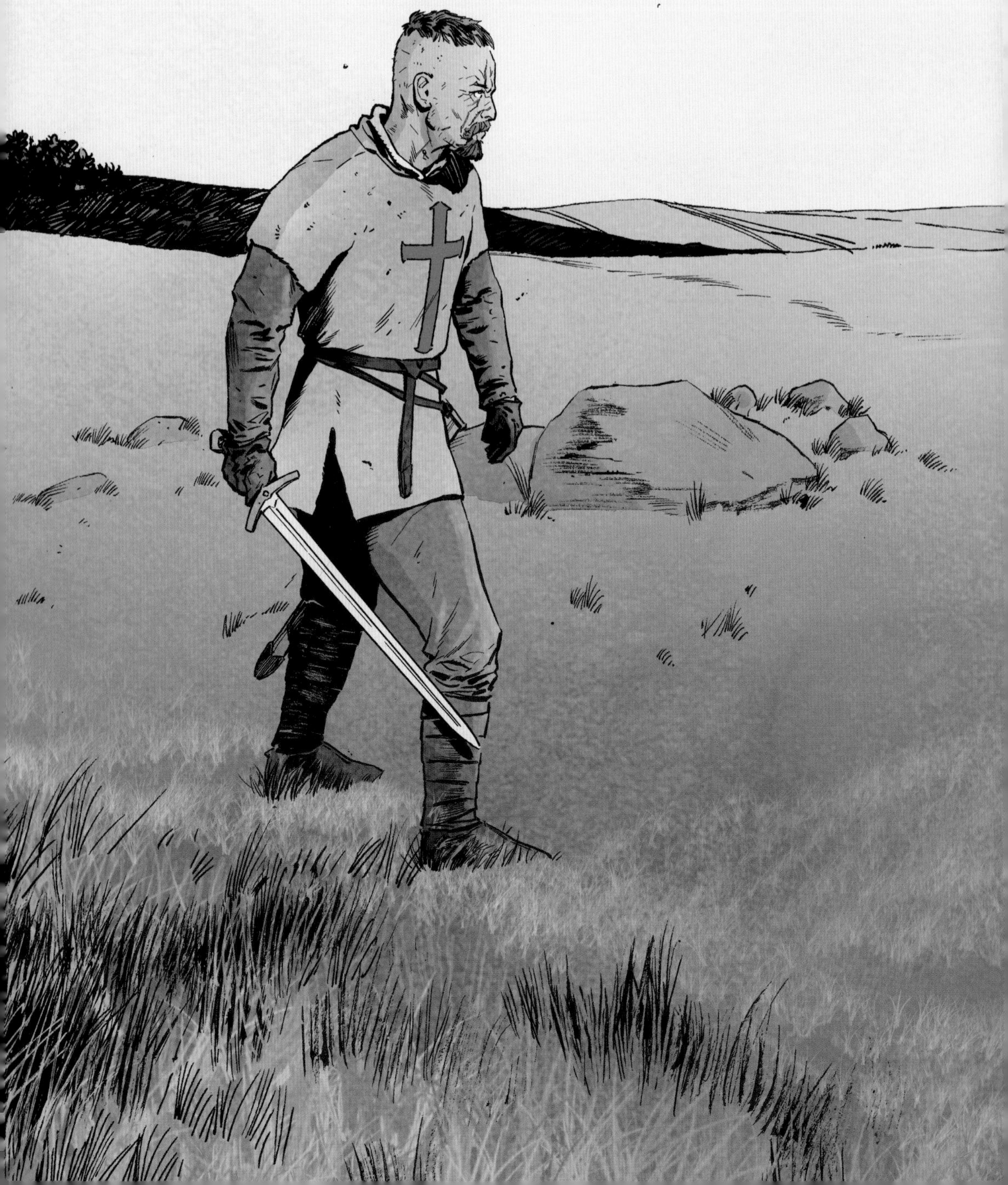

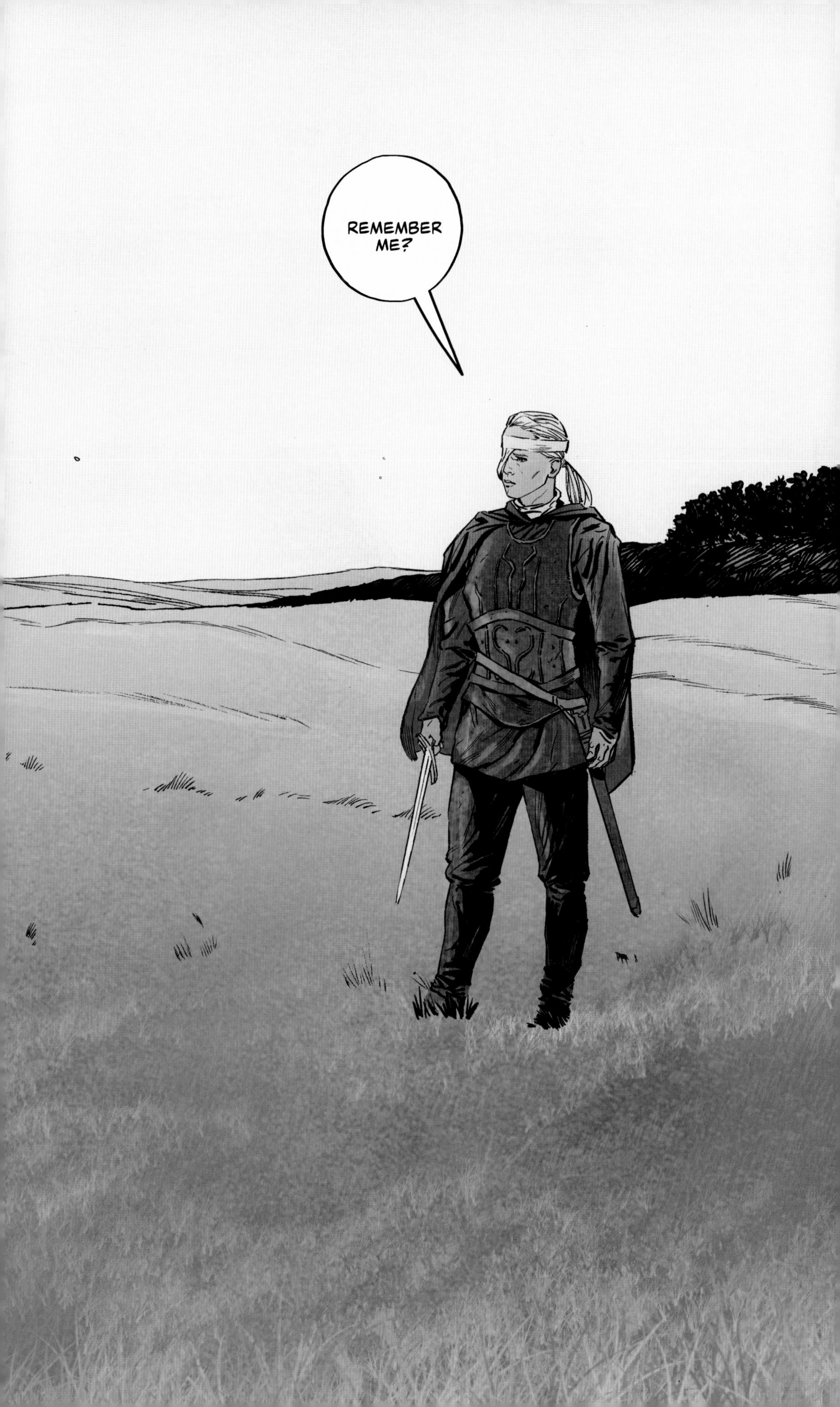
REMEMBER ME?

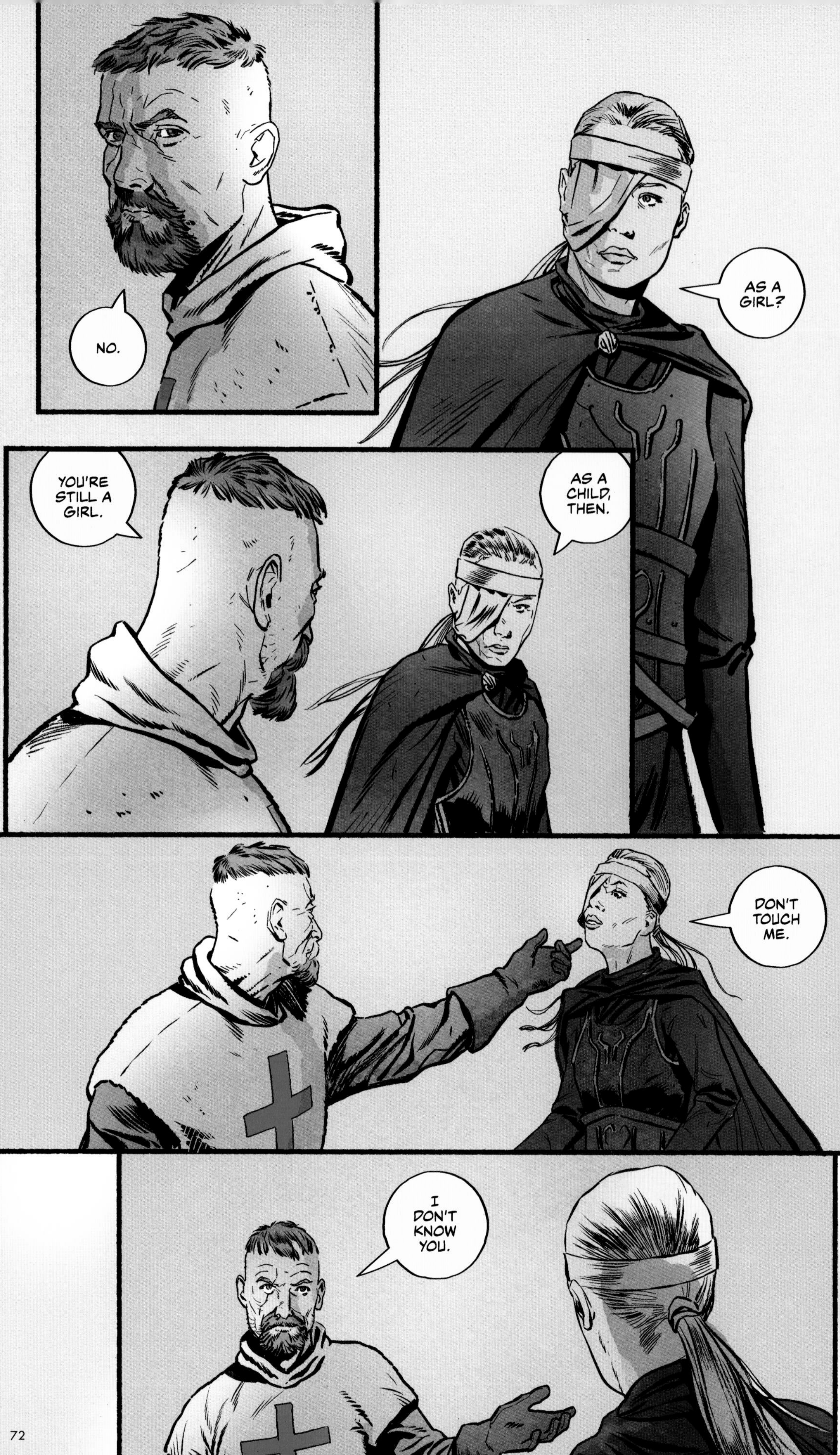
AS A GIRL?
NO.
YOU'RE STILL A GIRL.
AS A CHILD, THEN.
DON'T TOUCH ME.
I DON'T KNOW YOU.

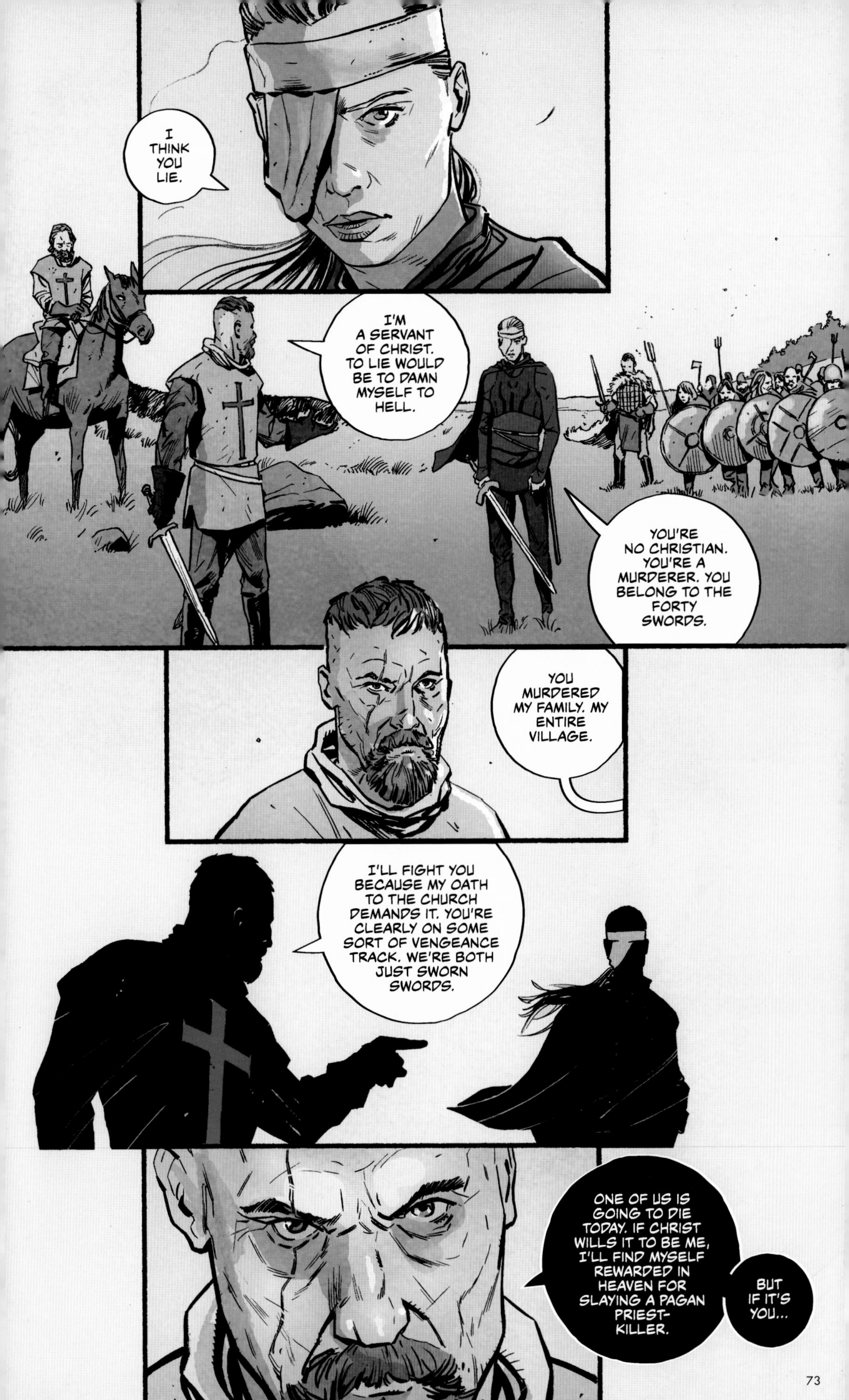
I THINK YOU LIE.
I'M A SERVANT OF CHRIST. TO LIE WOULD BE TO DAMN MYSELF TO HELL.
YOU'RE NO CHRISTIAN. YOU'RE A MURDERER. YOU BELONG TO THE FORTY SWORDS.
YOU MURDERED MY FAMILY. MY ENTIRE VILLAGE.
I'LL FIGHT YOU BECAUSE MY OATH TO THE CHURCH DEMANDS IT. YOU'RE CLEARLY ON SOME SORT OF VENGEANCE TRACK. WE'RE BOTH JUST SWORN SWORDS.
ONE OF US IS GOING TO DIE TODAY. IF CHRIST WILLS IT TO BE ME, I'LL FIND MYSELF REWARDED IN HEAVEN FOR SLAYING A PAGAN PRIEST-KILLER.
BUT IF IT'S YOU...

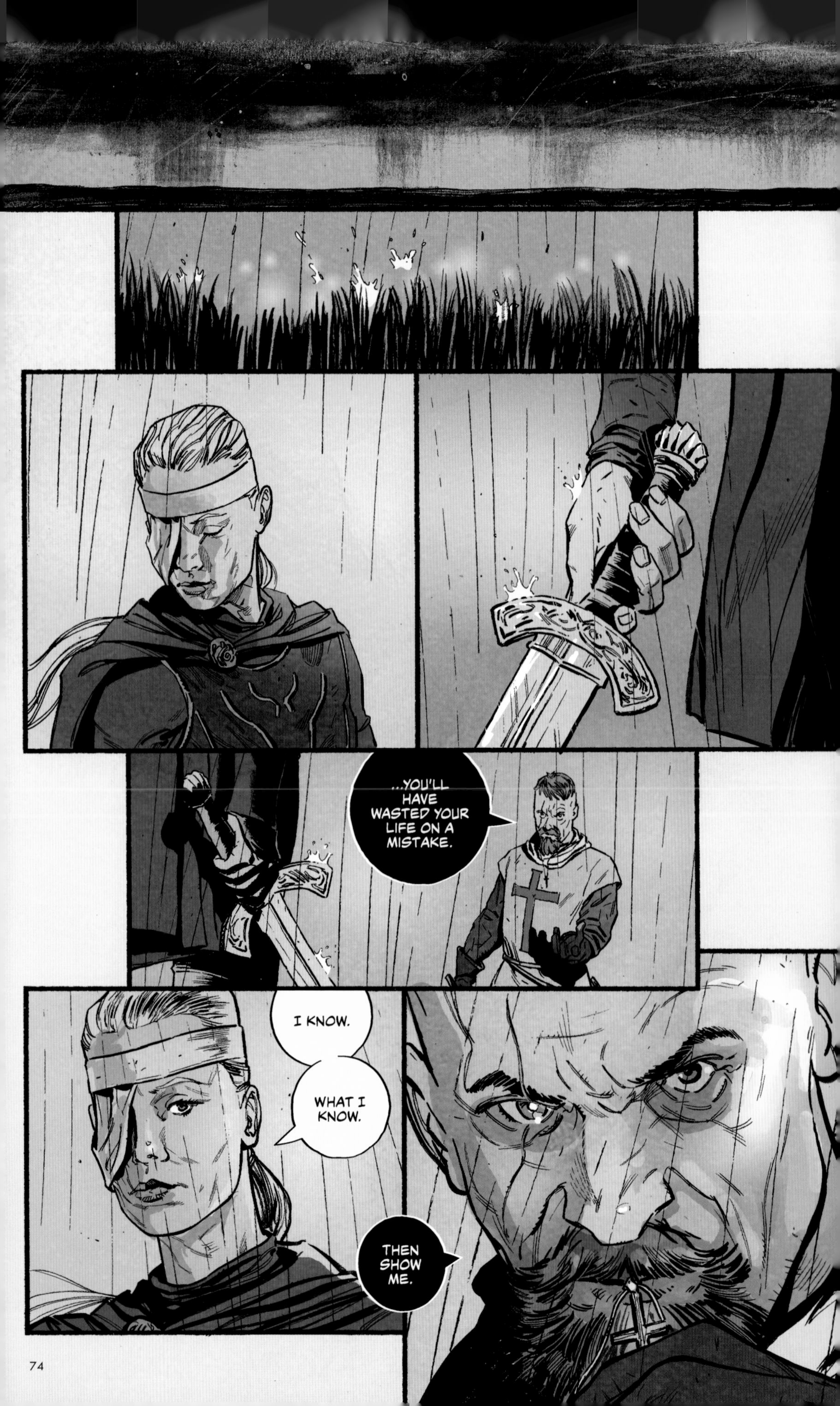

...YOU'LL HAVE WASTED YOUR LIFE ON A MISTAKE.
I KNOW.
WHAT I KNOW.
THEN SHOW ME.

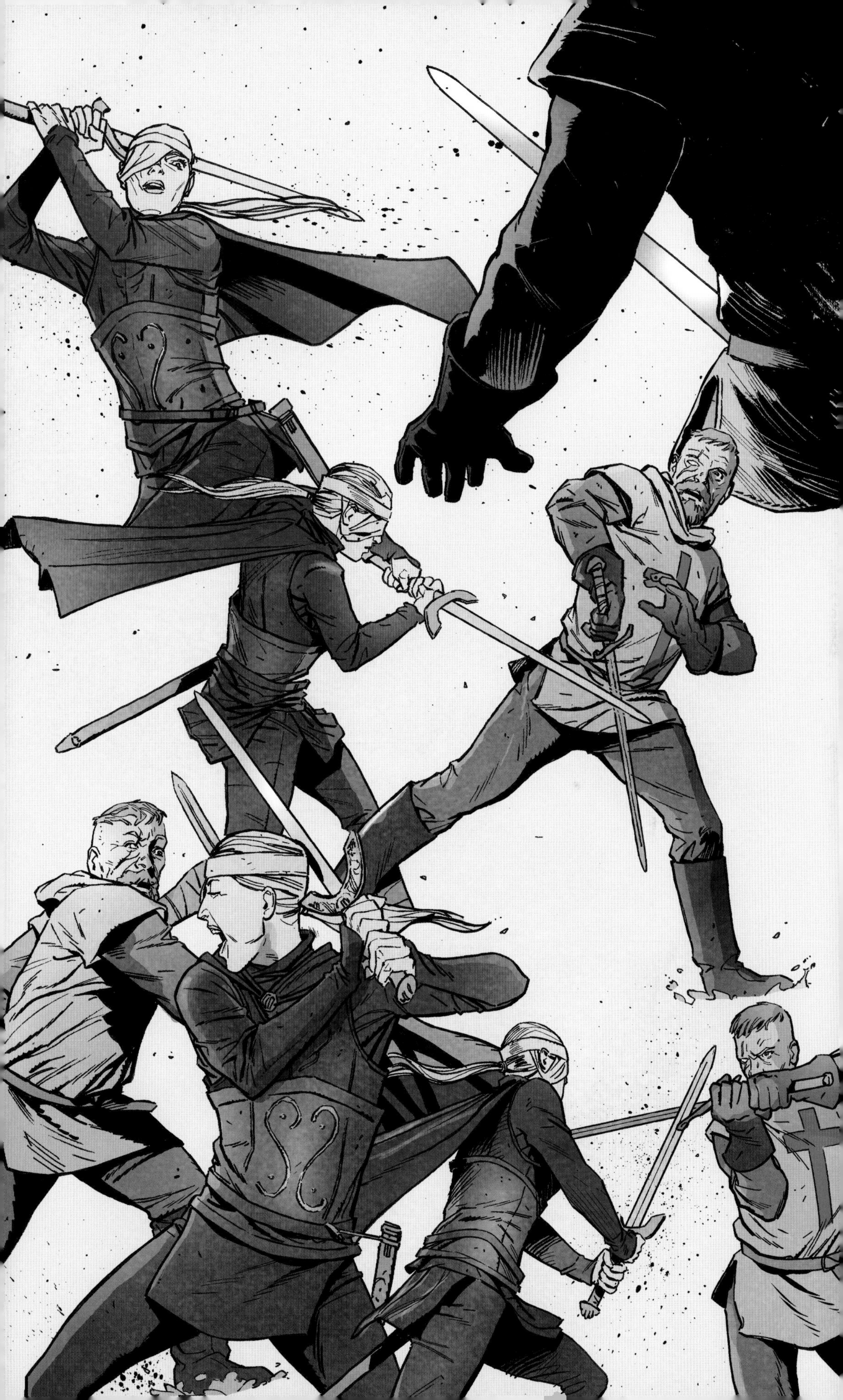

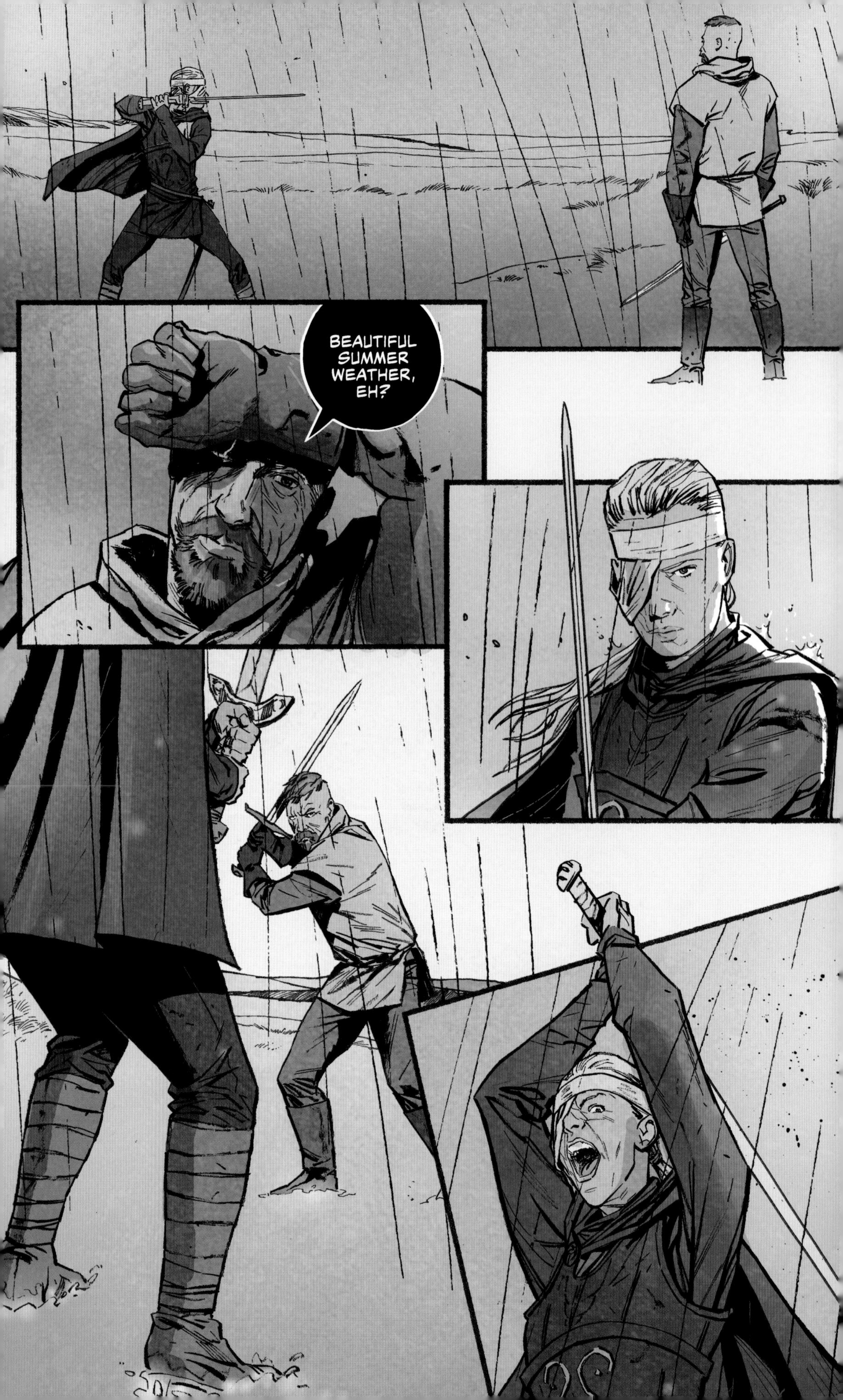
BEAUTIFUL SUMMER WEATHER, EH?

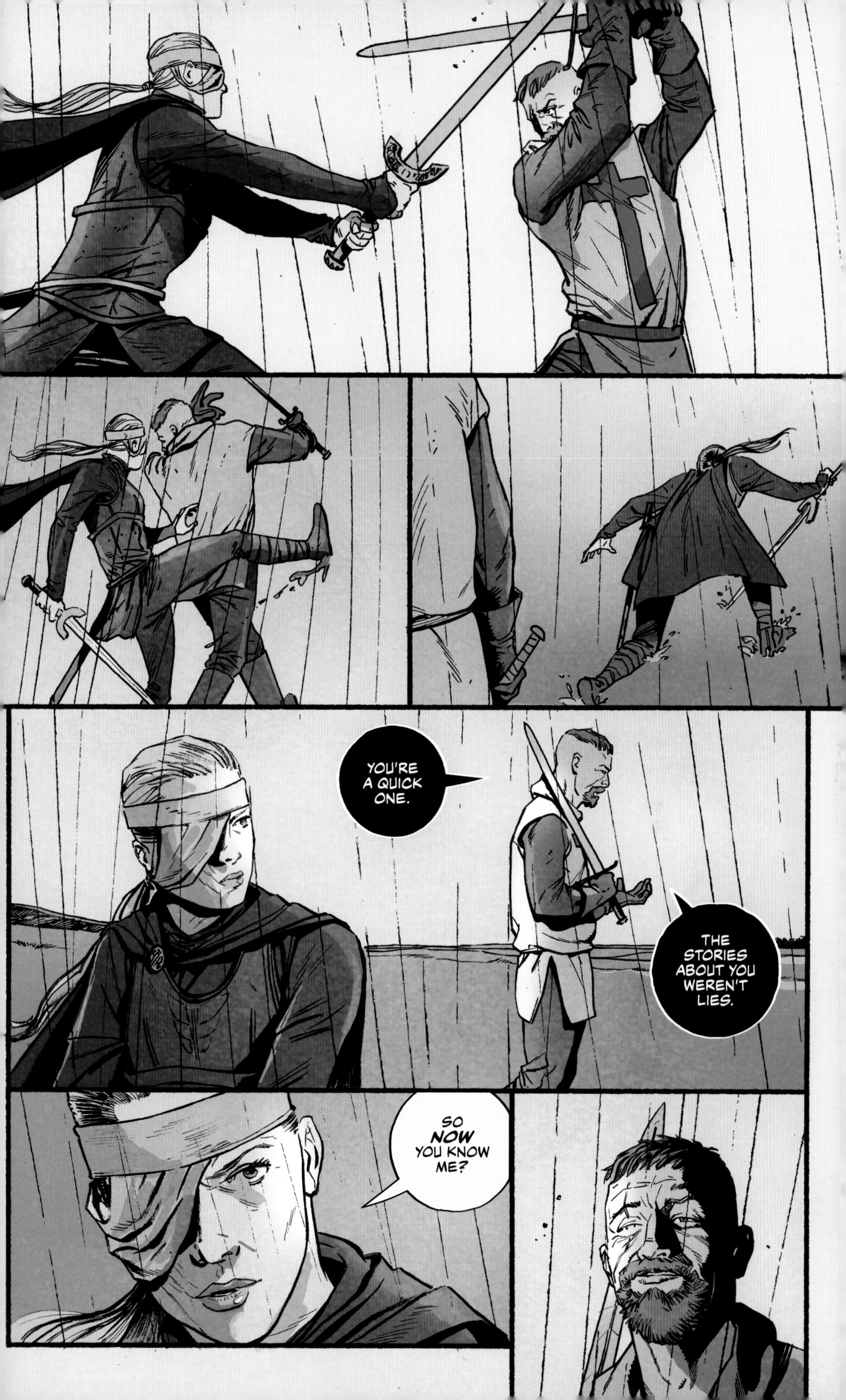
YOU'RE A QUICK ONE.
THE STORIES ABOUT YOU WEREN'T LIES.
SO NOW YOU KNOW ME?

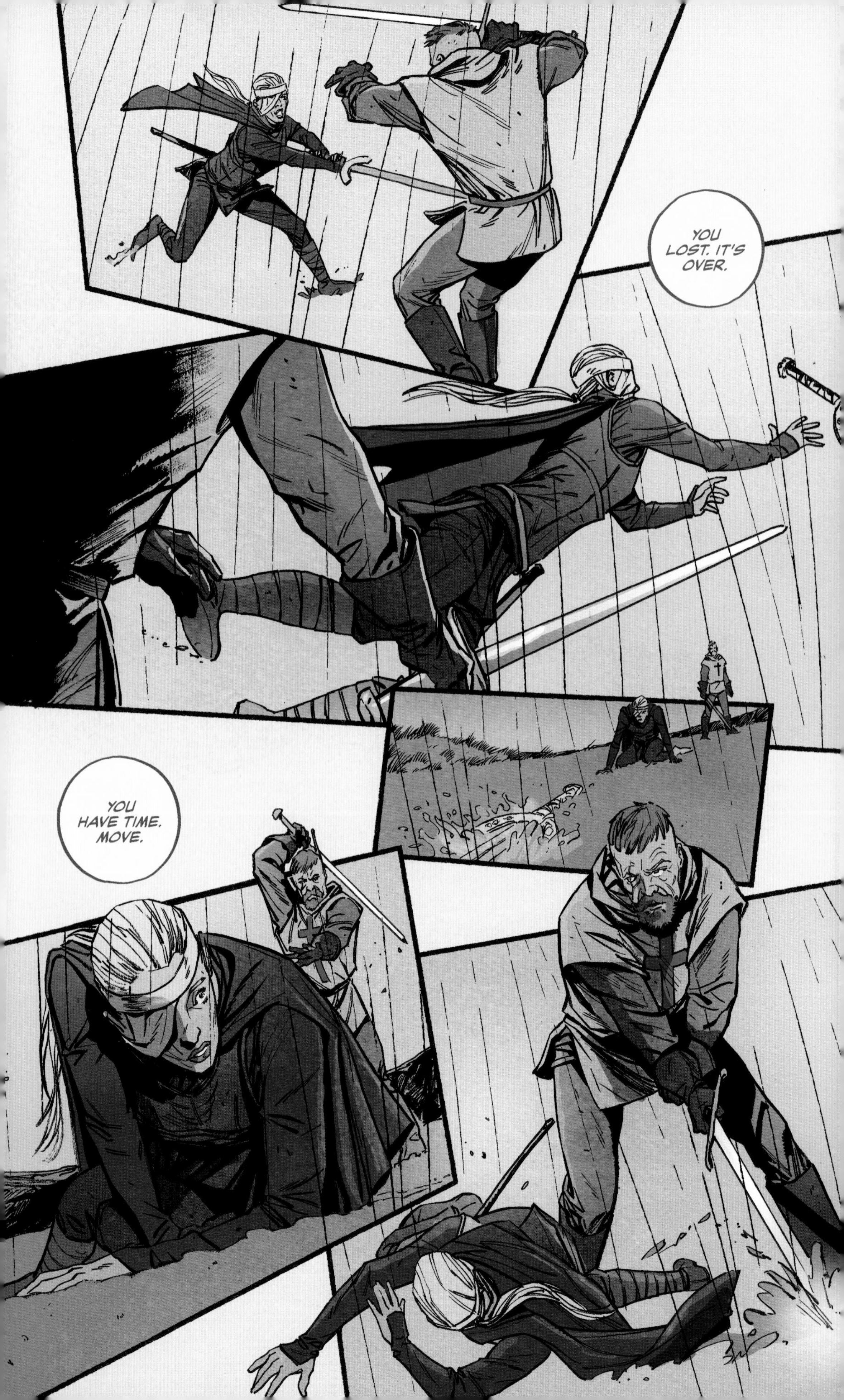
YOU LOST. IT'S OVER.
YOU HAVE TIME. MOVE.

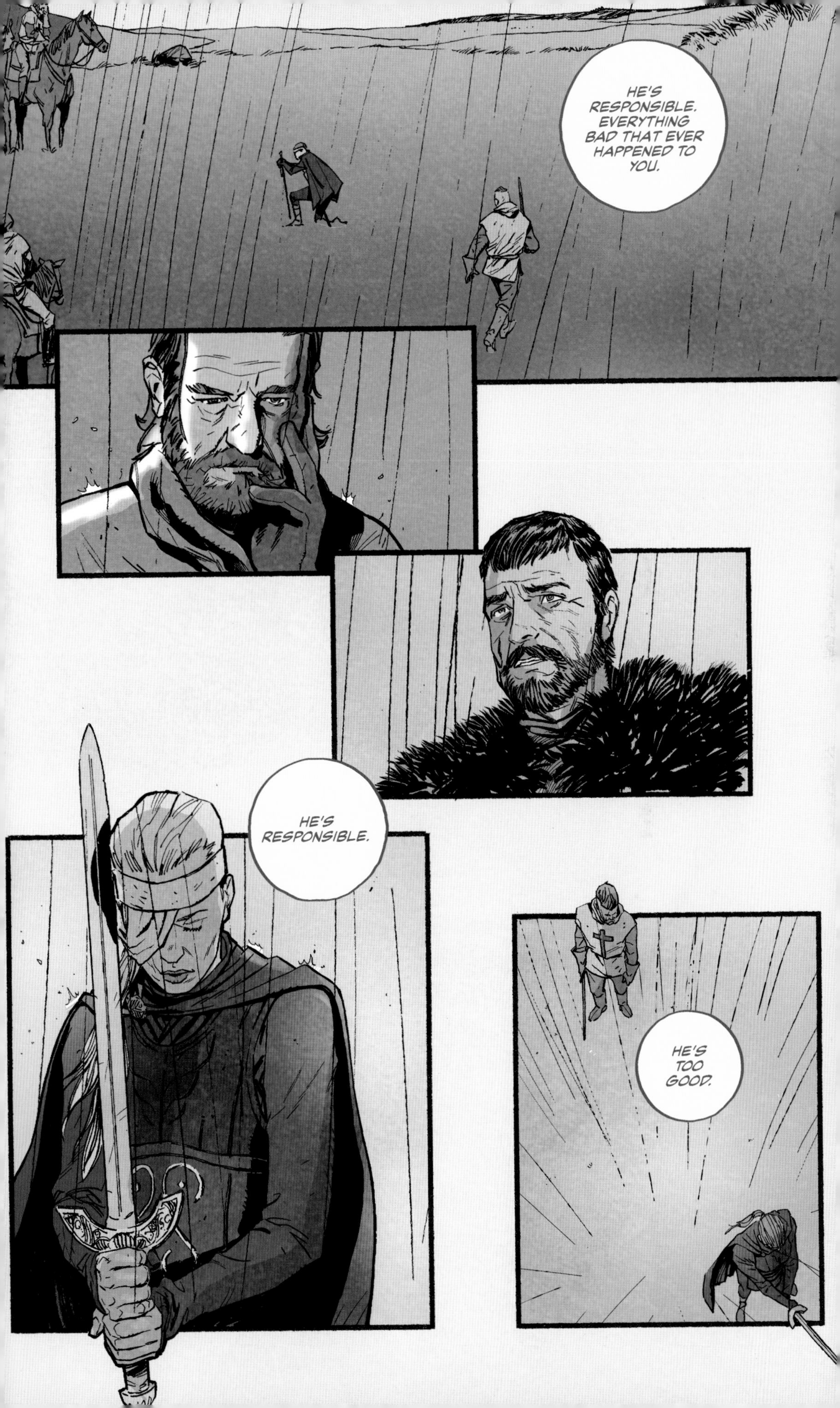
HE'S RESPONSIBLE. EVERYTHING BAD THAT EVER HAPPENED TO YOU.
HE'S RESPONSIBLE.
HE'S TOO GOOD.

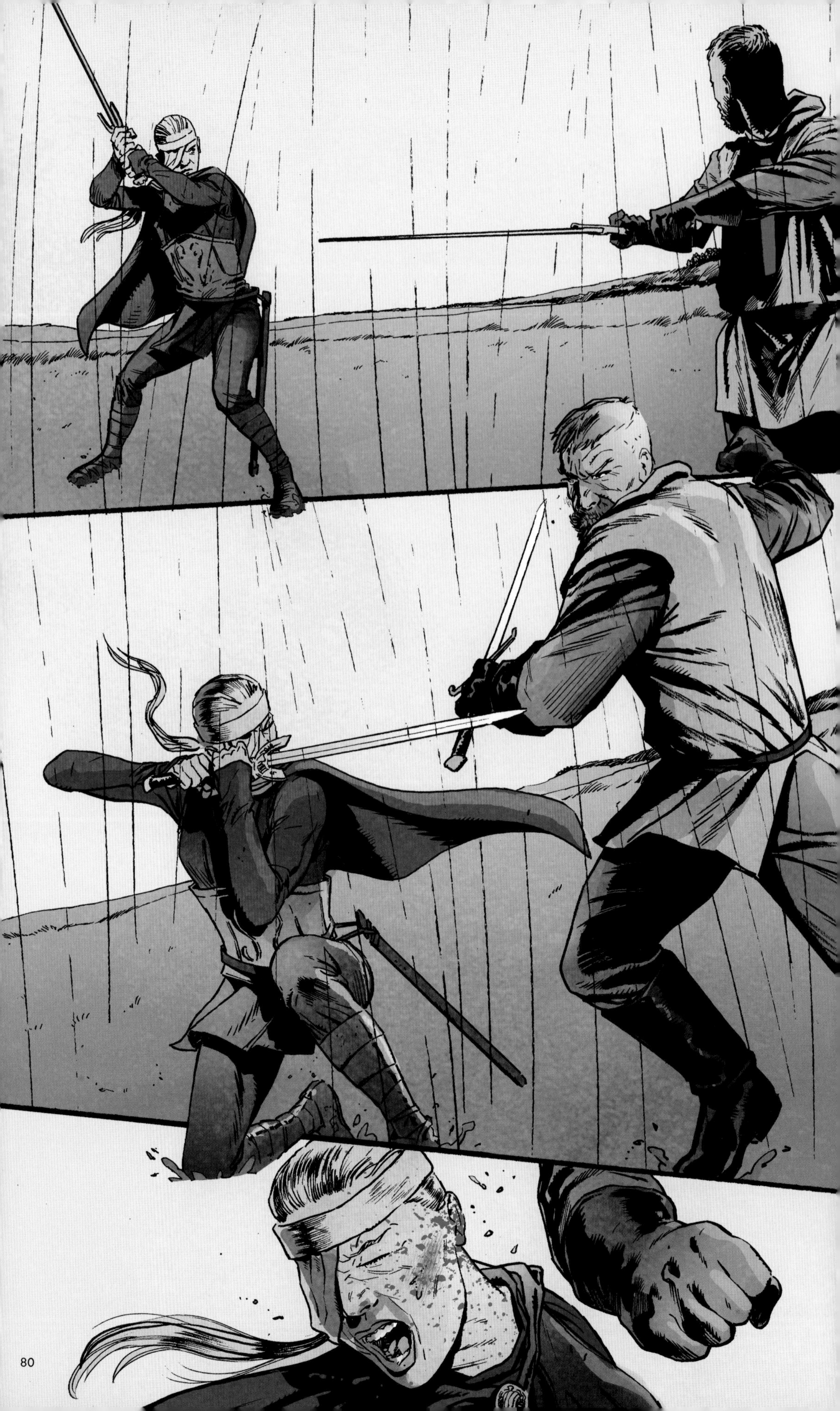

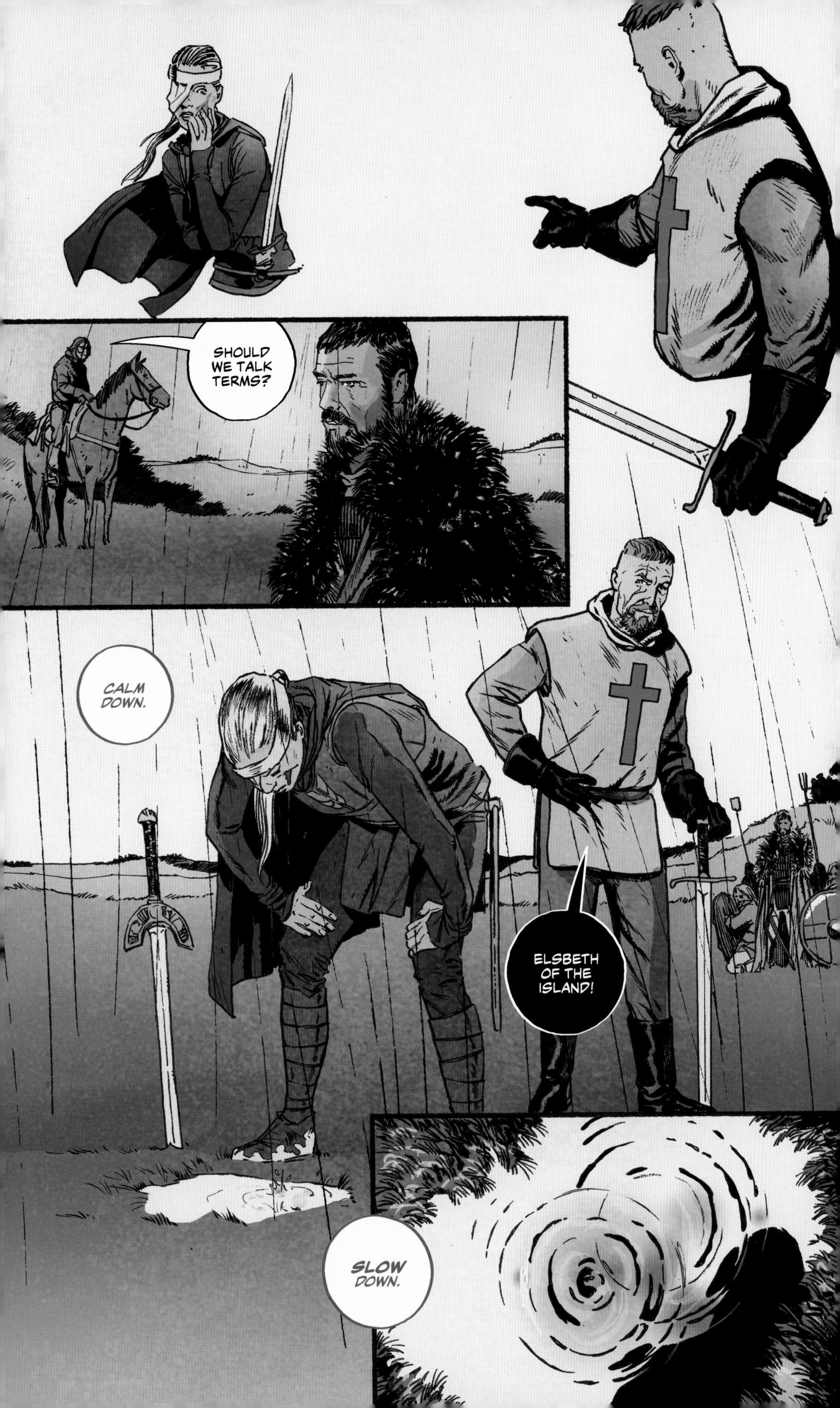
SHOULD WE TALK TERMS?
CALM DOWN.
ELSBETH OF THE ISLAND!
SLOW DOWN.

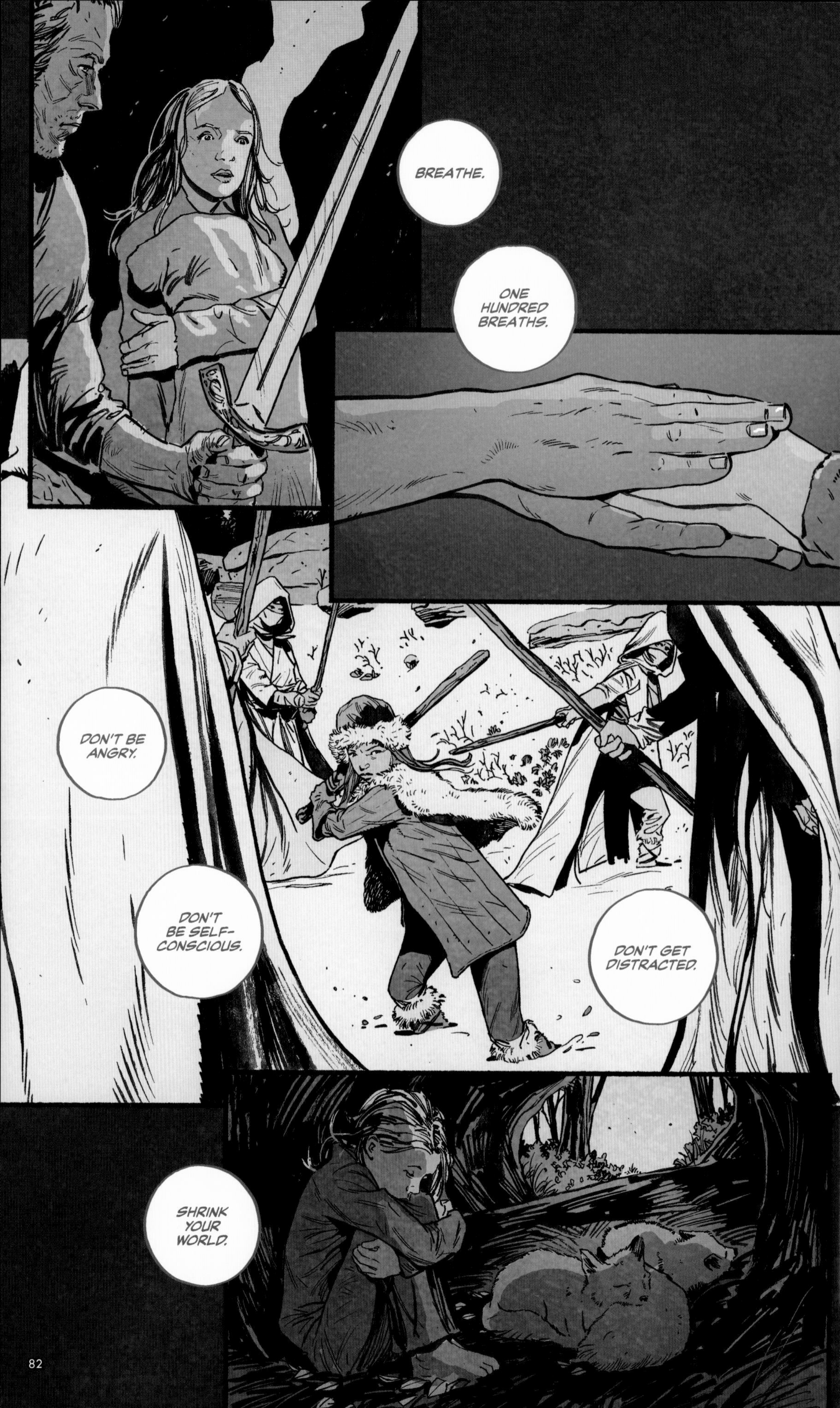
BREATHE.
ONE HUNDRED BREATHS.
DON'T BE ANGRY.
DON'T BE SELF-CONSCIOUS.
DON'T GET DISTRACTED.
SHRINK YOUR WORLD.

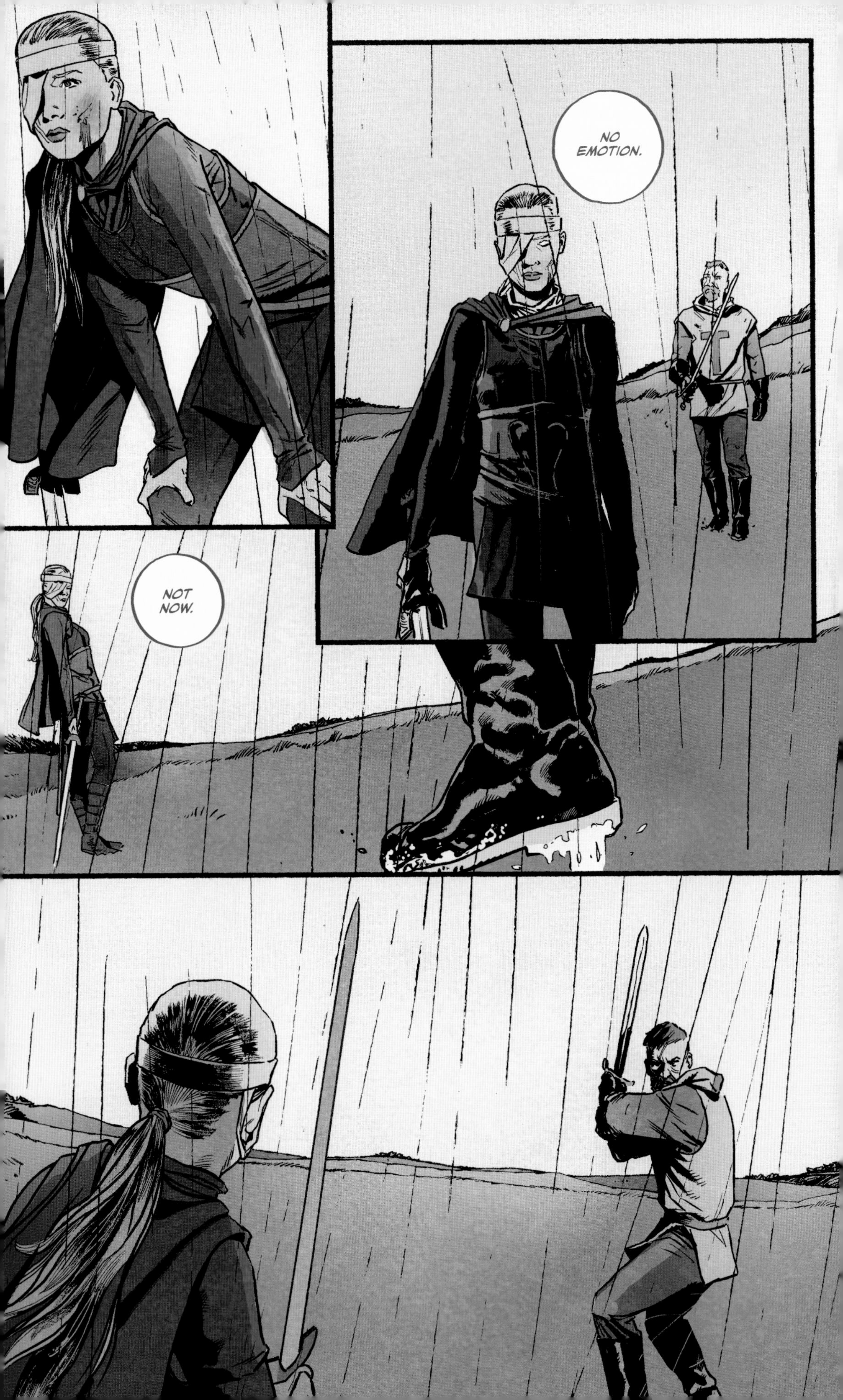
NO EMOTION.
NOT NOW.

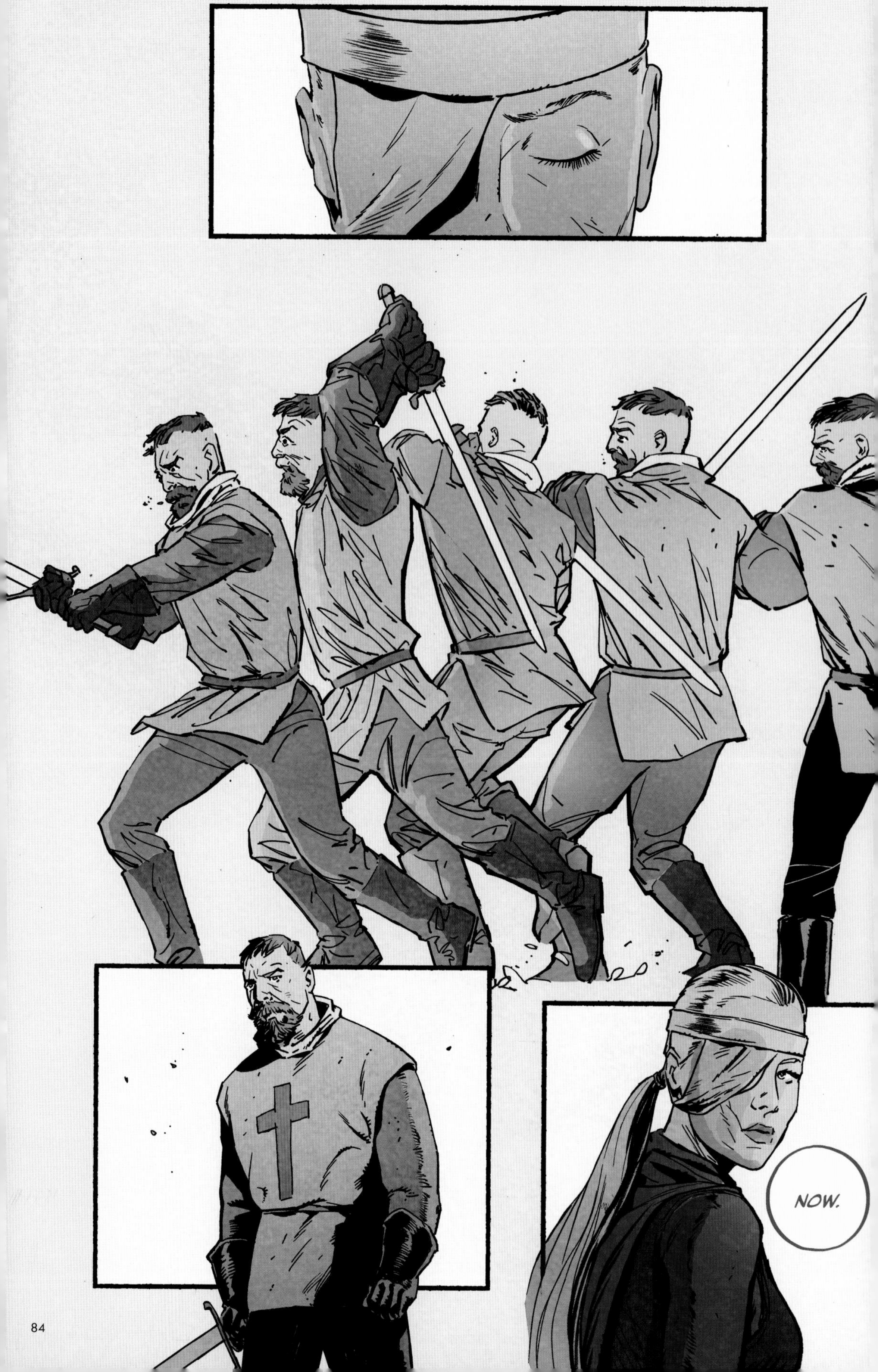
NOW.

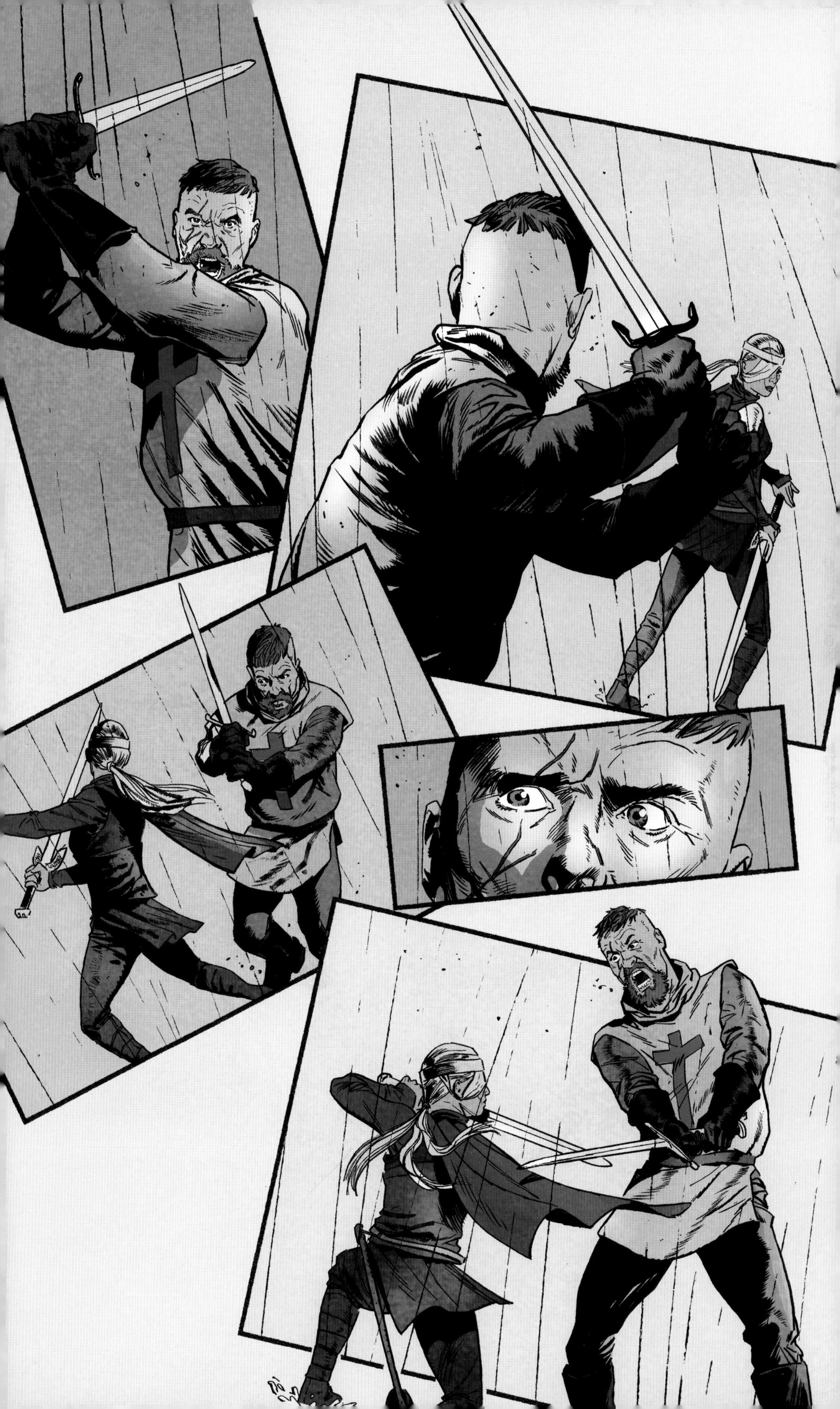

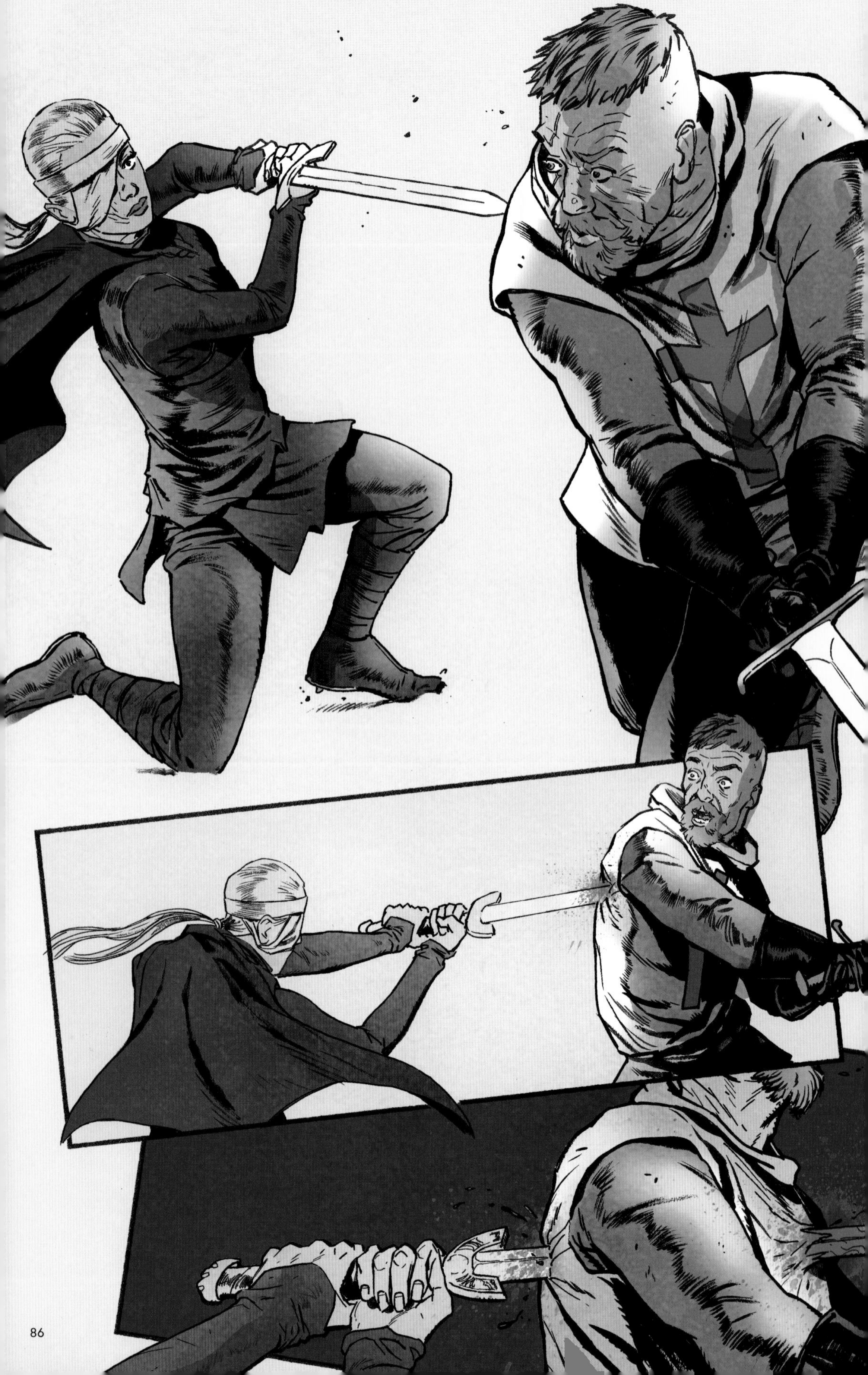

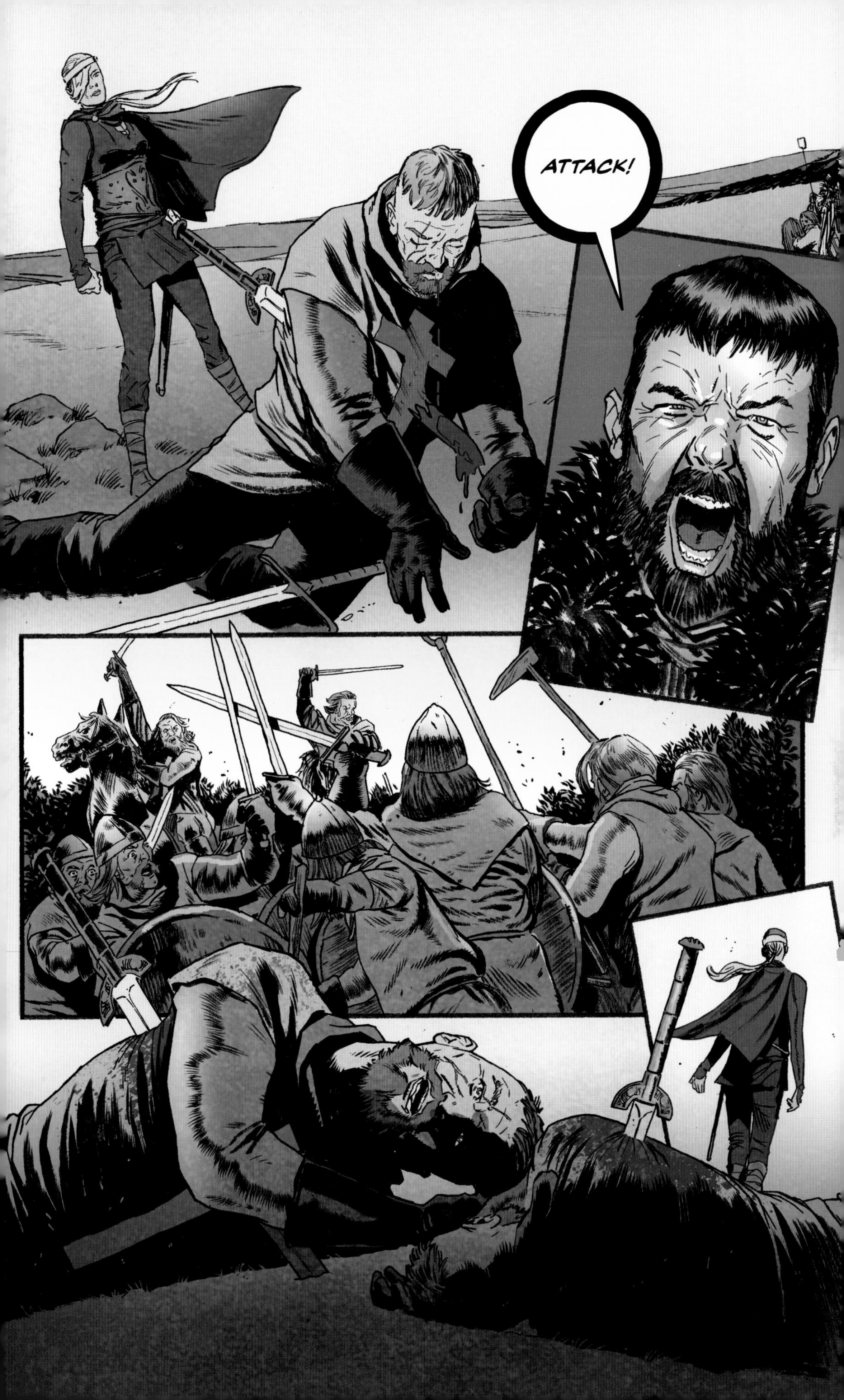
ATTACK!

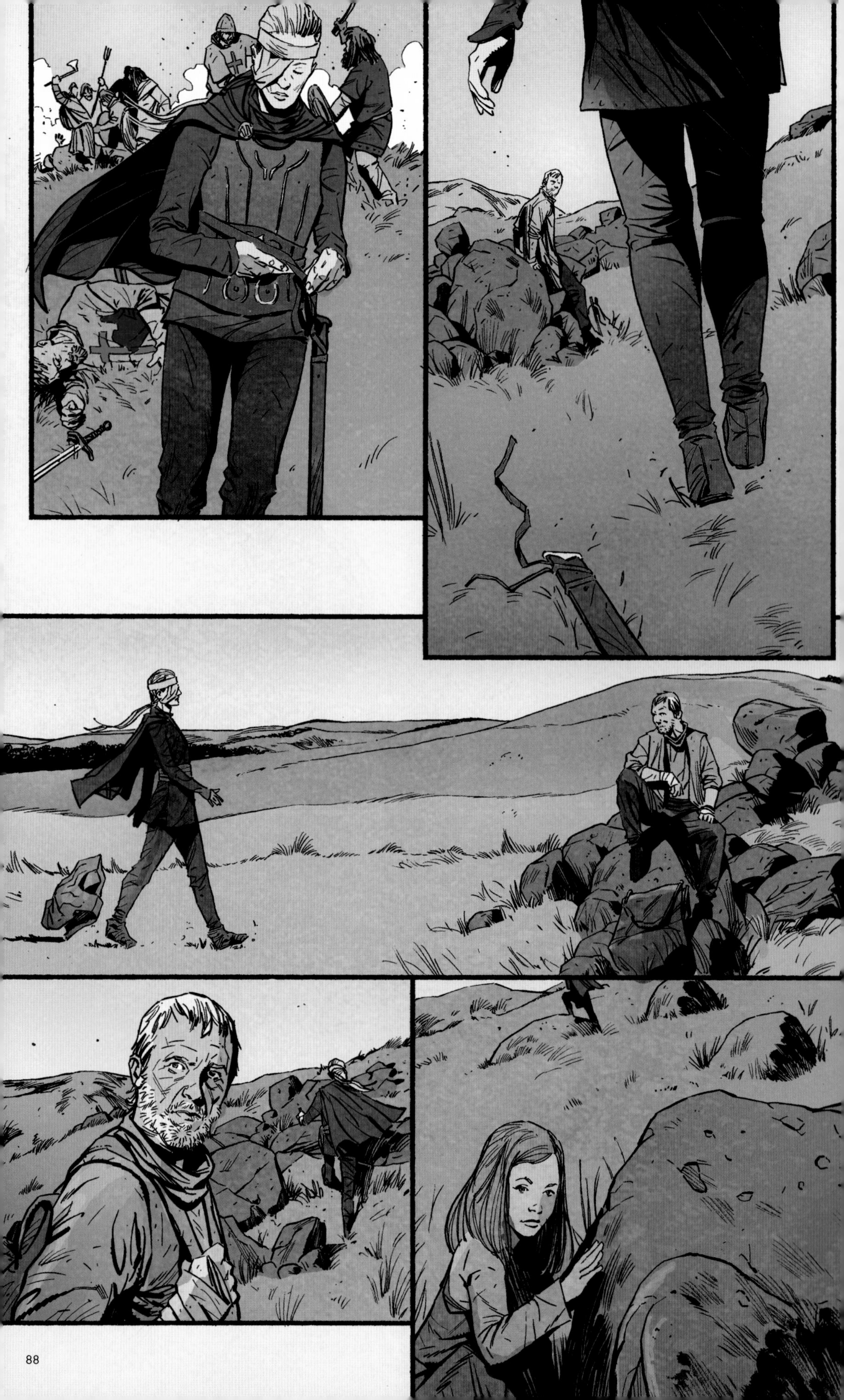

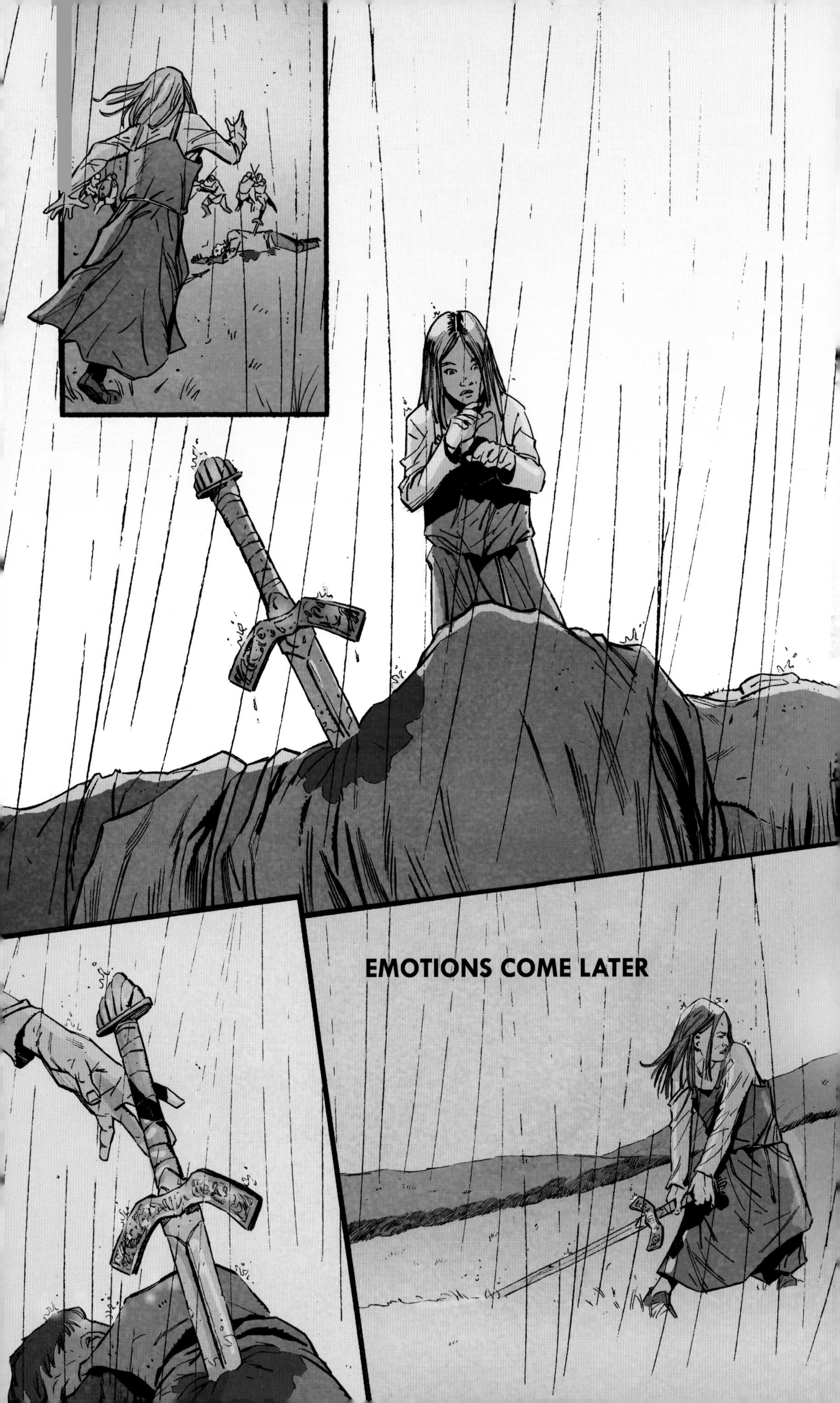
EMOTIONS COME LATER

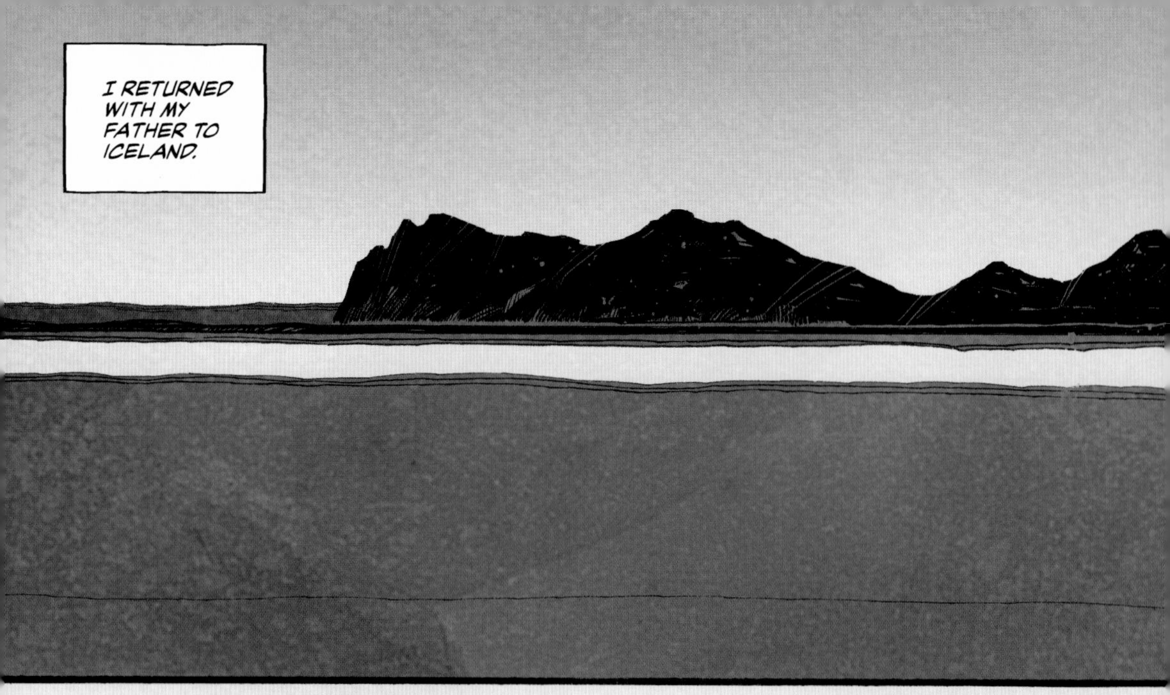
I RETURNED WITH MY FATHER TO ICELAND.

SUMARDAGURINN FYRSTI / FIRST DAY OF SUMMER / 1008AD

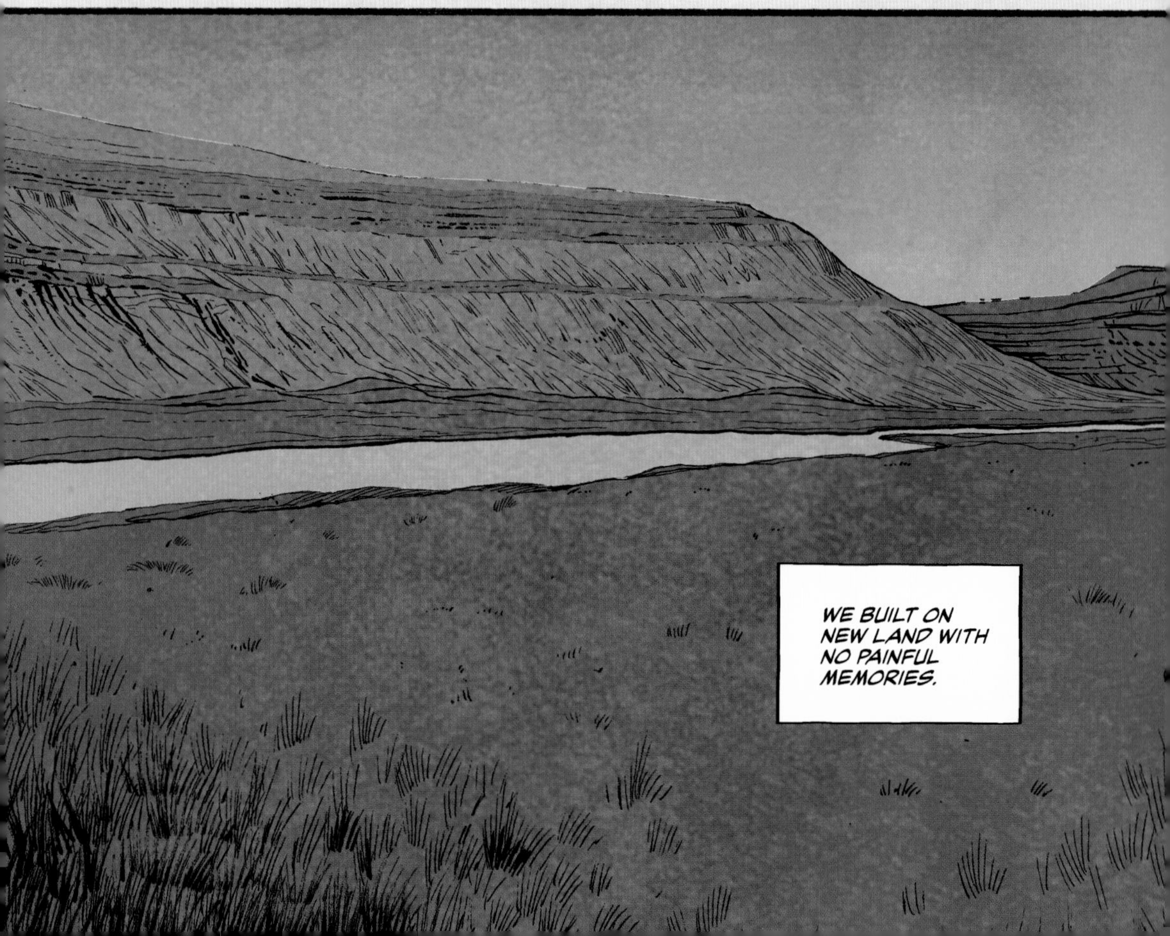
WE BUILT ON NEW LAND WITH NO PAINFUL MEMORIES.

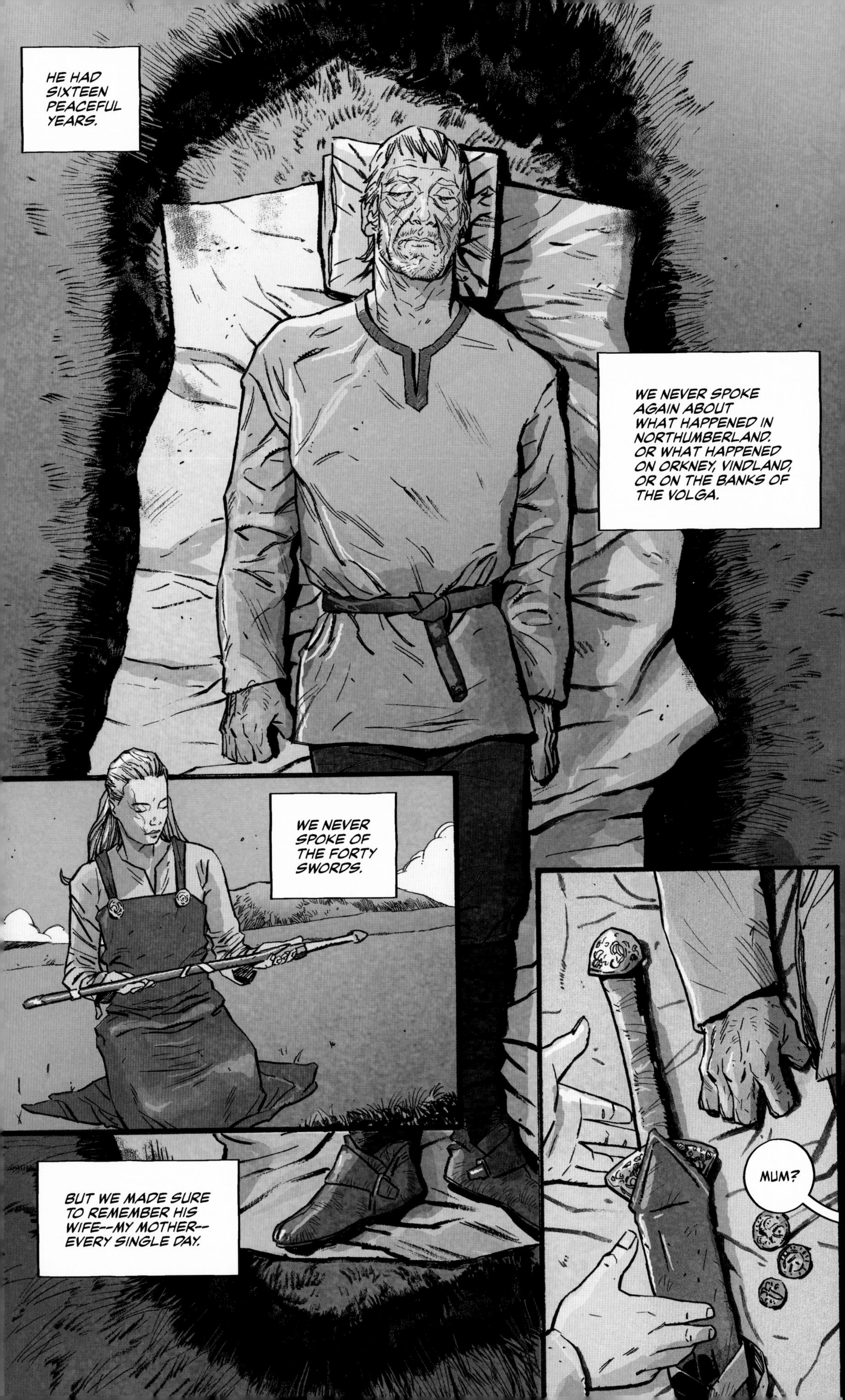
HE HAD SIXTEEN PEACEFUL YEARS.
WE NEVER SPOKE AGAIN ABOUT WHAT HAPPENED IN NORTHUMBERLAND. OR WHAT HAPPENED ON ORKNEY, VINDLAND, OR ON THE BANKS OF THE VOLGA.
WE NEVER SPOKE OF THE FORTY SWORDS.
BUT WE MADE SURE TO REMEMBER HIS WIFE--MY MOTHER--EVERY SINGLE DAY.
MUM?

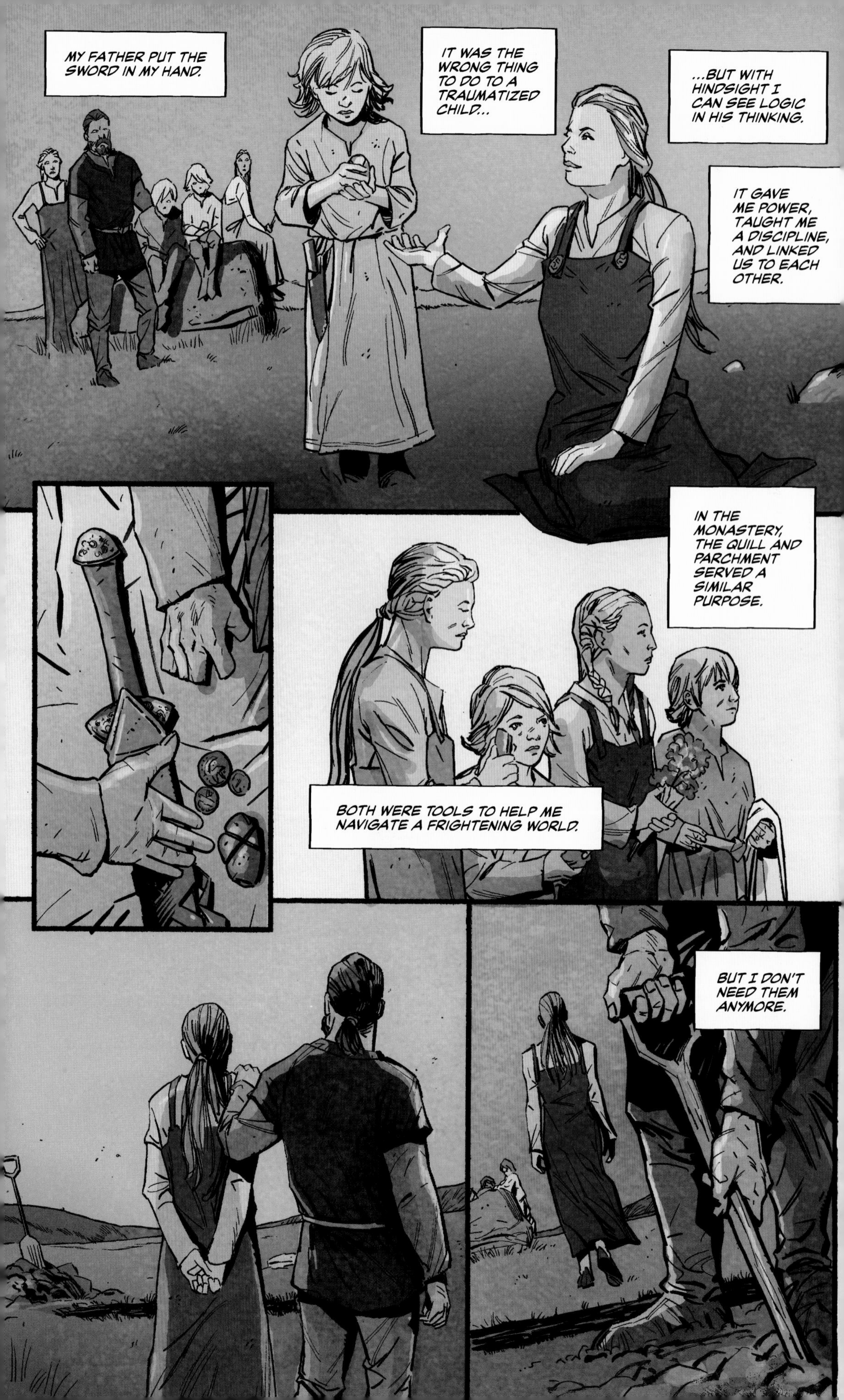
MY FATHER PUT THE SWORD IN MY HAND.
IT WAS THE WRONG THING TO DO TO A TRAUMATIZED CHILD...
...BUT WITH HINDSIGHT I CAN SEE LOGIC IN HIS THINKING.
IT GAVE ME POWER, TAUGHT ME A DISCIPLINE, AND LINKED US TO EACH OTHER.
IN THE MONASTERY, THE QUILL AND PARCHMENT SERVED A SIMILAR PURPOSE.
BOTH WERE TOOLS TO HELP ME NAVIGATE A FRIGHTENING WORLD.
BUT I DON'T NEED THEM ANYMORE.

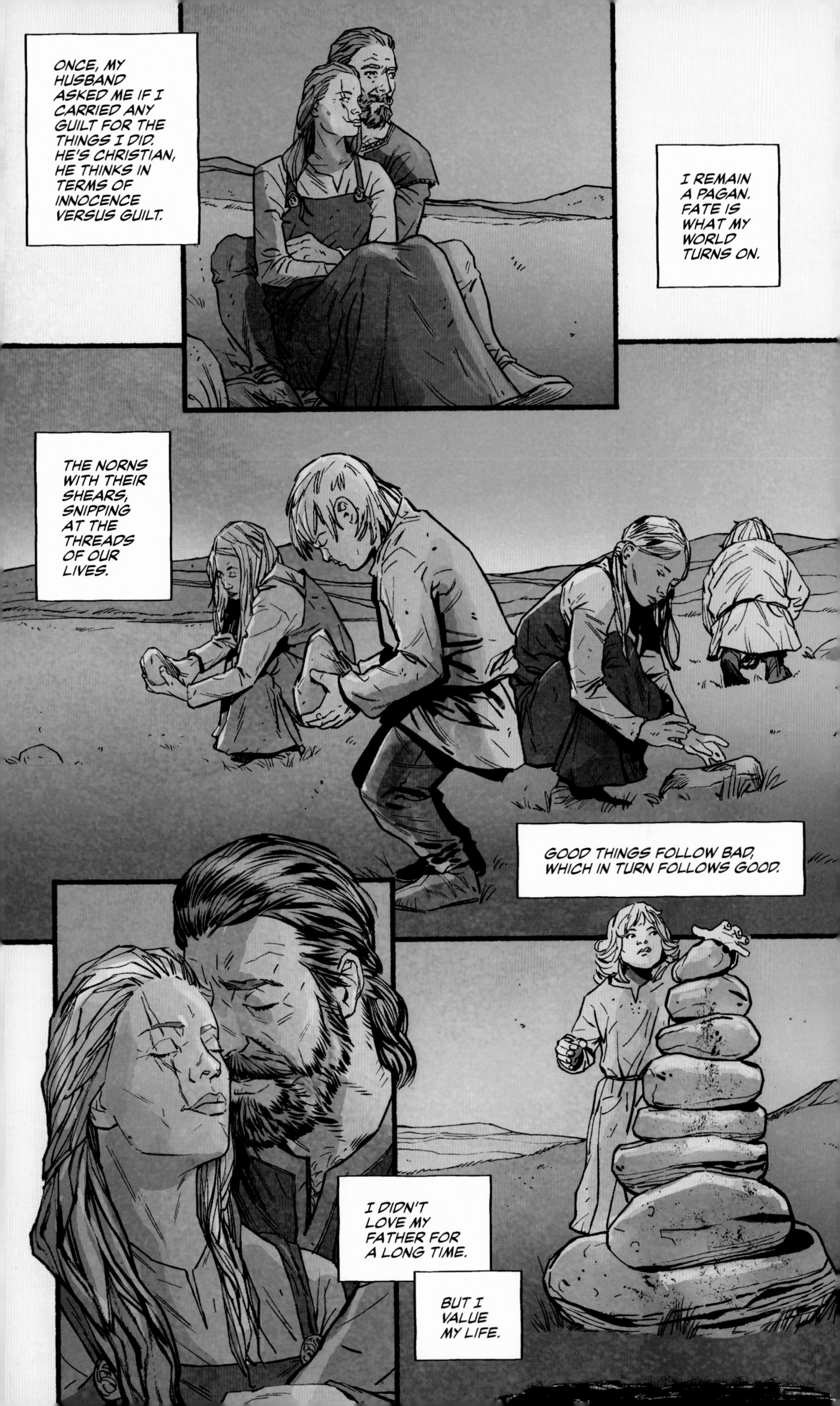
ONCE, MY HUSBAND ASKED ME IF I CARRIED ANY GUILT FOR THE THINGS I DID. HE'S CHRISTIAN, HE THINKS IN TERMS OF INNOCENCE VERSUS GUILT.
I REMAIN A PAGAN. FATE IS WHAT MY WORLD TURNS ON.
THE NORNS WITH THEIR SHEARS, SNIPPING AT THE THREADS OF OUR LIVES.
GOOD THINGS FOLLOW BAD, WHICH IN TURN FOLLOWS GOOD.
I DIDN'T LOVE MY FATHER FOR A LONG TIME.
BUT I VALUE MY LIFE.

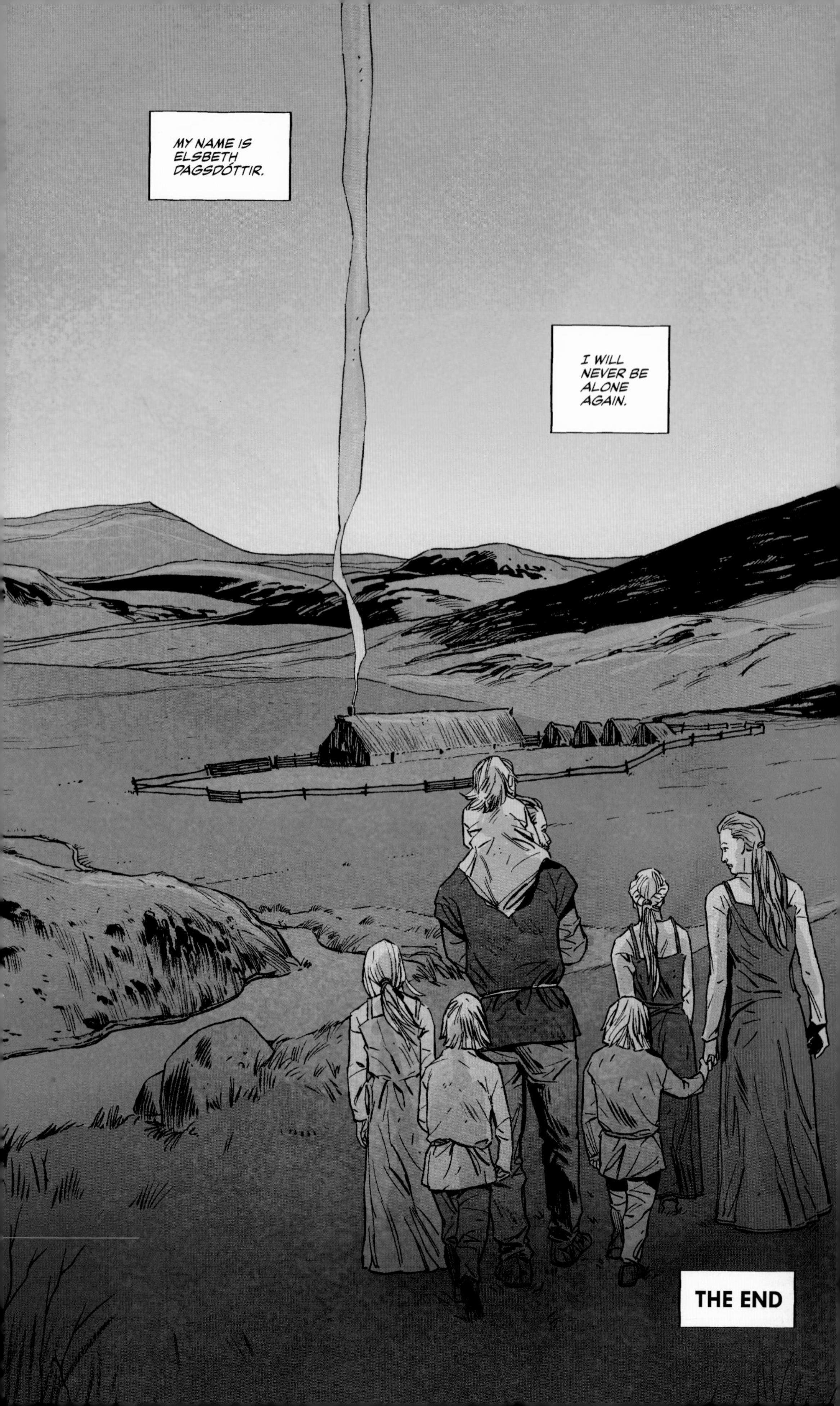
MY NAME IS ELSBETH DAGSDÓTTIR.
I WILL NEVER BE ALONE AGAIN.
THE END

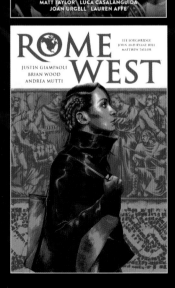

MORE EUROPEAN INTRIGUE FROM

DARK HORSE BOOKS

BLACKSAD
DÍAZ CANALES GUARNIDO
"As good as it gets!"

BLACKSAD

Juan Díaz Canales and Juanjo Guarnido

The *Blacksad* books first took Europe by storm in 2000 and sold over 200,000 copies in France alone. Now Dark Horse Comics presents the beautifully painted stories of private investigator John Blacksad, up to his feline ears in mystery, digging into the backstories behind murders, child abductions, and nuclear secrets.

Volume 1
978-1-59582-393-9 | $29.99
Volume 2: A Silent Hell
978-1-59582-931-3 | $19.99

VAMPIRE BOY
CARLOS TRILLO
EDUARDO RISSO

VAMPIRE BOY

Carlos Trillo and Eduardo Risso

Left nameless by his father and sentenced to eternal life by a trick of fate and fortune, the protagonist of Carlos Trillo and Eduardo Risso's *Vampire Boy* has spent fifty centuries in a body that never ages, locked in an eternal struggle with a rival as immortal as he. Acclaimed writer Carlos Trillo teams with legendary artist Eduardo Risso (*100 Bullets*) to produce a poignantly engrossing twist on the classic vampire mythos, now presented in English for the first time!

978-1-59582-562-9 | $24.99

STATION 16
HERMANN
YVES H.

STATION 16

Hermann and Yves H.

May 1997, Russia, north of the Arctic Circle: A border patrol rookie receives a distress call from the long-abandoned Station 16, uninhabited since the heyday of massive nuclear testing more than thirty years ago. When he and his squad fly out to investigate the call, they find an injured man who claims that the rookie was his attacker—and suddenly a nuclear explosion blasts the sky!

978-1-61655-481-1 | $19.99

ENTER A WORLD OF MAGIC AND FANTASY!
DRAGONERO
Luca Enoch • Stefano Vietti • Giuseppe Matteoni

DRAGONERO

Luca Enoch, Stefano Vietti, and Giuseppe Matteoni

Beyond the civilized lands of Erondàr, the Stone Towers are crumbling. The great monoliths are falling one after another under the wild thrusts of an evil force. The Ancient Prohibition that binds the Abominables inside their dark world is soon to be broken. Alben the Wizard will send for Myrva, a young follower of the powerful Technocrats; he will choose Ecuba, the fighting nun, to protect him; and he will call back Ian Aranill, a former Empire officer—followed by Gmor the Orc, his loyal friend—to use his scouting experience. Together they will face the Painers, the evil beings who still live in the barren Dragonlands. Can Ian prevail against the last, horrible threat they will be facing?

978-1-59582-291-8 | $19.99

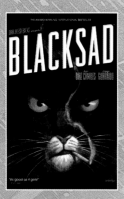